Routledge Revivals

European Advanced Technology

First published in 1969, *European Advanced Technology* expounds a programme of action for Europe to tackle the challenge posed by American technology in the 1960s. It analyses first the nature of the American predominance in science and technology and goes on to describe the efforts of the major European states to counter it on their own. It then explains the limitations of these efforts at the level of the nation state and shows how European countries have gone on to work together in certain key sectors: high energy physics, nuclear power, aircraft, space, electronics, transport and communications. The history of these programmes is examined carefully and the book describes a wider strategy. It deals with larger questions like how Europe can develop a common science and technology policy; what should be done to promote industrial integration and European companies, and what individual companies and the British government can and should do? This book will be an essential read for scholars and researchers interested in the history of European Union, European history, international organisations and European Politics and for European law makers.

European Advanced Technology

A Programme For Integration

by Christopher Layton

Routledge
Taylor & Francis Group

First published in 1969
by George Allen & Unwin Ltd

This edition first published in 2021 by Routledge
2 Park Square, Milton Park, Abingdon, Oxon, OX14 4RN

and by Routledge
605 Third Avenue, New York, NY 10017

Routledge is an imprint of the Taylor & Francis Group, an informa business

Publisher's Note
The publisher has gone to great lengths to ensure the quality of this reprint but points
out that some imperfections in the original copies may be apparent.

Disclaimer
The publisher has made every effort to trace copyright holders and welcomes
correspondence from those they have been unable to contact.

A Library of Congress record exists under LCCN: 76390719

ISBN 13: 978-1-032-04924-3(hbk)
ISBN 13: 978-1-003-19519-1(ebk)
ISBN 13: 978-1-032-04925-0(pbk)

EUROPEAN ADVANCED TECHNOLOGY
A PROGRAMME FOR INTEGRATION

BY

CHRISTOPHER LAYTON

PEP

12 Upper Belgrave Street

London

GEORGE ALLEN & UNWIN LTD

RUSKIN HOUSE . MUSEUM STREET

ACKNOWLEDGEMENTS

This book is the product of a study undertaken at PEP by Christopher Layton. He was assisted by Christopher Harlow, who brought his expert knowledge to compiling the main bulk of the statistics, often from elusive sources; and by Mrs Alex Morrison, who was secretary to the project. The study was financed by the Ford Foundation and by Britain in Europe, whose contribution resulted from a special appeal to British industry. A useful European trip was also financed and arranged by the Ariel Foundation.

The book derives, essentially, from several months of interviewing and discussion with those in industry, governments and the European organizations who have been struggling over the years to integrate Europe's efforts in science and technology. Our thanks are due to these many busy people, too many to list here, who contributed valuable time, experience and ideas.

CONTENTS

TABLES IN THE TEXT

STATISTICAL APPENDIX
TABLES

GLOSSARY

ABAP:	Association of Belgian companies for the Breguet Atlantic
AEA:	Atomic Energy Authority (UK)
AEC:	Atomic Energy Commission (USA)
AEG:	Allgemeine Elektricitäts Gesellschaft
AEI:	Associated Electrical Industries
AFVG:	Anglo-French Variable Geometry Aircraft
ASEA:	Allmänna Svenska Elektricität Aktiebolag
BAC:	British Aircraft Corporation
BEA:	British European Airways
BMC:	British Motor Corporation
BSE:	Bristol Siddeley Engines
CCITT:	Joint Committee for International Telephone and Telegraph
CDC:	Control Data Corporation
CEA:	Commissariat à l'Energie Atomique
CEGB:	Central Electricity Generating Board
CEN:	European Standards Committee
CENEL:	European Electrical Standards Committee
CEPT:	Comité Européen de Postes et Telegraphes
CERN:	Conseil Européen pour la Recherche Nucléaire
CETS:	European Conference on Satellite Telecommunications
CII:	Compagnie Internationale d'Informatique
CITEC:	Compagnie pour l'Informatique et les Techniques Electroniques de Controle
CNES:	Centre National d'Etudes Spatiales
CNEXO:	Centre National pour l'Exploitation Oceanographique
CNRS:	Centre National de la Recherche Scientifique
COSEM:	Compagnie Sémiconducteur
CSF:	Compagnie Général de Telegraphie Sans Fil
DGRST:	Délégation Générale à la Recherche Scientifique et Technique
DSIR:	Department for Scientific and Industrial Research
EBU:	European Broadcasting Union
ECE:	Economic Commission for Europe (United Nations)
ELDO:	European Launcher Development Organization
EMBO:	European Molecular Biology Organization
ENEA:	European Nuclear Energy Agency
ERA:	Electronic Research Associates

ESRO: European Space Research Organization
ESTEC: The Central Research and Development Laboratory of ESRO
GAAA: Groupement Atomique Alsacienne et Atlantique
GE: General Electric (USA)
GEV: Giga Electron Volt
GHH: Gutehoffnungshütte
GM: General Motors
IATA: International Air Transport Association
IBM: International Business Machines
ICI: Imperial Chemical Industries
ICL: International Computers Limited
ICT: International Computers and Tabulators (now ICL, above)
IEC: International Electrical Standards Committee
IRI: Istituto per la Ricostruzione Industriale
ISO: International Standards Organization
IT&T: International Telephone and Telegraph
ITU: International Telecommunications Union
MAN: Maschinenfabrik Augsburg-Nürnberg
MIT: Massachusetts Institute of Technology
MURA: Mid-west Universities Research Association
NASA: National Aeronautics and Space Administration
NASMO: Nato Starfighter Manufacturing Organization
NATO: North Atlantic Treaty Organization
NCR: National Cash Register
NRDC: National Research and Development Corporation
NSF: National Science Foundation
OECD: Organization for Economic Cooperation and Development
OST: Office of Science and Technology
RCA: Radio Corporation of America
SDS: Scientific Data Systems
SECBAT: Société d'Etude et de Construction du Bréguet Atlantique
SEPECAT: Société d'Etude et de Production de l'Avion école et d'appui Tactique
SGS: Societa Generale Semiconduttori
SNCF: Société National des Chemins de Fers
SNECMA: Société National d'Etudes et de Construction de Moteurs d'Aviation
SST: Supersonic Transport
WMO: World Meteorological Organization

PART ONE

EUROPE AND AMERICA

CHAPTER 1

EUROPE'S FEARS

From the iron age sword or pot, to radar and nuclear reactors, military power and prosperity have both been dependent on technology. It is not surprising that Europe, which for four centuries dominated the world through its technology, is worried by the growing technological predominance of the United States.

Ten years ago, as Europe emerged from its wartime agony, it was the European 'economic miracle' and European growth rates which caused astonishment. 'Catching up with America' was a favourite slogan of politicians. In the early 1960s the American economy achieved a new and astonishing burst of expansion—averaging growth of some 4-5 per cent per year. European growth, by contrast, faltered; the economic lead of the richest continent seemed to be growing wider than ever. America's prosperity brings great advantages for all. It is in no one's interest that the main motor of the world's economy should slow down. The trouble is that the imbalance in world development has other more alarming consequences. Just as, in a nation, say Italy, or Britain, the concentration of wealth and power around London or Milan drains strength, in the form of men and women, capital and jobs from Scotland or Sicily, so the far more gross imbalance in world regional development brings cumulative economic disadvantages to the poorer regions, as well as explosive political problems. In his book *Le Défi Américain*, Jean-Jacques Servain Schreiber[1] has expounded the problem. This book sets out to outline the response: how Europe can effectively combine its resources to form a counterpole of growth and development comparable to the United States. And because the

[1] J.-J. Servain-Schreiber, *Le Défi Américain*, Denoel, 1967.

crucial resource for economic growth is becoming, increasingly, not raw materials, nor even capital, but knowledge and social as well as individual skills in using it, this pole must be partly concerned with technology and its use.

Even wider than the gap between Europe and America yawns the gulf between all the rich nations and the poorer southern hemisphere. A stronger Europe would provide an additional reservoir of wealth and skills to help close this gap—the great task of the next three decades.

What are the symptoms of the technological imbalance of today? One is the growth of American direct investment in Europe. As Table 1 shows, American direct investment in Europe grew from $4,151 mn. in 1957 to $13,894 mn. in 1965[2]; it is still growing fast and is financed increasingly by European capital harnessed to American energy and skills. American direct investors, who once provided the bread and butter industries of Europe's new affluence —from sewing machines to razor blades—now play a central role in the new industries, from computers and microcircuits to many pharmaceuticals. Seventy-five per cent of the computers sold in Europe and an even larger proportion of the integrated electronic circuits come from American companies. One third of Europe's telephones are produced by a single American firm. All the carbon black in Europe, a key material in tyre production, is produced by American companies. So are half the pharmaceuticals bought by Britain's national health service. American companies have also been the first to take advantage of the emerging Common Market. Already expert in the techniques of marketing and producing on a continental scale, they have been the first to integrate output and research in several countries, pooling brains multinationally and reaping European economies of scale.

In the short run, all this has made a striking contribution to Europe's own economic growth and productivity; for direct investment is often the most rapid and efficient way of transferring a technology or skill. If a discovery is made in IT & T's American laboratories, for instance, it takes only a telephone call, a letter, or an air flight, to transfer it to their European laboratories.

But if direct investment is, in the main, a one way traffic, there can be adverse consequences. It can mean growing world control of an advanced industry by a single country (the USA) or even a

[2]Christopher Layton, *Transatlantic Investment*, the Atlantic Institute, Paris, 1967.

single company (IBM). Uncontrolled, this can mean, in turn, that the most advanced research and development continues to get done in the one, powerful country, pre-empting the future—especially if, as with some US companies, the bulk of research and hence the best men are concentrated in the parent company while their European research centres mainly monitor[3]: small potential rival enterprises may be bought up and nipped in the bud. An investment which, in the short run, accelerates development, can, in the long run, limit potential growth and indirectly damage the balance of payments.

This concentration of economic power and knowledge has political implications and not merely in such obvious ways as the monopoly of a key weapons system. The best-known example was the American refusal, since waived, to allow France to buy a large computer in 1962. There could one day be even bigger implications if America retains a technological monopoly of communications satellites in the western world.

The brain drain is a second symptom of America's technological predominance. If the best research facilities and the most exciting work are available in the United States, many of the best and most enterprising brains in Europe will tend to go there too. In the year July 1965 to June 1966, 30,000 professional and technical brains emigrated to the United States, and of these 70 per cent came from Europe, Japan, Canada, Australia and New Zealand. The drain from poorer countries was smaller, but the emigrants formed a large slice of a tiny and more desperately needed skilled elite.

Table 2 shows the place of advanced technology in emigration. It is true that motives for the exodus vary, and are often concerned with society and its attitudes, as well as with income or technology. For the British, whose language encourages the flow, the biggest single motive, according to a study on scientists emigrating in 1964,[4] was sheer frustration. Both in American universities and in companies, young able men find they are given, not only more pay, but challenging responsibilities which they see no hope of getting in Britain. Lack of opportunities for promotion, upper management opposition to new ideas and methods, unwillingness to embark on bold commercial initiatives to sell new products, all play a part in the drain

[3]Stanford Research Institute, *Research and Development in Europe*, Long-Range Planning Report No. 198.

[4]James A. Wilson, The depletion of national resources of human talent in the United Kingdom. A special aspect of emigration to America, *Minerva*, Autumn 1966. Also, *The Brain Drain*, Cmnd. 3417, HMSO, London, October 1967.

B

from Britain. Elsewhere in Europe, similar frustrations operate. In West Germany, the young academic researcher finds himself at the base of a ponderous hierarchic structure; the free interdisciplinary study of an American university can be a liberation.

The international market for skilled managers and technologists is becoming highly sensitive. In the immediate postwar years, when European laboratories could not offer physicists the expensive advanced equipment they needed, there was a large-scale exodus of bright physicists. When, at Geneva, Europe built the largest particle accelerator in the world (described in Chapter 7), the outflow stopped. When the British Government slashed TSR2 and other advanced air projects in 1964 there was a similar wave of emigrants from the aerospace industry.

Of the major European countries, only France has so far succeeded in almost wholly avoiding the brain drain. The French, it seems, put good living, French style, highest in their priorities. They have also been encouraged to stay in Europe by nationalistic feeling and France's growing national effort in advanced technology (see Chapter 4). But whether France will remain permanently immune is open to doubt.

The loss of 10,000 men, trained at a hypothetical cost to Europe of say $50,000 each, is equivalent to the annual transfer to the United States of an investment of $500 mn. It is not a massive sum, especially when compared with the catastrophic continuing drain of brains from the poorer developing countries to the rich ones. There is also a reverse movement; the chance to travel is an important opportunity for the individual to widen his horizons. Nonetheless, the net movement westward, like the net movement of direct investment eastward, reduces Europe's research and development potential for the future. It reflects and magnifies the shift in the centre of gravity of technological power.

A third symptom of America's emergent technological predominance is the recorded flow of payments for industrial knowledge, such as patents and licence fees for knowhow. As Table 3 shows, the United States has a massive and growing surplus with European countries (as the Europeans do, incidentally, with the rest of the world). These figures are no more than the tip of an iceberg, for they do not show the massive flow of industrial information which is exchanged without payment under reciprocal arrangements and which is included in other forms of interchange such as sales. However, they do suggest a trend. Like direct investment, the flow of industrial knowledge is a cheering sign of the transfer of technology, a means by which Europe can, in some measure, keep pace with America's advance. Indeed, in one sense, a high level of import of technology is a sign of industrial strength and vigour. Yet the ideal industrial structure both imports the maximum amount of foreign technology and generates and sells a large quantity of new technology of its own. All the evidence from successful companies is that effective application of bought technology depends on a strong 'in-house' research effort. Licensing arrangements cannot guarantee the complete transfer of knowhow learnt from hard experience, and often require the purchasing firm to invest heavily to get the bugs out of the process. Above all, a powerful 'in-house' research and development (R & D) effort is needed if a firm is to get the best terms of trade in knowhow—to buy licences or patents at good prices and be strongly placed in the market-place. Europe's adverse trade balance in knowledge is not, in itself, an economic malady. But it, too, reflects a major shift in the hub of development and bargaining power. In one major sector, chemicals, as Table 3 shows, Europe has a relatively favourable trade balance with America. We shall see, later, that much other evidence—size of company, trade patterns, research and development expenditure—confirms that view. But the contrast between chemicals and other sectors is revealing.

Europe's growing net need to buy and import advanced technology has another major implication. The time taken to develop and apply innovations is steadily decreasing—from some 56 years for the introduction of the telephone in the last century to 14 years for television and a mere five years for transistors. Over half of the products traded by American industry did not exist 20 years ago. So time gains in importance. The company which is first or at least close second in the field with a highly marketable product makes the highest monopoly profits. Those which follow, say by buying the technology, only come into the market in time to see competition bring down prices and cut profit margins; by the time the market has stabilised, a new product may be ousting the old. Integrated circuits in the US, colour television tubes and many chemicals illustrate this cycle. Time thus places a premium on internal innovation in a company, and on carrying out that innovation fast.

The best-known indicator of America's predominance in this crucial process are the statistics of research and development (R & D) shown in Table 4. In 1936, Europe and America each spent perhaps $150 mn. on research. By 1963-64 America was spending

$21 bn. on research and development each year compared to Western Europe's $6 bn.[5] America, in other words, spends nearly four times as much on research and development as Western Europe, even though Western Europe's population is larger; the US employed 2·5 times as many scientists and engineers on R & D. Total incomes in Western Europe, it is true, are only two thirds of America's. But even as a proportion of total income, Western Europe as a whole spent only 1·7 per cent compared to America's 3·5 per cent. In their classic study on research in the Atlantic area, Freeman and Young suggest that higher American costs make the real comparison between the research efforts in the two continents some 2·5 to 1. But very many people in industry believe that higher US costs are compensated by less efficient European use of manpower. If that were true the comparison between US and European R & D efforts would be less favourable.

The bulk of America's research and development was concentrated in the crucial sectors (aerospace, electronics, chemicals) where the challenge of US competition and direct investment is particularly strong. The trade figures bear out the dynamic commercial impact of the US research effort. A study by Donald Keesing[6] shows a remarkable correlation between intensive research and development in the United States and a large American share in world trade (see Table 7).

The three US industries with the largest research efforts (aircraft, machinery, drugs) were also those with the best export performance, compared with other competitors in the North Atlantic world; they had between 30 and 50 per cent of the trade of the ten richest nations. In nine other industries, however, where less than 1 per cent of the labour force was employed in R & D, the US exported less than 20 per cent of the exports of the ten richest countries. The research-intensive industries also happen to be those in which Britain and West Germany have a favourable trade position. Research and development plainly pays off in Europe as well as America, but the United States does more of it.

From all this, many Europeans conclude that there is a growing 'technological gap' between Europe and the United States, and that

[5]C. Freeman & B. Young, *The Research and Development Effort*, OECD, Paris, 1965. Also *The overall level and structure of* R & D *efforts in the* OECD *member countries*, OECD, Paris, 1967.

[6]Donald B. Keesing, *The Impact of Research and Development on United States Trade*, Columbia University, 1966.

something should be done to close it. Strong words like 'industrial
helotry' have been used, and a variety of measures, from restrictions
on American direct investment to a Marshall Aid Plan in technology have been proposed to close it.

Americans retort that the real problem is not in pure inventiveness.
Europe, after all, produced the jet engine, radar, the first operational
fast-breeder nuclear reactor, polythene, air-cushion vehicles and
many other new discoveries. The real problem is that many of these
ideas have been applied more swiftly and more effectively in the
United States. The trouble is not a 'science and technology gap', runs
the American thesis, but a lack of skill and enterprise in Europe in
the whole process of innovation; caste systems in Europe separate
the scientist from the engineer, the industrialist from the professor
and the politician. An elite system of education in Europe starves
industry of the broad mass of technicians who are available in the
United States to develop and apply discovery. The man on the shop
floor does not, like his American counterpart, have the feeling he
can rise to the boardroom. The gap, above all, is one of management, a failing of professional skill in applying, developing and ex-
ploiting an invention efficiently and fast. There is all too much
truth in this picture, as those who know both the Old and New
Worlds will agree.

A second American thesis runs a little differently. The 'technology
gap' it is argued, does exist in a few industries, but not in most. And
in some industries the gap is even in Europe's favour. A paper by
Charpie and Shoup[7], for instance, argued that in steel, chemicals
and nuclear power, Europe was America's equal. Only in computers, electronics generally and aviation was the United States
dramatically ahead. International trade, the argument goes on, has
the function of distributing to everyone the benefits of such comparative advantages. Technological 'gaps', it is argued, are the normal stuff of economic life.

This argument is superficially attractive, but it begins to wear
thin when one takes a close look at the sectors examined in the
paper.

In steel, it is true that the American industry is on the defensive,
and America has a big trade deficit. Technically, oxygen steel, for
instance, has come from Europe. The largest US company, US Steel,
suffered for some years from what can only be called the 'paralysis

[7]A. Charpie and Charles S. Shoup, unpublished paper presented to Deauville
Conference on Technology Gap, North Atlantic Assembly, Paris, 1967.

of scale'; bad management and lagging technology made it highly vulnerable to competition from foreign manufacturers and energetic domestic rivals like Bethlehem Steel. But today even us Steel is beginning to recover technologically. An injection of new management, plus the massive financial resources its scale has given it, are making possible a large R & D programme which is paying off. The demanding metallurgical requirements of the space and defence programmes are spilling into the steel industry. The us steel industry is still on the defensive; but the balance is shifting, thanks to the stimulus of advanced technology provided by the us Government.

The chemical industry is always quoted as the one major sector in which Europe is America's match. In scale, the nine largest European companies have a turnover almost exactly equal to that of the American top nine. In the exchange of licences, patents and know-how the balance in chemicals is far better than in other sectors. Giants like Unilever, ICI, the three IG Farben successors and Rhone-Poulenc, can meet Du Pont and Union Carbide on equal terms.

Yet even in chemicals there are some disquieting signs for Europe. Profitability of the nine top European companies is only half that of the us top ten. Professor Knoppers, head of research at Merck, Finck and Dohm, believes that, while there is a real balance in the heavy chemical industry, Europe is beginning to lag behind in certain important fields.[8] Advanced instrumentation, for instance, helped in part by federal programmes in other fields, is improving the rate of chemical research. Small but vital shifts are occurring in basic research. The European chemical industry is more of a match for the Americans than any other major advanced industry; it demonstrates that where Europeans can muster financial resources for research, development and investment on the American scale, they can match the commercial vigour and success of us companies. The trouble is that in many sectors they cannot.

Nuclear power is a good example. Here, two European countries, Britain and France, have invested large sums of money in the development of reactors for peaceful power production. The British had, until recently, more nuclear power in operation than the rest of the world combined; they and perhaps the Russians are ahead of the Americans in the construction of fast-breeder reactor prototypes —probably the crucial type of reactor of the 1980s. But in the last

[8]Anthonie T. Knoppers, *The Role of Science and Technology in Atlantic Economic Relationships*, Atlantic Institute, Paris, 1966.

five years this rosy picture has faded. Somehow or other American nuclear reactors have begun to sweep world markets. In the United States itself, power stations to produce at least 40,000 megawatts of electric power are now on order; in Western Europe the American-type water reactors threaten to conquer the West German and Italian markets and perhaps even France. In the world as a whole, Britain has so far succeeded in selling abroad two nuclear power stations (partly exported, partly built under license) of the gas-cooled type and one (in Japan) has not been a success. Once more, it seems, European inventiveness has not been matched by skill in commercial development and application.

In some sectors, it is clear, America has no predominance. In shipbuilding, for instance, Japan is far ahead. Even in nuclear power, the picture could change quickly. But it is plain that there are certain general American advantages which have importance: the social factors—management and education; the sheer size of the American market and of American companies; and the role of the American Government. Let us look more closely at the American model to see what makes it tick.

CHAPTER 2

THE AMERICAN MODEL

The challenge of American technology is not a new phenomenon, and is based in part on qualities long present in the American scene. As far back as the Great Exhibition of 1851, British manufacturers were surprised and disconcerted by the technological prowess shown by American exhibitors of advanced machinery. At the turn of the century, and again between the two world wars, American direct investors were playing a major part in creating in Britain, and other European countries, the new industries of an affluent society—tractors and motorcars, refrigerators and vacuum cleaners. The Hoover, the Singer and the Frigidaire were already synonyms for whole new industries, as well as for a new and easier way of life for the ordinary man and woman.

Those industries developed first in the United States because the mass market developed there first. As far back as the 1920s Henry Ford was selling far more cars than were being sold in any single European country. Already new production processes, methods and products were being engendered by this first mass market of continental scale. And already corporations of continental stature were emerging to exploit the market. It was hardly surprising that such companies were well placed to transfer their new skills and products to Europe by direct investment, when, later, the mass market developed there. The snag for Europe is that this process inevitably has certain harmful consequences. The highest profits tend to go to the market leaders. A majority of the great international corporations are based in the United States.

If Europeans have been slow to react, that is because the process has only lately been gathering speed. For today the accelerating advantages of continental-scale industry do not need underlining. Large-scale operation, important 30 years ago in industries (like cars) where mass production was of critical importance, is becoming vital for other functions: research and development, marketing, and the finance for these activities. The faster technology advances, the more size becomes important in the innovation process. 'Lead times', discussed in the previous chapter, can be shortened drastically if unlimited skilled manpower can be thrown into a development project. This, plus tighter scheduling and control, is one of the reasons why some American aircraft companies take less time to develop a prototype than the Europeans do. Again and again, British aircraft designs, conceived before their American rivals, have been beaten in the race to the market-place by their faster moving American rivals.

In the initial phase of research—that of creative ideas—ideas are only in part a function of the numbers of able people on the job. In the next phase, that of exploration and development, size matters much more. An idea conceived by one or two men in a laboratory may need 30 men to elaborate it scientifically and 600 men to develop and engineer it and work out marketing strategies. Expensive instruments, and computer installations, may save months of development time. Size, of course, matters vitally again when it comes to launching a new product on the world market and reaping high profits before other competitors come in.

Size is not everything. Indeed, later in this chapter we shall see that the small, dynamic company plays a vital part in the American 'miracle'. Yet where innovation means large and complicated plants or prototypes, where marketing and servicing are expensive and must be widespread to be profitable, scale counts. If, of course, the 'threshold' or minimum size required is large for some individual products and processes, it is a great deal larger if a company is to develop a whole range of products enabling it to diversify its profit centres, and ensure that if one line flops, another succeeds.

In his study on the electronic industry, Christopher Freeman[1] worked out 'minimum threshold' sizes for the development of various products. At European costs, he suggested, it might cost $80-$110 mn. to develop a communications satellite over say five years and $20-$40 mn. for a range of computers over a period of four

[1]C. Freeman, C. J. Harlow and J. K. Fuller, Research and Development in Electronic Capital Goods, *National Institute Economic Review*, No. 34, London, November, 1965.

years. To support such an effort a company must plainly have a high turnover. It will need to spend more, quicker, if it wants to pursue an 'offensive' strategy accelerating development time sufficiently to get there first. A company wishing to develop several such products would have to be far larger. It is not surprising that many relatively small European electronic companies have not been sufficiently large to be able to stay in this race. One could add that developing the Dragon high temperature gas-cooled nuclear reactor has cost $70 mn., while Britain's fast-breeder reactor prototype and research and development programme may cost $250 mn.; a modern aero-engine can cost $150-$200 mn. to develop and a supersonic transport $2·5 bn. In all such cases there must be a powerful background of research and development. In such industries, in other words, both very large companies, and indeed big government financial assistance are needed if development is to be possible. It is not surprising that America's big battalions tend to win.

In Britain and other European countries, tears are often shed for the European inventions—from the swing-wing aircraft to holography—which have been exploited first in the United States. This process is not merely due to accident, or to bumble-headedness on the part of European governments and industrialists. It is due in part to scale. In a study of the innovation process, a team set up by the US Department of Commerce has suggested that pure research accounts for only 5-10 per cent of the cost of inventing and developing a product to the production stage. The rest is accounted for by engineering and marketing development.[2] No problem of limited financial resources, in short, inhibited Dr Barnes Wallis from imagining swing-wings on aircraft, or indeed Pierre Curie, Enrico Fermi, Niels Bohr, and Rutherford from making the theoretical advances that led to the atomic bomb. But so far only the US Government has felt it could command the massive resources to translate the swing-wing principle into an operational aircraft, the F-111. And only the continental giant could amass the resources to develop the atomic bomb within four years (1941-45).

In the size stakes for companies, there is no doubt of America's lead. Of the 500 largest industrial companies in 1966 shown in Fortune's list,[3] 304 were American, and 146 European. The 25

[2]US Department of Commerce, Technological Innovation, its Environment and Management, Washington, 1967.

[3]Fortune, The 500 Largest US Industrial Corporations; The 200 Largest Industrials outside the US. See also Transatlantic Investment, Atlantic Institute, Paris, 1967.

largest American companies had over twice the turnover of the 25 largest Europeans, and nearly twice the assets. In certain sectors the balance is far less uneven. Chemicals are the best case; and in some other industries, such as cars, vast size does not seem to have led to any technological predominance in either products or processes. In this case the oligopolistic structure of the American market (there are only a few firms which maximise profits and compete only in certain limited ways) may well be the reason. Research and development expenditures have been a smaller proportion of turnover, and have gone so heavily into promotional remodelling and marketing variations, that it is only when a major new change is forced on the industry, perhaps from outside (safety, the electric car) that size really tells. All the same the potential is there. And in many other relatively unexciting industries (like agricultural machinery, or photographic films), larger American size, springing from a larger market, has conferred larger financial resources for marketing and research and development. In the electronic industry five American companies each spend as much on research and development as France or West Germany alone. In aviation, the turnover of the six leading European companies (BAC, Rolls Royce, Sud-Aviation, Dassault-Bréguet, Saab and the airframe branch of Hawker Siddeley) is roughly $2,000 mn., or about the same as the annual turnover of Boeing.

When one considers that Western Europe's total income is a mere two thirds of America's and that it is still divided economically into 18 separate states, the Europeans do remarkably well. The fact remains that an industrial system born from a continental market has inevitably produced larger corporations, better able to reap the benefits of large scale than the structures of the smaller European nation states. And, because of their size, as well as their skills in large-scale marketing, these American-based giants inevitably provide the bulk of the companies with operations and subsidiaries throughout the world.

Management skills, and training in them, are a second factor in America's technological predominance. For 40 years management has been taught systematically in the United States, while in Britain men like Urwick pressing for training in management were voices crying in the wilderness. These specific skills are backed up by a system of education which provides higher education for the broad mass of the population and in particular a far larger output of qualified scientists and engineers. As Table 8 shows, at least every other young American boy or girl (and one in three Russians) can expect to get some kind of higher education. By contrast higher education in West European countries is still the privilege of a small elite (between 15 and 20 per cent). Some Europeans still like to point out that their higher education makes up for quantity by quality and certainly some European 'centres of excellence' match up to their equivalents in the United States. What Europe lacks is the broad output of managers and engineers who can apply discovery in development and production. The two exceptions outside America —Sweden, which has the highest living standards and the largest proportion of national income going into education, and Japan, with the highest growth in both education and economy—only underline the weakness of the rest of Europe.

Socialism without ownership

In the last 20 years a new advantage has been added to America's structural advantages of scale and mass education—the drive from government. In the 1939-45 war the Federal Government for the first time embarked on a massive programme of applied research, above all in the nuclear field. In 1944, in a report to President Roosevelt, Vannevar Bush[4] propounded the theme that 'basic research is the pacemaker of technological progress' and that US Government funds should be used to back research in universities and other private institutions. In both the institutions and the government a new era of partnership began, which broke sharply with the accepted tradition that government should stay out of science and business, and elevated research to the status of a national goal.

The challenge of Russian power soon gave a new and dramatic impetus to the federal role in technology, first in nuclear power, then more widely in defence, and then, from 1957, when the Sputnik shook America, in space. Between 1953 and 1966 American expenditure on R & D multiplied fourfold, or by an average of 12 per cent per year from $5·2 bn. to $22·6 bn., compared to an average economic growth of 5·3 per cent per year (4 per cent in real terms). The Federal Government's contribution, a mere $2,750 mn. in 1953, had rocketed to $14,070 mn. in 1966, or two thirds of the total. It was this drive which swung the balance of research and development from Europe to America.

Careful scrutiny takes some of the sting out of these dramatic

[4]Vannevar Bush, *Science, the Endless Frontier: A Report to the President*, US Government Printing Office, Washington, 1945.

figures. As we have seen, higher salaries and costs may mean that the real value of each dollar spent on research in Europe is higher than in America. And a larger proportion of America's spending has gone to aerospace and defence, where it has less impact on commercial performance than more earthbound research has. All the same, the dramatic growth of the US Government's spending on research and development is a fact. It has been concentrated in two sectors—aerospace and electronics—where the 'gap' between America and Europe is most pronounced.

The method by which the American state promotes research and development is remarkable. From an early stage the bulk of federal research and development spending has been carried out by grant and contract to private industry and universities. The system began in the 1939-45 war in the nuclear programme and in other military research and development. When the Atomic Energy Commission (AEC) was set up in 1948 to develop both peaceful and military applications of nuclear power, the system was made permanent. Thus nine tenths of those employed under AEC programmes work in private corporations; even key military plants like the Oakridge fuel enrichment plant are managed and operated by private firms (in this case General Electric). It is a sharp contrast with the British and French decisions to place the bulk of nuclear research, development and production in a government body. Prodded by political bodies like the two Hoover Commissions, which vigorously urged the principle that government functions be contracted to private firms whenever there was no need for the government to undertake them, the lion's share of the mounting federal development expenditure is carried out by private industry. Each of five industrial corporations now spends more than a billion dollars a year from federal taxes—more than any one of the five smallest executive departments. In aerospace the corporation least dependent on government business had only a third of sales to non-military buyers by 1960 and the Martin Corporation less than 1 per cent. In this industry development work has so eclipsed production that production workers dropped by 17 per cent between 1954 and 1959, while scientists and engineers almost doubled till there was 'roughly a one-to-one relationship between production workers and scientist-engineers'. As Don Price[5] has put it in his book *The Scientific Estate*, America has discovered 'how to socialize without assuming ownership'.

[5]Don K. Price, *The Scientific Estate*, Belknap, Harvard, 1965, especially pages 34–56.

The state did not become a main promoter of industrial research and development merely through big business pressure. After all, America's traditional private enterprise philosophy regarded government-run business as anathema. But other American traditions played a part. In the age of Thomas Jefferson the division of powers meant the splitting of legal and political authority between executive, judiciary, legislature and states. In an age when technology is a growing source of power the federal instinct encouraged congressmen to resist the concentration of this massive new bonanza in the hands of some giant central authority and to urge its distribution to firms and universities throughout the nation. After all, the practical industrial knowhow already existed in the main in industry and there was a traditional belief that private firms, spurred if possible by competition, would be more efficient spenders of public money than government bodies. A systematic version of this philosophy was propounded in a speech in 1967 by Secretary of Commerce Holloman,[6] who listed the following order of priorities if government wished to fulfil an economic purpose or obtain a product:

1 See if the market provided the product already.
2 If not, see whether the removal of obstacles to the market (obsolete laws, tariffs, restrictive practices) would do the trick.
3 If this failed, make use of government purchasing power. For instance, to promote the development of pollution-free vehicles the Federal Government is simply requiring that the 30,000 vehicles it buys in 1968 be non-polluting.
4 If purchasing power fails, place a research and development contract with private industry.
5 Only as a last resort, do the research yourself.

There have been critics of the pumping of massive new resources into private industry, including President Eisenhower, who on his retirement spoke of the danger of subservience to a new 'technological elite', which he later explained meant military and industrial power groups. Nonetheless, America's new technological explosion has been guided by something like the Holloman doctrine. The result is that while two thirds of American R & D expenditure is financed by the Federal Government, over half this is spent in private industry: a contrast with the European scene. (See Table 4.)

Public money has also been injected into research and development in the universities, mainly by four departments (Defence,

[6]Speech at OECD Conference on Technology, Paris, 1967.

Space, Atomic Energy and the National Institutes of Health). The Massachusetts Institute of Technology, Caltech, Chicago and Johns Hopkins, for instance, all administer special military or atomic energy programmes and, consequently, draw three fifths to five sixths of their budgets from government.[7] As the soldiers, in particular, have recognized that the key weapons of the future may not be familiar ones or even derivations of them, but could spring from fresh research, they and other agencies have poured growing resources into pure scientific effort, which is recognized as a national goal. Thus it was the Navy's research programme, under Emmanuel Piore, which first backed America's brilliant postwar effort in high energy physics—the purest of pure science. At MIT Project Mac, a giant experimental multiaccess computer system is being financed, without strings, by the Department of Defence.

In 1950 the purely functional distribution of funds from the four great departments was supplemented by the creation of the National Science Foundation (NSF), which some of its creators hoped would 'create a body of thought and planning which would produce a good and growing synthesis of directions and resource estimates', in other words the brain-box for a national science policy. In practice funds were swallowed up by soaring defence R & D. The NSF was weak, new, and merely one of many competing agencies with smaller funds than the giant defence agencies. As one key administrator put it: 'it found it could not make its way effectively with all the tough kids on the block'. It has, however, developed a vital supplementary role. The NSF finances a wide range of scientific research and education in universities and other institutions, concentrating on programmes of the kind not backed by the giant departments, and making use of the incentive principle that more than half the finance for a programme must be provided by the university itself. Its $480 mn. dollar budget in 1966 thus generated and guided projects worth more than a billion dollars, ranging from $50 mn. of research projects in biology and medicine to a programme of college teacher training.

New types of institution have also been set up to carry out research and thinking for government in an independent atmosphere. The Rand Corporation, set up by the Air Force to analyse defence problems, and the private Stanford Research Institute, are archetypes of the non-profit-making Think Tanks, which government has

[7]*Government Contracting for Research and Development*, Bureau of the Budget, 1962.

found it wise to use as organs for analysis of its problems outside the limitations of the bureaucratic machine. There has been an immense inventiveness in institutions to match the scientific and technological response to the real or imagined Russian challenge.

The massive spending of public funds outside government has brought a sea-change in political and economic attitudes. Industrialists, who once regarded government intervention as anathema, now work in close partnership with it. Most of them are coming to take it for granted that government must share the funding in industries where massive development expenditure is needed before an industry takes off. Liberal congressmen, for whom 'big business' was once the bogeyman, and anti-trust, perhaps, the main weapon against it, must now concentrate increasingly on questions of control—on, say, 'How can efficiency be ensured when 60 per cent of government contracts are not fixed price contracts and advertised bids are the exception rather than the rule? How can a proper balance between competition and scale be achieved? The sheer complexity of some programmes require a relationship of partnership between government and the giant executive companies. It is more like the administrative relationship between an industrial corporation and its subsidiary than the traditional relationship of buyer and seller in a market.'[8]

There is no doubt of the impact of these giant programmes on certain areas of technology. In aviation, Boeing developed the 707 commercial jet, side-by-side with a similar military tanker; both programmes benefited from each other. In communications, the combination of space programme and defence gave birth to the communications satellites which now span the world. In computers, where the first machine was working in Germany during the 1939-45 war and where workable computer systems existed on both sides of the Atlantic in the late 1940s, us military demand for the control of complex systems provided a massive impetus to the transformation from an inventor's dream to a \$4 bn. industry. Miniaturization for space purposes accelerated the development of the integrated circuit: those chips of silicon no bigger than a pinhead containing enough circuits to run a radio and which are now transforming much of the technology of the electronics industry. In such areas government provides not merely development contracts but a huge market (\$10 bn. or roughly half the us market for

[8]Don K. Price, *op. cit.*, p. 36.

electronic equipment in 1967, or more than the entire European market).

The government role in stimulating innovation and development in industry has, nonetheless, often been a delicate one. It would rarely have been adequate without the partnership of a dynamic private enterprise. In electronics almost all the blue chip companies with a spectacular recent record in world markets have a tale to tell of this blend of entrepreneurial skill and energy with government support. The original germanium transistor, parent of the electronics revolution of the last 15 years, was developed in the private Bell Laboratories, a spin-off from government work. Texas Instruments, the medium-sized firm which seized on Bell's discovery of the transistor in 1952, developed it and rocketed upward from this launching pad to become the world's largest manufacturer of electronic components. Originally a small instrument firm dependent on government and the oil industry, it was rejuvenated by four ex-Navy engineers. When the germanium transistor appeared, they took a bold commercial risk and backed the first transistorized radio in the United States, challenging the giants GE and RCA. They soon went on to capture an important part of the government avionics market. Since then formidable management techniques have kept Texas Instruments (TI) on its expansionary course. The development of integrated circuits was once more helped by development contracts; so was their application to radar. Today a timely defence contract for nearly $2 bn. is financing the development of a 'fourth generation' computer, in which tight-packed circuits will compress two million bits of logic into a computer little larger than a fist. IBM's world predominance in computers stems in part from its command of the punch-card market, but it too was helped forward at a critical stage by government contracts for the 600 computer.

In some cases, like Boeing's jet tanker, the company conceived a key product, sold it to the government for development, and later exploited it commercially. In others, like nuclear power, a masterful federal administrator (in this case Admiral Rickover) drove the programme, though it was executed by private enterprise (Westinghouse and later General Electric), and eventually produced products (light water reactors) which turned up trumps in the commercial market.

The nuclear example, indeed, deserves further consideration: why has America been so successful in advancing from a relatively laggard position to an apparent commercial lead?

c

The American pressurized water reactors were developed, essentially, for the submarine programme which required relatively small reactors. Of the $2 bn. spent by the Atomic Energy Commission on water reactors by 1967, the great bulk has been spent in the Navy programme, most of it in industry, but some of it 'in house'.

The major companies in the power business, Westinghouse and General Electric, were already interested in nuclear power and had been given the chance to share in nuclear work at Oakridge. But all also recognized that since nuclear power was a long-range strategic investment, not yet economic, it needed government support. When the Navy programme got under way, Westinghouse, in particular, saw its chance. Initially, the national laboratories were supposed to carry out the R & D, and Westinghouse the manufacture. But the company became increasingly involved in the development work. Its Atomic Equipment Divison assumed total responsibility for production of components: pumps, turbines, steam generators, control drive mechanisms, and instruments; work which the Navy would have been unable to perform. The Westinghouse work on the Navy programme was done, essentially, by good engineers brought in from other departments. The Navy, under Rickover, also had a first class team, but their task, apart from some initial research, was, essentially, to monitor, organize, make sure time-scales were met, impose rigorous quality standards and enforce the Admiral's leather-necked contracts.

Halfway through the highly successful five-year programme which launched the *Nautilus* on its voyage round the earth under the sea, Westinghouse began to appreciate the commercial possibilities of their experience. Strong backing from the Congressional Committee on Atomic Energy led to the Shippingport demonstration power plant, financed by the Federal Government, but built by Westinghouse. This awoke the interest of public utilities, which began to work with Westinghouse on plant design. In 1955 Westinghouse set up its own commercial department and began to carry a share of the risk itself. Another $5 mn. R & D grant plus free fuel helped it on its way. Later, a few key men were to come over from the Navy (General Electric's nuclear sales manager was the chief engineer on the *Nautilus*).

The transfers of men from the Navy itself have not been large. Since the mid-1950s, a growing proportion of development funds has come from the company itself. At last, in 1963, the commercial market began to break open. The two large companies were able at this crucial stage to use their massive financial strength to quote prices which would have been hopelessly unprofitable if only a few plants had been ordered. The picture that emerges is of partnership in which both partners were indispensable. Westinghouse and General Electric would not be where they are without the experience and the massive government finance funded in the Navy programme. But neither the Navy programme nor the present US nuclear power sales drive would have been successful if the management, engineering, sales and financial capabilities of these companies had not been to hand. The American Government's policy of fostering technological advance in industry is deliberate and clear. In fast-breeder reactors, for instance, the Atomic Energy Commission takes the clear-cut view that its task is to nurture an outside industrial capability. It does this by placing contracts and imposing stringent disciplinary conditions on the contractors, in terms of both technical requirement and competition in price. In each field it deliberately seeks to bring into existence three or four competitors.

Outside nuclear power, electronics and aviation, the stimulus of the US Government has been far smaller. In the chemical industry, the Federal Government paid for only 18 per cent of research and development expenditure in 1964, and in all other industries the proportion is far smaller. All the same, government spending has had some effect elsewhere. The demand for advanced metals for the space and aircraft industries has advanced the whole science of metallurgy, and played a part in giving the US steel industry—and even the gigantic, but long backward US Steel Corporation—a new lease of life. Advances in physics and the new computer technology have helped accelerate some branches of chemical research and molecular biology.

A whole new range of management techniques—operations research, systems analysis, statistical quality control and so on—of crucial importance in the management of very large projects (like the Polaris programme) have also been developed in defence and space programmes, and increasingly applied elsewhere. The need for high performance, reliability, and speed in development have called for and stimulated the development of new management skills.

The skills are not always those required in the commercial market (where cost may matter more). Companies skilled at probing the moon have yet to show that they can efficiently transfer their skills to more mundane problems, like that of organizing rapid and comfortable commuting between Brooklyn and Manhattan. The 'technological gap' within America, between the new, esoteric, space-age industries and the humdrum suppliers of many consumer needs, from railways to leather goods, remains immense. All the same, if US Government spending has had uneven effects, they have still been big. Work on the frontiers of technology and management has sharpened the edge of the American economy.

Crucial to the dissemination of knowledge in Federal Government programmes has been its open patent policy. The Atomic Energy Commission, after an early policy of secrecy, can now require publication of all work done under contract for the AEC. The National Aeronautics and Space Administration (NASA) has a similar arrangement. Controversy comes from those who think that these departments have published, not too little information, but too much. Non-exclusive licences, runs the argument, have discouraged industry from investing in the development of defence or space patents,[10] so that only 10-15 per cent of them have been taken up by industry. The figures are interesting evidence of the limits of 'fall-out', but they have not deterred the Space Administration from pursuing an essentially liberal policy. One interesting modification has been made; where a NASA patent is not taken up within two years a three-year exclusive licence can be given to encourage a firm to develop the discovery, and removed again if it does not succeed. NASA is also making more systematic efforts to disseminate its technology by identifying technology that may have a civilian application, and setting up a statistical storehouse of, for instance, engineering characteristics of new metals. Regional dissemination centres communicate the knowledge, free, to industrial concerns that want it.

In defence the system is only marginally less liberal. Companies are given patents on their developments under contract, with government reserving the right to use them or pass them on. The Defence Department as yet has no rights to 'march in' to companies to ensure that it gets back all the information, but it is trying to get these. Security, of course, also places a 'classified' barrier round much defence information. However, inside the barrier—between defence companies, universities and government—there is great freedom of discussion and movement of ideas. In defence and space, in short, there is something like a government encouraged open

[10]Peter Berger, Utilization or Dispensation—Suggestions for the Government's Patent Procurement Programme, *Journal of the Patent Office Society*, Vol. XLVIII, No. 7, July 1966.

market for information, a sharp contrast to the secrecy surrounding much commercially financed research.

Perhaps the most decisive difference between us and European practice is the allocation of 5 per cent of all government contracts to cover company overheads and 'independent research'. Companies are legitimately able to use federal resources to build laboratories and improve their research and development effort as a whole. The Bell Laboratories' development of the germanium transistor was a classic example of this process. The idea germinated in a team that had been involved in radar research and which was working full-time for the government. Bell took the two inventors off the government work and set them working on the sideline—just the kind of use for which these funds are meant.

Where does this generous attitude to research and development come from? Why, it may be asked, are there no abominable no-men in the us Government machine? One explanation is political pressures. The congressional urge to respond to Russia's technological challenge, or even to research into health, encouraged by the powerful American Medical Association and the drug companies, is far greater, it seems, than the urge to campaign against poverty or provide public health insurance. Thus President Eisenhower, who had started by cutting down research and development expenditure with the aim of balancing the budget, ended by quadrupling it.[11] During his eight years in office Congress multiplied appropriations for the National Institutes of Health more than ninefold, giving him each year more than he had recommended. The separate functional congressional committees—for Atomic Energy, for Space, etc.—have often combined a valuable supervising function with lobbying for the interest of the sector concerned, with the natural proviso that key members get a healthy slice of development contracts, or a large government establishment in their constituencies.

More interesting perhaps, and more important, as a reason for the Federal Government's wider role in research and development, is the high place scientists have in the government machine. In the nineteenth century, while Britain was installing the arts trained 'administrative class' civil servant in the commanding heights of its bureaucracy, the United States was developing a public service with no comparable permanent elite and in which the most permanent posts tended to be technical in character: the Coast and Geodetic Survey; the Public Health Service. The best paid grades in the us

[11]Don K. Price, *op. cit.*, p. 11.

civil service today are the 'supergrades' created above the normal administrative grades to attract top scientific and engineering talent from industry. It is quite a contrast with the British situation, where a first class technical consultant at a public enquiry may be paid one sixth as much as the QC on the same bench. A study in 1958 showed that 26 of the top 63 bureau chiefs in Federal Government had a scientific or technical training; only 17 were lawyers and economists; the remainder came from miscellaneous business or administrative careers.

There is remarkable mobility between the key posts in government, industry and the universities, especially at the top level. Thus Herbert Holloman, after a period as a leading businessman, became Secretary for Commerce before moving on to the presidency of a university. Richard Blumenthal, one of America's two key negotiators in the Kennedy round, reversed this order of experience: from university to Geneva, and on to a key industrial post. This mobility within the new elite goes together with the mobility of ideas: the professor running a consulting firm, serving industry and government; or the phone calls between friends in all three estates to discuss a new development. A government in which scientists and engineers have top jobs is far more likely to be creative and alert to new scientific ideas than one in which scientists are underpaid boffins and the top decision-makers are arts trained arbiters between different scientific groups.

Mobility of people and ideas has conspired to produce such unique social institutions as Route 128 in Boston, where some 200 new advanced technology companies have been created by the movement of scientists and engineers out of the Massachusetts Institute of Technology. At MIT, teaching staff are not merely encouraged to work in industry. Ownership of a small company has become a veritable academic status symbol. These companies thrive on both the government and commercial markets, drawing bright people and ideas from that formidable matrix of talent, MIT. According to the Department of Commerce study on innovation, the total net *personal* worth of a dozen of these new entrepreneurs is some $500 mn. Similar industrial firms have been spawned by Caltech in Palo Alto and the great space centres in Texas.

The Role of the Dynamic Small Firm

The initially small, but fast growing advanced technology firm is, indeed, as crucial to the US 'miracle' as the established giant. Many studies have shown that a disproportionately large share of key inventions have started with independent inventors or small companies:[12] power-steering, the ballpoint pen, penicillin, Xerox reproduction, and the jet engine are a few examples. While large size is important for large-scale production and marketing or in expensive development processes, it can also be slow moving, negative in its attitude and planning systems, and cramping to the creative mind. The small firm may suffer from lack of finance and management skills. But the original innovator has a free hand and the chance to stake all on success. It is not surprising that giant American companies (in chemicals and glass for instance) are now setting up venture-capital subsidiaries to finance small and thrusting innovative firms; or that there are many cases of inventive engineers learning a business in large companies and then breaking out to start up on their own.

The special character of these small innovative companies is shown by their uneven distribution on the American map. Boston and Palo Alto have spawned them but Chicago and Philadelphia have not. Evidently, a very special kind of graduate institution as well as exceptionally helpful suppliers of venture capital are needed to give birth to them. Intangibles, like the social climate of a place and the quality of its leaders, may be crucial. In Britain, after all, taxation of capital gains and hence of venture capital was for many years more favourable than in the United States. There are large numbers of small firms run by graduates in instruments and electronics. But most stay small. There is not the same market, or, it seems, the same ambition to grow as in the United States. Europe has its own dramatic exceptions in the form of once small high-technology growth firms such as Grundig and Solartron. But it has tended to be more successful in consumer goods than in products for government and industrial application. Once more the size of the market tells.

All this is not to say that the large company has no role, though sometimes American apologists tend to give this impression. If the small firm plays a key role in invention, the large is essential for mass marketing and production, for development in industries where plant is expensive, and for fast development on a broad front. Sometimes the transfer of an innovation from small to large firms takes place by imitation and competition; sometimes by takeover; some-

[12]See, for instance, J. Jewkes, S. Dawyers, and R. Stillerman, *The Sources of Invention*, London, St Martin's Press, 1958.

times it takes quite a time. In computers, a classic example, more than one small group of boffins (the Electronics Research Associates, or ERA Group, for instance) developed an effective product in the late 1940s, with the help of the Defence Department, but could not at first sell the product in the commercial world. IBM, for instance, which commissioned the 650 computer from the ERA Group in 1948-49, put it on the shelf for the next five years. In 1952-53, the Group was taken over by Univac, which, by installing a computer in the Metropolitan Life Insurance Company instead of a floorful of punch cards, at last succeeded in awakening IBM. The original ERA boffins, however, were increasingly frustrated by Univac's 'big firm' inertia, and in 1957 ten of them broke away, borrowed $600,000 from local investors in Minnesota, and founded the successful Control Data Corporation (CDC). It now has a turnover of $200 mn. and markets the most successful large computer in the world.

The strength of America's advanced technology industries lies in the remarkable dialectic between large and small companies, in a ring where the anti-trust ringmaster is always promoting competition, and where there is a massive public as well as private market for advanced ideas. It is a strength that lies in the whole process of innovation, in the translation of new ideas into marketable products. The state has provided much of the market; society with its management methods and attitudes, the innovation skills.

The Machinery of Choice

This remarkable new industrial order appears to have been devised unconsciously. Certainly there is nothing in Washington which can be described as a preconceived 'science policy'. Agencies have emerged pragmatically, starting with the Coastal Survey and the Geodetic Survey in the nineteenth century, and moving on to The Space Administration (NASA), and the National Institutes of Health in the mid-twentieth century. Today, with awareness of the potentialities of the oceans and of the problems of mass transport, a commission and council on oceanography and a Department of Transportation have emerged. The promotion of scientific research and development has been organized functionally, with each agency doing the research and development necessary to fulfil its own goals, and with a scientist in the post of number two. If the strength of America is its practical men, its skill in carrying out specific tasks, its weakness perhaps lies in the absence of a philosophy for policy. It has been called a reservoir of undirected power.

The shift from development of specific technologies to support of pure science as well was as pragmatic as the choice of functional fields for action. A climate of opinion was set by specific actions such as the report of Vannevar Bush[13] to President Roosevelt. But implementation was initially a matter for individual agencies: first the imaginative Navy Department, then the Institutes of Health, NASA, and so on. Even when the National Science Foundation was created, it was not able to develop a national science policy. One among many agencies, it was not in a position to impose its will on the other great feudalities. The Foundation contented itself with publishing statistics and information, pushing techniques of research management, and developing its own programmes to fill the gaps left by the Big Four. The NSF is a balancing wheel in an engine driven by defence and space.

In 1962, however, President Kennedy set up the Office of Science and Technology (OST), as part of the President's Executive Office; it was headed by a Special Assistant to the President whose status enabled him to report to Congress. For the first time a key executive figure (like the Secretary of Defence, or the head of the Bureau of the Budget) could report to Congress on science policy as a whole. The Special Assistant was also made chairman of the National Council of Scientific Advisers, a body of eminent independent scientists who have counselled the President (usually through sub-committees) on issues as diverse as nuclear test detection and the control and use of pesticides. The Special Assistant is also chairman of the interdepartmental Council for Research and Development, where the heads of the agencies meet. This body, like many other similar interdepartmental committees, has not been a driving force. But an informal 'Saturday morning meeting' of key men is a real generator of new directions and ideas. If the NSF may be called a mere balancing wheel, the OST is the steering wheel.

The OST brings in eminent outsiders to help to look at programmes that are not functioning well, or at their organization, and promotes action. The first Special Assistant to the President for Science and Technology, for instance, participated in studies that initiated a major reorganization of military research and development and created the post of Director of Defence Research and Engineering. One panel examined, on a sampling basis, the quality of 17,000 research grants of the booming National Institutes of Health. It raised important questions on the balance between pure and applied

13Vannevar Bush, *op. cit.*

research. When research is spattered across a number of agencies, the OST pulls the work together. In oceanography, for instance, an inter-agency committee developed a unified programme covering some 20 agencies, eliminating duplication and guiding the work towards planned goals; a vital preparation for the new Oceanography Agency which has now been set up. The OST has also developed a central service for the road research laboratories of the different states. Most important of all, perhaps, together with the President's Science Advisory Committee, it has exercised leadership in the creation of new programmes as new needs have emerged.

Yet even the OST does not pursue a science policy based on some careful central calculus. Cost-benefit analysis, and the new technique of planned programming and budgeting, are increasingly applied in the execution of programmes and the pursuit of agreed goals, and the OST and Bureau of the Budget make sure that they are used in the agencies where possible. But when it comes to making choices between programmes and value judgements on the pursuit of various goals, those involved recognize that these techniques lose value. In the words of Theodore Sorensen, one of President Kennedy's new frontiersmen: 'White House decision-making is not a science but an art. It requires not calculation, but judgement. There is no unit of measure which can weigh the substantive consequences of a decision against the political consequences, or judge the precise portions of public opinion and Congressional pressure, or balance domestic against foreign, short-range against long-range, or private against public considerations.'[14] Or as David Beckler of the OST put it, 'We do not have a Federal research and development budget', or 'a master plan for research and development, nor is there a systematic valuation of alternative goals in a strategic planning sense.'[15] The OST provides the President with the best technical advice, on which the broad political and economic judgements about public spending on research and development are made. The OST, in short, is a loose, but on occasion powerful, coordinating force. Staffed by men of high quality it supports the President in injecting into America's decentralized federal science and technology policies an element of leadership.

This federal structure is very different from the technological monolith which many Europeans envisage as they look fearfully

[14]Theodore Sorensen, Columbia University lecture, Columbia.

[15]David Beckler, Strategic Federal Decision-Making on R & D, paper presented at National Conference on Administration of Research, 1965.

across the sea. Indeed, the problems of managing it have much in common with the problems of developing common policies for Europe. In it, regional pressures, the power of different agencies, and of different congressional committees and members, all play a part. Take for instance the long-delayed decision as to whether and where the United States should build a 200 Giga Electron Volt (GEV) accelerator for experiments in high energy physics; an incredibly expensive tool for pure research into the nature of the elementary particles which compose the universe. The decision, as we shall see in Chapter 7, is one of interest to Europe, for Europe, in turn, has still to take a decision on whether it is to embark on the construction of an even larger accelerator of 300 GEV.

The decision to build the 200 GEV accelerator first began to emerge in 1963, when a panel under Professor Ramsey rejected the view that there should be some six to eight smaller units comparable to the existing Brookhaven 33 GEV accelerator. Instead, it said, the money should be spent, over the next 20 years, on building one or more accelerators at high energy. A proposal for a 100 GEV accelerator in California was rejected on the grounds that the Russians were already constructing just such an accelerator at Serphukov.

Proposals for a world effort (including Europe and Russia) to construct a 1,000 GEV accelerator were, it was felt, premature. A suggestion for a much smaller high intensity accelerator, put forward by the Midwest Universities Research Association (MURA), was left aside. The proposal to build the larger 200 GEV accelerator seemed a logical sequel to the experience at Brookhaven with a smaller machine. It was given added impetus when President Johnson specifically rejected the MURA accelerator, on the grounds that a 200 GEV accelerator would soak up most of the funds.

Design money for a 200 GEV accelerator was then granted by the Atomic Energy Commission and in 1965 the subcommittee on research, development and radiation of the Joint Congressional Committee on Atomic Energy held hearings which illuminated the choice to be made and confirmed the decision to go for a 200 GEV accelerator. One of the interesting facts thrown up by the hearings was that the price of the machine might vary between $200 mn. and $400 mn., depending on what equipment was included in the bill. Nor could Congress adjudicate on the fiercely contested question of where the accelerator was to be built, a question which aroused as much feeling and pressure as the comparable decision on a European installation, which we shall discuss in Chapter 7.

So the National Academy of Sciences was brought in to make a technical judgement on the site, and came up with six potential contestants, leaving it to the OST to make the final choice.

In 1966 the money was brought into the budget of the Atomic Energy Commission. If the demands of the Vietnam war do not raise new difficulties, the odds are that the 200 GEV accelerator will be built, helping to raise expenditure on high energy physics from some $160 mn. per year to perhaps $350 bn. per year in 1975. Throughout the argument, the executive showed caution, and was anxious not to take on excessive commitments. But the AEC mounted a systematic and well argued case for the 200 GEV machine, and in the last analysis Congress seemed determined that in high energy physics, America must stay in front.[16]

A second development which throws revealing light on the Jeffersonian battlefield between the different powers of American government was the emergence of a national oceanography programme in the early 1960s, beautifully described in Don Price's book. Oceanography, he tells us, was the first large-scale federal scientific programme; it began in 1807 when Thomas Jefferson founded the Coast Survey and employed a Swiss scientist, Ferdinand Hassler, to bring scientific instruments from Europe and begin to chart the seas round America. By March 1961, 24 federal bureaux, ranging from the Navy to the Public Health Service, plus many small state agencies concerned about pollution, had some sort of programme. But for many years their claim on funds was weak. There was no lead agency to push the interests of oceanography. There was little university pressure, because there were no strong university centres; it was not a major discipline. In 1956, however, pressure began to build up for a bigger and more imaginative effort, coordinated at national level. An unofficial group of government marine scientists worked up the idea, and then gingered five of the leading agencies to commission the Academy of Sciences to set up a committee to prepare a programme. 'This committee engaged the interest of a widening circle of leading scientists, and did its job with such despatch and energy that by the time President Kennedy presented an administration programme in March 1961, the Academy's programme had been under discussion by Congressional committees for almost two years.'[17]

[16]David Robinson, 'Problems of Resource allocation in High Energy Physics', unpublished paper, Office of Science and Technology, Washington, 1965.

[17]Don K. Price, *op. cit.*, p. 209.

At first the drive in government came mainly from the Navy, which was confronting difficult technical problems in anti-submarine warfare. When the OST first picked up the subject, its aim was, essentially, to bring order into chaos, find out who was doing what, and make informed judgements on the options over the next ten years.

Soon, however, pressures grew to increase the programme. The scientists had begun to awaken informed opinion to the biological interest of research beneath the oceans, the untapped mineral resources, the vast potential of food from the seas. Congressmen from the maritime states were pressing for a larger national programme. In March 1961 President Kennedy responded by proposing an enlarged oceanography programme in his first budget.

A prolonged bout of manoeuvre between executive and legislative then began. Early in 1961 Congress passed a bill setting up a new National Oceanographic Council headed by the heads of six operating agencies, which was to report annually to Congress with an annual programme of appropriations. In a series of actions and shifts of position on both sides the executive fought the establishment of a new body, in a form which would have had the effect of shifting the balance of control towards the Congress. In 1962 President Kennedy vetoed the Oceanography Act. By 1966 the space industries, concerned at the prospect of two successive years of lower space expenditure, were looking about for new fields to apply their advanced technology and a new source of federal contracts. At last, in 1966, both a National Council on Marine Resources and Engineering Development containing five cabinet members, and an independent advisory commission, were set up, responsible to the President, who was required to present to Congress a national programme with annual reports and proposals for expenditure and action. The debate on oceanography still goes on, as well as the battle for control and guidance of the expanding programme.

New Directions

The programme of research in and round the oceans illustrates not only America's federal structure, but the new directions American policy is beginning to take. While Europe is worrying about the effects of the great American space and defence programmes begun in the 1950s, America is becoming fascinated by new areas of endeavour, which may have an equally large impact ten years hence. Expenditure in oceanography, under $100 mn. in 1959, was budgeted to rise to $462 mn. by 1968. A first programme includes a pilot programme to produce enough cheap protein to feed a million people in a selected developing country; a programme of mineral exploration; a study of pollution in the Chesapeake Bay which is blackened by industrial effluent; promotion of the technology of work at great ocean depths; and sea grants to universities to promote training and research.

For the future there is vast potential. Harnessed by control of ocean currents, and systematic farming, the sea could provide man with perhaps ten times more food than the land does today. Its mineral resources, unknown and untapped, seem to be boundless. Skilled manipulation might one day adjust the climate and thus make more habitable barren regions of the globe. No one knows the life of many of the creatures who live in the deepest parts of the oceans. The depths are less explored than outer space itself. By nature the oceans are international, encouraging cooperation. The exploration and wise exploitation of the oceans offers a challenge to science and technology which could, one day, yield huge returns. But like space, it is a challenge which requires both massive government spending in the early stages, and industrial engineering skills; a classic opportunity for America's new-style partnership between state and private enterprise.

As America experiences the backlash of random technological advance—the congested city streets, the silent spring, the seashore and river polluted with industrial and agricultural chemicals and oil—a consensus of opinion and growing political pressure have emerged for systematic federal programmes of research and development to defeat them. Air travellers, used to circling for hours in the congested air above New York's airports, will not be surprised to hear that in the north-east corner of the United States the airlanes and the airfields are now so jammed to capacity that they have small prospect of carrying the heavier traffic expected.

The railways have changed little since 1900. So the new Department of Transportation has commissioned a broad study of the north-east corridor (from Washington to New York to Boston) to find out the implications of different types of new ground transport system: more highways, with their effects on the vehicle population; spinal rail or other fast systems, which might concentrate industry along the communications cord. The study is also to work out the implications of different methods of financing and organizing:

private enterprise, the Federal Government, consortia of states, or some or all of these together.

Work on new types of hardware is also to go forward: commercial tests with fast electric trains between Washington and New York, and gas turbine trains, powered with aero-engines, from New York to Boston, to test the market for fast ground transport; research and development on conventional railway problems like smoother suspension at higher speeds, studies on electric contact problems, and even contracts with American Telephone and Telegraph (AT & T) to improve train telephones. Finally, new high speed systems are to be developed: the aircushion train, an air-gulping tube vehicle developed by the head of the Aeronautical Engineering Institution, New York; and the linear electric motor. As with space and defence, the development work will be done in industry (GM, Westinghouse, Budd, AT & T, United Aircraft), and the Federal Government will buy ideas from France (the aircushion train) and Britain (the linear electric motor) if it can.

At the end of three years $35 mn. will have been spent. The entire programme might cost $100-$200 mn. The hope is that development will then take off into private industry.

The Department of Housing and Urban Development has also placed $45 mn. of contracts for experimental transit systems in the cities, including computer controlled trains, aircushion vehicles, lifting vehicles by helicopter, and so on. These projects fit into a broad research programme designed to investigate the possible future shape of the city, the impact of different patterns and plans. The research serves the 'model cities' programme, under which a billion dollars of Federal Government money is to be pumped into redevelopment programmes in America's slum areas.

These new directions in America's research and development policy have not been followed far. And, in many cases, they do not involve investment of massive government funds. Air pollution from vehicles, for instance, is being fought by stringent regulation and by the skilful use of government purchasing. Many other pollution problems, from pesticides to noise, are being dealt with by regulation and incentives of this kind.

But when and if the Vietnam war comes to an end, the possibility opens up for a far wider application of technology to deal with the problems of America's backyard. Inside the administration thought is already being given to the great opportunities that will emerge, when some of the $26 bn. annual 'Vietnam costs' become available for other more constructive tasks. What new goals can be given priority? Improving the cities and the quality of life? Helping the poor through a negative income tax? More higher education? More space research? Or more deliberate investment in civilian technological innovation to promote full employment and growth? Some key administrators believe that the end of the Vietnam war could present the greatest single ' opportunity for national investment planning; the question is whether America's remarkable federal machinery of government, though good, is good enough to match the power behind it.

America's new directions should give Europe further food for thought, pointing as they do to whole new areas of technological advance with far more relevance to human needs than moon probes. The Vietnam war, draining American resources, inhibits these developments and in a sense gives Europe the chance to take the lead. But if Europe sleeps, or concentrates on emulating the American technologies of the last decade, America's new-style 'socialism without ownership' may generate new 'technological gaps', and advances of greater practical significance than those of today.

Morals for Europe

What, then, is the significance for Europe of America's technological lead in certain fields, and of the role of the Federal Government in promoting it?

The American Government's huge expenditure on research and development has plainly had the Keynesian effect of creating jobs and economic expansion, though whether the space programme has been more of a stimulus to the creation of wealth than if the government had financed the digging of holes in the ground is arguable. After all a billion-dollar hole digging programme would have a dramatic 'fall-out' in the construction industries; if holes were being dug in competition with the Russians, and at top speed, materials research, the control and management of large projects, and knowledge of physics and the nature of matter and the earth, would no doubt be rapidly advanced.

But even all this sounds very different from Maynard Keynes's original notion of a bunch of men digging with spades. What distinguishes American support for advanced technology is the pursuit of difficult goals, under competitive conditions, at high speed, and in an economy which already possesses a huge highly skilled labour force and powerful industrial firms. The effect has been a tremendous devotion of energy and skill to improving methods and products. In short, this Keynesian expenditure has increased not only production but productivity as well.

Powerful arguments can be advanced to prove that, in sheer economic terms, more effective ways could have been found of increasing productivity. Half of America's scientists and engineers are engaged in defence and space work. They might well have been more productive in other industries, or if a larger proportion of engineers were employed on production instead of on R & D. Socially, while the space effort laps up talent, the City of New York cannot find or pay competent administrators to administer the poverty programme. The growing desire of young Americans to work in social fields instead of in technology is good news.

Yet, though alternative policies might have achieved more, or other things, America's technological explosion has had its effect —and notably on Europe.

Trade, international investment, growth, have all been affected. In the fields where the American Government has provided a massive stimulus, a series of 'technological gaps' do exist. The moral for Europe is not that they should all necessarily be closed, duplicating the efforts America has made. It is that systematic efforts by European governments to promote research and development are needed, and that these must be concentrated on areas which promise to yield the right balance of scientific, economic and political returns. Europe, indeed, has an immense opportunity, not to emulate America's goals, but to make use of similar tools to pursue objectives of its own. Europe is a far more crowded society which cannot afford to squander natural resources, or the heritage of its natural and man-made environment, as America has done. Europeans are perhaps more individualist and less intellectually conformist too. They may wish, justly, to give more attention to making technology serve good living than to the conquest of the stars.

In education and management training there are also many morals. For Europe needs more of both, and fast. It needs systematically to break down the barriers between academic subjects, between industry, universities and government.

Europe needs also to break down the barriers between nations. For there is, above all, a general moral concerning scale. Obviously, if European companies are to enjoy the benefit of a continental market and grow, naturally, to continental scale, the Common Market must be completed rapidly and joined by Britain and other

D

countries. While the Common Market is already a customs union, a plethora of barriers inherited from the past—separate capital markets, different standards, taxes, patents, and an abiding nationalism—still inhibit the formation of a European industrial structure and a fully single market. The sooner these are harmonized, permitting European companies to operate freely throughout Europe, as American companies do in the United States, the quicker European companies will emerge which can compete with IBM, Westinghouse and Ford. Indeed, if European companies do not take shape simultaneously with the emergence of the Common Market, the customs union will simply be an irretrievable gift to the giant American companies which are already operating in Europe on a continental scale.

The emergence of an enlarged common market in the private sector, however, will not pool the resources of Europe in that whole vast area where the American state plays its new dynamic part. The European public market absorbs a third of national income, as much as in America; but nothing whatever has been done as yet to unify it. As for research and development, West European states spend only a quarter as much as America, and a smaller proportion of national income. Yet their efforts are still divided between 18 different policies and administrations. The same applies to the universities. There is some movement between European countries; but far less than within America, and probably less than between individual European countries and the United States. While modern communications have diminished physical distances, different languages, rules and regulations, and academic career structures impose bigger barriers to movement between European universities than in mediaeval times.

As one leading European research director has put it: If America wishes to close the 'technological gap' all it needs to do is erect 51 different sets of customs barriers, laws, tax systems, space and defence programmes, science policies and public buying arrangements; the gap will be gone in a year.

This book sets out to explore a more constructive solution: the pooling of Europe's resources in science and advanced technology, especially in those expensive fields where the state must play a major role. But first, let us look more closely at the organization of science and technology in the major European countries, and at some of the pressures which deter them, increasingly, from trying to go it alone.

PART TWO

THE LIMITS OF THE NATION STATE

CHAPTER 3

BRITAIN LEARNS THE HARD WAY

Britain has far the largest research and development effort of any country in Western Europe; 2·3 per cent of its national income compared with 1·4 per cent by West Germany, and 1·6 per cent by France in 1963-64. Its total research and development expenditure was valued at some $2·2 bn. in 1963-64, compared with $3·5 bn. in the Common Market as a whole. But even Britain's significant effort was a mere tenth of America's in 1963-64, in terms of money, and about one eighth of America's in terms of qualified men.

Over half Britain's spending (54 per cent) came from the government in 1964-65, less than in America and France (64 per cent) but more than in most other European countries. Above all, the state provides a major share of Britain's effort in aviation, electronics and nuclear power.

Defence—the Motor

Britain's strength in these advanced fields is due, in the main, to massive defence expenditure, and a continuous effort in advanced technology ever since the last war. In the late 1940's, with Germany shattered, America disarmed, and Russia still struggling to recover, Britain may for a short period have had the strongest military production system of any of the powers. Certainly, for a few years after the war, it was the largest exporter of military equipment and aircraft.[1]

For much of the next 20 years she continued to try to maintain the all-round military capability of a mini-superpower; a national

[1]C. J. E. Harlow, *The European Armaments Base*, Institute of Strategic Studies, London, 1967, provides much material on which the next three pages are based.

nuclear armoury and national production of every form of military aircraft, tanks, ships and ordnance. By 1967, despite diminished ambitions, Britain's defence expenditure was still the largest in Western Europe (with a projected ceiling of $5,600 mn.). About $700 mn. of its research and development effort of $2·1 bn. was concerned with defence.

In 1964, Chris Harlow estimates, Britain's research and development spending in defence industries broke down roughly as follows. The figures show the major impetus given to aircraft, engines and electronics by defence:

TABLE A

United Kingdom: Spending on Defence R & D

	$ million	% of all R & D in the industry
Aircraft and aero-engines	200–300 }	80–90
Missiles	40–70 }	
Nuclear	15–40	10–20
Electronics	110–130	60–70
Ships	30–50	90–95
Vehicles	30–40	20–40
Ordnance	15–30	100

(*Note*: $ figures throughout this chapter are converted at $2·8 to the pound)

Though the distribution of this spending between the sectors of industry was similar to the United States, there was a difference in the type of organization which carried the work out. In the United States, as we have seen, a large proportion of federal research and development expenditure in aviation and electronics has been spent in private industry (58 per cent of total government research and development spending). In Britain, a rather larger proportion of government-backed work was in government research establishments and less in industry (49 per cent). Of the Ministry of Aviation's expenditure, about $300 mn. is spent in the aircraft industry, and another $85 mn. in the electronics industry on defence work. But a further $130-$200 mn. is spent in government establishments like the Royal Radar Establishment at Farnborough, which maintain large and expensive equipment, such as wind tunnels, and large staffs. Work in these official enterprises does not 'spill' out into commercial activity as easily as does comparable research done in American private companies.

With one notable exception, no major government defence establishment is managed by a private enterprise company, as are so many in America. The exception is the Spadeadam missile development establishment, where Britain's Blue Streak intermediate-range ballistic missile was developed in the late 1950s. Later, this became the first stage launcher for ELDO's rocket. The company which manages Spadeadam is Rolls Royce; the British company with the most successful, continuous record in advanced technology. The exception proves an important point. The concentration of British advanced technology in government establishments owes something to the fact that, when the effort began 25 years ago, it was thought that there were few British industrial companies with a management capable of rapidly taking on these tasks. Clearly, if the work remains inside government establishments, it does not help industry to grow stronger.

This difference of emphasis between Britain and America does not mean that the defence effort has not stimulated British industry. Britain's aircraft industry, employing a quarter of a million people, is easily the largest in Europe; so is its electronic industry, whose turnover grew from $560 mn. to $1,120 mn. between 1955 and 1964. Defence accounted for 25 per cent of the turnover in electronics in 1955 and 20 per cent in 1964. But there was no space programme to provide a stimulus, as in America, no deliberate attempt to foster industrial competence; and no research funds, like America's 5 per cent on every research contract, which a company could use, openly and freely, for whatever research it chose.

The Problem of Scale

Britain's ambitious defence programme also ran, in the late 1950s, into a disastrous conflict between ambitious ends and limited means. Between 1955 and 1964, Britain made efforts to develop nuclear weapons and ballistic missiles to deliver them; a low-level strike supersonic bomber; Mach 2 interceptor aircraft; strike and interceptor aircraft for fleets in the Mediterranean, Alantic and Far East; and an increasingly complex range of missiles and electronic equipment for use by all three services. If all these programmes had been carried out in the early 60s, together with other conventional programmes, they could have absorbed double the R & D funds (some $700 mn. annually) actually available.

The result was a whole series of cancellations, and opportunist shifts in policy, as government after government struggled vainly to spread the funds available, without radically cutting back the ambitions they were designed to serve. Blue Streak, the British ballistic missile, was cancelled in 1961, when the massive costs of launching sites and facilities became apparent. It was replaced by the American Thor missile and then by Polaris. Blue Water, a surface tactical nuclear missile, was also cancelled, as were six different interceptor developments, five transport aircraft, and a number of engine programmes. In aviation, not one of the new developments begun in 1950-55 reached service. A final wave of cancellations in 1965 knocked out the TSR2, HS681 short take-off transport and the P1154 vertical take-off fighter.

All this provides a classic illustration of the inability of a medium-sized European power to keep in the front rank with a full range of weapons. Soaring development costs are far beyond the means of a single European country. And the tiny market, say for modern military aircraft, makes production costs exorbitantly high. Of course, if British governments had been more selective and more consistent in their policies, a limited number of successful projects might have emerged. A timely willingness to produce under licence, too, would have avoided the extremity of having to buy American planes. But the fact remains that Britain is a supreme illustration of the limitations, in the most advanced defence technology, which scale imposes on the European nation state. It still has the greatest technological potential in Europe in advanced defence industries. But its small size has made it quite unable to bring that potential to fruition.

At first its reactions to this new situation were confused and disorganized. In the 1950s Britain was the despair of its neighbours who were trying to develop joint requirements and weapons in NATO. When Blue Streak was cancelled, the missile was made the basis of a European space club (ELDO). But the weapon was eventually replaced by an American one—Polaris, and in April 1968 the British Government announced its withdrawal from ELDO after all.

By 1967, a more consistent pattern was emerging, at least in aviation. Since Britain could no longer develop the most advanced aircraft alone, it must try to do so in collaboration with its European neighbours; a strategic political decision was gradually taken during 1965 to try to pool resources with similar sized European powers.

Nuclear Power

A founder member of the nuclear club, Britain was the first

European country to enter the race for nuclear weapons and for peaceful nuclear power. It decided to develop its own bomb programme late in 1945, and exploded its first atomic bomb in 1952. In 1956 the world's first nuclear power station, at Calder Hall, went into production, and by 1965 Britain had eight more large nuclear power generating plants in operation. With a plentiful stock of bomb-plutonium and the test ban in operation, Britain's military spending on nuclear matters is now well below its former peak, and may be no more than $60 mn. per year. But civil research is still running at some $120 mn. annually from government resources, far and away the largest government research investment in any civil technology.

Britain's civil nuclear programme, however, suffers far more than its defence industries from the policy of entrusting the research and development effort to government establishments. While the American Atomic Energy Commission was deliberately set up as a foster parent for industrial development, the British Government's view, in 1941, was that this vital source of power 'must not be allowed to fall into the hands of private business'.[2] After the war peaceful nuclear research and development was entrusted first to the Ministry of Supply and then to the Atomic Energy Authority (AEA). When its designs for power stations were complete, they were simply licensed to five and later three consortia of industrial firms.

The Atomic Energy Authority's design and scientific work has been good. Britain's atomic power programme grew out of its military programme; so it made sense, initially, to develop a stream of gas-cooled, graphite moderated reactors, using natural uranium. As a next development, in search of lower costs, it was equally sensible to move on and develop an advanced gas-cooled reactor using partially enriched uranium. The only mistake here was that the development was rather slow. Today the AEA is pushing ahead fast with the first prototype fast reactor in the western world. The anxiety of American companies to emulate is a tribute to the correctness of its judgement.

But while the AEA's basic strategy has been sound enough, the machinery for applying all this knowhow in the market-place has been disconcertingly unsuccessful. Despite Britain's two firsts (the first peaceful power station; and the first fast reactor), in the world market for nuclear power stations, American reactors are sweeping

[2]Margaret Gowing, *Britain and Atomic Energy 1939–45*, Macmillan, 1964, pp. 98–99, 105.

the board. Where the American AEC systematically develops the capability of American nuclear companies by development contracts, the Atomic Energy Authority charges British industry licence fees and royalties for the knowledge it sells. The AEA retains a monopoly of fuel supply, dividing responsibility in a critical matter. Again this is a contrast with America, where industry can supply both fuel and reactor. The supply of fuel during a reactor's life can be twice as expensive as the plant itself. The relatively poor initial capabilities of the British companies have fostered arrogance and a 'do it ourselves' mentality in the AEA, instead of a systematic endeavour to put industrial weakness right. In nuclear instruments, for instance, the AEA has tended to design its own instruments to suit its own requirements, subcontracting their manufacture to small jobbing firms. Since the AEA is almost a monopoly customer in Britain it is not surprising that when it has a more ambitious requirement there are no strong British nuclear instrument firms about. Usually, the AEA then buys American, giving the vicious circle one more twist. The design relationship with the industrial companies is also ludicrous. In the fast-breeder prototype at Dounreay, for instance, the basic reactor is by the AEA. The sodium pumps have been contracted to component manufacturers, in this case English Electric. But parts of the pumps are designed, in detail, by the AEA—though manufactured by English Electric. A worse management formula for development could hardly be imagined. The problems of the British nuclear industry have been compounded by the very detailed specifications of the Central Electricity Generating Board (CEGB). Three teams of engineers, the AEA, the consortia, and the CEGB have in fact been entangled in reactor design. It is not surprising that sharp cuts have been possible in the costs of advanced gas reactors (AGR) when they have been designed abroad under licence (for instance by Brown Boveri).

In his racy and provoking study of the nuclear industry,[3] Duncan Burn concludes that these weaknesses can be shown to result in low productivity in the AEA compared to its US counterpart, the AEC. Britain's Atomic Energy Authority has 40,000 employees, to America's 6,000—though of course, the AEA is doing a bigger research and development job. In 1964, the United States, including both industry and government, spent $535 mn. on reactor development compared to Britain's $134 mn. He argues that Britain's effort

[3]Duncan Burn, *The Political Economy of Nuclear Energy*, Institute of Economic Affairs, London, 1967.

placed a disproportionate load on small resources with slim results.

The argument should not be carried too far. By 1966, us spending had risen to $707 mn., as much as the Common Market (see Table 15). Over the years, the AEC spent $2 bn. on developing the pressurized water reactor, mainly through the Navy programme—compared to some $750 mn. in Britain's gas reactors. Britain's nuclear effort has, nonetheless, been disproportionately large compared to its efforts in other fields of research. It is the organization and management that have failed to produce results in the market-place. Moreover, this weakness has been compounded by the size and structure of the market compared to the United States.

Though British firms gained experience in civil power reactors before the Americans, American companies were able to break into a new and lower level of costs, in the early 1960s, by producing and marketing on a far larger scale. The two leading American companies, Westinghouse and General Electric, both had the resources to loss-lead on their first reactors. General Electric cut the price so low at its plant at Oyster Creek that an avalanche of orders rolled in for over 30,000 megawatts of nuclear generating power. Prices have risen since.

The British nuclear consortia, by contrast, have so far obtained home orders for eleven 'Calder Hall' gas-cooled reactors, and three AGRs. They are plainly not in the same position to write off any development or overhead costs over a wide market. This has affected their competitiveness, compared to the Americans, in third markets.

British nuclear technology, in short, is as advanced in its own type of reactor as its American rival. But the small size of the home market, and shortcomings in organization and management, have led to disproportionately slim results.

These weaknesses have prompted vigorous discussion in Britain on new ways of creating a more viable industrial structure. The Atomic Energy Authority proposed the formation of a single mixed company, merging its own efforts with those of private industry. An alternative suggestion was to create a single design authority, with the actual construction work done essentially by subcontractors. These solutions might overcome some of the communications problems within the industry, but would they engender a commercial dynamic comparable to that of American firms?

In July 1968 the British Government, advised by a new team in the AEA, decided on a third and better solution. The AEA's reactor development teams were to be gradually transferred to two private industrial groups which would be given the contracts for development work in future, as in America. This should produce a healthy change. The signs are, for instance, that efforts made so far to adapt AEA teams, who have worked in the military field and on reactor development to other different civilian technologies, like ceramics or desalination, are not yet producing useful results. The scientists ought to be in industry itself. To make the most of the work done so far, it would make sense to try to transfer the team which has worked on fast breeders complete to one of these enterprises, and to concentrate the expertise in gas reactors in the second. How this fits into a European structure is described in Chapter 8.

Computers: Development without Market

Defence and nuclear power take the lion's share of the British Government's contribution to research and development. But other industries have of course helped as well. In the late 1940s, for instance, a grant from the Department for Scientific and Industrial Research (DSIR) backed the development of a computer at Manchester University; this later evolved into Ferranti's successful Argus and Atlas, and the research team which formed the nucleus of ICT. Ferranti financed Atlas with excess profits made from the Bloodhound missile. Thus the British computer industry, in which Prime Minister Wilson later took much pride, only existed thanks to the inefficiency of Britain's system of defence contracting. The trouble was that for some years no British government department was prepared to try to buy computers until they had been tried in private industry; a stark contrast to the American scene. The British commercial market was relatively slow to develop, even though the first commercial application in the world was by J. Lyons and Company in 1951, when they developed a computer to handle bakery orders. In other cases neither the developers of computers, nor the potential users, grasped the possible applications. Thus, while computers were as advanced in Britain, in the 1940s, as in America, it was in America that their application first exploded ten years later. By the late 1950s IBM was invading the British market vigorously from its burgeoning home base; the many infant British computer companies were far too small and weak to compete with its giant research and development spending and marketing strength. Mergers followed, which left the British computer industry slimmer and healthier. ICT was formed from a merger of Powers-Samas and

Hollerith (IBM's former punch card distributor) and soon absorbed the computer divisions of GEC and AEI, plus Ferranti's crucial research and development team. English Electric Leo, which in 1967 absorbed Elliott Automation, formed another group, linked with the Radio Corporation of America.

In 1965 the new Ministry of Technology lent $14 mn. to ICT and later lent $20 mn. to English Electric. With this marginal assistance at a tricky time ICT at least has become a successful enterprise, sharing the British market equally with IBM and rapidly expanding. It is the only successful, profitable European computer enterprise. The trouble is that even ICT is diminutive compared with IBM, with a turnover comparable to IBM's research and development expenditure. ICT could provide a solid British contribution to a European computer industry, but will have a hard task in the long run to match the giant. In March 1968, a further British merger combined ICT with English Electric Computers to form a single company, International Computers Limited. A further $30 mn. of government money was put in.

A similar picture of advanced technology inhibited by lack of market, lack of financial strength, and lack of judicious government support can be seen in numerically-controlled machine tools, which the Ferranti company was ready to market in 1952. In the United States it was blocked by the Buy American Act. In Britain neither private buyers nor government showed much interest. Only in 1967 was more substantial government backing forthcoming, prompted by the Ministry of Technology.

These examples do not mean that there have been no British successes in peaceful advanced technology industries. Decca and Marconi set off, after the war, to capture a major part of the world market for radar equipment. They have succeeded. So has Rolls Royce in aero-engines. These firms succeeded through excellence. But many other British technological successes were smothered by the small home market and the failure of the government to provide the kind of creative backing to enterprise found in the United States.

In pure science, as well, the limitations of scale have caused difficulty and waste. At the Culham laboratory, a major effort has been going on for some years to harness nuclear fusion—the power of the H-bomb—to peaceful power production. The work at Culham has stimulated a wide range of new technologies, from computer applications to the use of very powerful magnets. The work on magnetic and other properties of hot gases has other wider applications, for instance in space.

But the Culham centre of excellence, probably the most advanced in Europe in its field, costs the British taxpayer some $10 mn. per year. In July 1967, the British Government announced a decision to cut it back over a period of years.

Obviously $10 mn. could be found to maintain such a centre, if it were felt to have high enough priority. The difficulty is that its claims do not seem to come so high as those of some other more immediate applications of technology. Yet Europe can ill afford to lose one of its leading scientific enterprises. The larger West European nation states can afford individual big science enterprises, but they cannot, separately, afford such efforts in all fields at once.

Too Pure for Profit?

The Culham dilemma illustrates a deeper British problem. As Prime Minister Wilson has emphasized, Britain has a contribution to make to European science and technology. It is also the classic case of failure to translate high scientific achievement into rapid innovation, development and marketing. Its weakness, like America's success, has been in management skills and in the absence of a market of sufficient scale in which to apply its knowledge.

In 1966 Professor Blackett, a key elder statesman of Britain's science policy, declared that in his view Britain had made a strategic mistake after the war when it placed the main emphasis of research policy on government laboratories. The American way—to contract research to industry—led, he believed, to better results.

It can, indeed, be argued that if a country spends heavily on research and development merely for the gratification of intellectual curiosity or for reasons of prestige, its efforts add a heavy burden to the economy, rather than a stimulus. Certainly Britain's fine research and development effort present a paradox. It is the largest in Western Europe. And yet the country has the worst economic record, in terms of growth of production, exports and wealth.

Britain's research and development effort has also been coloured by deep-rooted social characteristics, typical of Europe. The British educational system has prized academic achievement for its own sake. The result has been high status for pure science, and less for the industrial application of discovery. The caste system in British education, and in British society, has produced many Nobel prize winners, but given few rewards and opportunities to the applied engineer and still fewer to trained managers.

Britain's heritage in pure science could be valuable in the long run. The United States is today expanding its effort in pure science rapidly. But the number of British pure scientists may still be too large in relation to the ability to use their knowledge. The brain drain figures, and the other evidence, even suggest that industry does not know how to make use of the huge increase in numbers of engineering graduates emerging from the colleges. Run as a business, research can well be a paying proposition. But it can absorb too high a proportion of a country's top trained brains. And it does, of course, bring in no economic return at all if it is conducted in government laboratories which are cut off from commercial applications in the market-place.

Power in the Ministries

Britain's governmental machinery for organizing science and technology is dominated by a number of powerful ministries. Outside defence, these are the Department of Education and Science and the Ministry of Technology. One (concerned with science) has a long history; the other (industrial technology) has not.

The Department of Scientific and Industrial Research was set up in 1916. It set up a number of laboratories and later became the main government instrument for promoting science and technology, outside defence. In 1961 a new Ministry of Science was set up; it was merged in 1964 with the Ministry of Education to form the Department of Education and Science. This Department is responsible for a number of research councils: the Science Research Council; the Natural Environment Council; the Social Science Research Council, which guide research grants and government laboratories in their respective fields. Others, like the Medical and Agricultural Research Councils, are under their respective ministries. The councils spend over $140 mn. per year and are thus the main source of finance for basic research. The powerful University Grants Committee, which backs research in the universities, also comes under the Department of Education and Science, which is thus the main executive department responsible for pure research.

The Ministry of Technology was set up in 1965 to promote the application of technology in industry. It has absorbed the Ministry of Aviation, which has the responsibility for aircraft development; it also supervises the Atomic Energy Authority. It is responsible for the National Research and Development Corporation, which gives grants and loans to promising inventions to help development. This Council has been the agent for the Ministry's lending to the computer industry and for the development of Hovercraft. The Ministry of Technology is also responsible for standards, and it has teams responsible for different industrial sectors such as computers and machine tools. It has brought a useful new awareness of the need to apply Britain's research capability more effectively to industry, a healthy shift away from the old emphasis on pure inquiry, towards research and development that yield practical returns.

This British set-up has one major disadvantage: the separation between pure science and applied technology. It emphasizes and aggravates a classic British weakness, namely, the failure to translate scientific discovery into marketable applications. The divisions are often transferred to the European scene. Two British ministers, for instance, faithfully appeared at the European Space Conference in Rome in 1967 (see page 172) to wave flags for British science and British technology, and for the two departments concerned.

In Britain, the great government departments or ministries thus play an even greater role in science and technology policy than in the United States. Not only defence, but pure science and education, technology, medicine, each have a separate ministry. Nor is there an effective steering wheel, such as the OST under the White House. An attempt is being made to strengthen the Cabinet Office where the Prime Minister's scientific adviser, Sir Solly Zuckerman, has a small staff. But, as yet, Britain's policies on science and technology evolve more as a result of the interaction of the great departments than from a conscious central choice. There is no central body charged with the creation of new agencies to cover a new area of endeavour when this is necessary, or with the investigation of an agency that does not work well. The only overall responsibility of this kind, indeed, lies with the Treasury, which can be guaranteed to approach technology from a negative and sceptical point of view and on occasion even welcomes a division of authority between the executive departments. In space, Britain's efforts are still split between seven ministries. In oceanography, fourteen departments have some kind of stake. Combining Britain's efforts with other European countries in such fields thus poses real administrative problems. Who are the other partners to integrate with?

Britain, in short, brings a formidable scientific and technological dowry to Europe at a time when it has come, increasingly, to recognize the limitations of national scale. Cooperation might also open new opportunities to apply Britain's heritage of pure scientific discovery. But there is still much to be done at national level to organize science policy effectively and accelerate the transfer of skills and brains to practical commercial applications.

CHAPTER 4

FRANCE SEEKS
TECHNOLOGICAL GREATNESS

In the years between 1870 and 1945, French science and technology, like French military power, was eclipsed on the Continent by Germany's rising star. The postwar years have seen a determined attempt to redress the balance, first under the Fourth Republic, and then, with greater urgency, under President de Gaulle. France was the first European country to recognize how American technology is challenging the power-base of European nations. President de Gaulle has sought deliberately to halt the process, by making France an independent 'technological great power'.

The French effort in research and development is still smaller than Britain's and it is only a twelfth of the spending in the United States. But it has been growing fast, guided by clear political aims (from 1·6 per cent of national income in 1963-4 to 2·1 per cent in 1968). The French state, like the American, provides 64 per cent of the resources for French research and development. But, unlike America, where industry spends two thirds of the money, enterprises spend only half the money in France and the state the rest.

Defence

As in Britain and the United States, defence is the major driving force of French advanced technology. During the 1950s overseas commitments drained resources; there was heavy expenditure on and a deep preoccupation with conventional forces for colonial wars. Since the ending of the Algerian war, however, the emphasis has shifted and a massive effort has been made to build up France's *Force Nucléaire Strategique*. The Mark II Supersonic Mirage IVA bomber was developed and bought into service in the early 1960s.

An intermediate range solid fuel strategic missile is now in service. A first nuclear-powered missile-firing submarine was launched in 1967. After ten years of Herculean effort and expense the Pierrelatte enrichment plant began to produce highly enriched U235 in 1967 for the French bomb.

In all this France, unlike Britain, had barely any help from America, despite requests in the case of missiles, submarines and nuclear fuel. A number of brilliant French scientists spent the war years as part of the Allied nuclear endeavour, which gave them valuable experience. But, though there have been significant industrial licensing agreements, American governments have done all they could to discourage the development of a French *force de frappe*. Yet France is, it seems, succeeding at last in producing a range of strategic weapons (submarines, missiles), where Britain has abandoned the race or turned to the United States. It has done so only by giving clear and over-riding priority to the nuclear objective.

Where Britain is still in the process of withdrawing from its overseas military commitments, France has cut the bulk of hers. And where, in conventional weapons, Britain has struggled to develop the most advanced systems conceivable (like the abandoned TSR2), France has been content with less ambitious, but more workman-like aircraft, like the Mirage III, which has proved saleable throughout the world.

The French defence programme has been far more selective than the British and many people would disagree with the decision to put the bomb first. It has had its share of cancellations, for instance when the Algerian war came to an end. But since then it has been less erratic and wasteful, in terms of cancelled projects. Moreoever, it has succeeded in building up a fine capability in certain specific fields.

The French aerospace industry (employing 100,000 people) is less than half the size of the British but its sales (some $1,000 mn. in 1965) and range of work make it comparable. The airframe industry, in particular, has at least three major successes to its credit: the Caravelle; the series of helicopters developed by Sud Aviation; and the Mirage III fighter from the Dassault company, the major producer of military planes. Yet for some ten years the French Government has recognized that the small French military market was too small to justify development costs of all types of advanced military aircraft, and has sought cooperative projects as a remedy. The Mirage IVA itself was scaled down because of cost while Ameri-

E

can tanker aircraft were bought to refuel it and extend its range. The variable geometry aircraft, which was to be developed with Britain, was dropped in 1967 partly, it was said, because the budget, burdened by other things, could not take the strain. Today, every major aircraft under development by the French industry with government backing (Concorde, Jaguar, Airbus) is a cooperative project. And though the Dassault company in particular is still putting its own money into its own developments and has indeed succeeded in twisting the arm of government to persuade it to back Dassault's own VG aircraft, the policy may not outlive the 72-year old owner of the company himself.

Unlike the airframe industry, the French aero-engine industry does not compare with Britain's. SNECMA, the largest company, has a mere 10,000 employees compared with around 70,000 in Rolls Royce. SNECMA's technology is based essentially on Pratt & Whitney, which has an 11 per cent holding in the company. Turbomeca, a small private company, has a remarkably successful record in small engines, but it is too small to provide effective servicing support for its sales.

France has, however, developed a strong missile capability, which produced a range of national missiles before 1960 and is now involved increasingly in cooperative schemes. She took part in the NATO-backed consortium for joint production of the Hawk surface-to-air missile, is now developing the Martel air-to-surface missile with Britain, and anti-aircraft and anti-missiles with the West Germans.

TABLE B

France: Spending on Defence R & D (1962)

	$ mn.
Nuclear Weapons	204
Aircraft	153
Missiles	82
Electronics	61
Other	20
Total Defence	520
Total including others	1,108

Source: C. J. E. Harlow, *The European Armaments Base*, Institute of Strategic Studies, London, 1967.

Space

Since 1961 France has been developing a small and well-conceived national space programme, which is now the third largest in the world. Under it the Diamant rocket has been developed, which has put four scientific satellites successfully into low orbit. There is a programme of sounding rockets, balloon experiments, a computer centre, and a network of telemetry stations around the world. A major launching base for putting satellites into equatorial orbit is being built in French Guyana. The civil space programme is, of course, closely linked to military strategic missile development, where France is now the most active European power.

France recognizes that it is not possible, alone, to develop the largest launchers and satellites, and though US Scout launchers have put up French satellites, the French are determined to become as free as possible from the United States. France, therefore, plays an active part in the European space organizations and will buy European launchers when it seeks, with West Germany, to put up a first communications satellite. The French Coralie rocket, the second stage of Europe's three stage launchers, has run into trouble. But its powerful national programme has enabled it to win the lion's share of orders (for instance for telemetry stations) in the European bodies. It sees Europe, in short, both as necessary because of the out-dated scale of the nation-state, and as an arena for pursuing national ends,

TABLE C

France: Spending on Space ($ million)

	1962	1963	1964	1965	1966	1967
National	10	22	32	39	44	70
International	9	13	20	21	28	29

Source: Centre National d'Etudes Spatiales, *Rapport d'Activité 1965–66*.

The Fourth Nuclear Power

At the heart of the French effort to achieve great power status in technology has been research on nuclear power. The French Commissariat à L'Energie Atomique was set up in 1945 by President de Gaulle's provisional government. It embarked in the 1950s on the development of a stream of gas-cooled, graphite moderated reactors similar to Britain's. France, like Britain, had no easy access to American supplies of enriched uranium. It chose to develop reactors using natural uranium (which France had in abundance), despite their larger capital cost; these could also provide plutonium fuel for an atomic bomb.

Because of its late start, however, French nuclear development remained behind British. Britain's first Calder Hall reactor was in service in 1956; France's first similar reactor (built at Marcoule) in 1958. By this time Britain, anxious to match American progress, was moving to the new advanced gas reactors; with luck and effort these might just succeed in matching their American rivals, the water reactors from GE and Westinghouse, in terms of cost. The French electricity authority, however, is still struggling to bring into service its original Magnox reactors which might be 10 per cent more costly to run than either the American water reactors or Britain's AGR. It is therefore pressing to be allowed to buy American reactors, a damning comment on the huge sums spent in France's own programme.

The French Atomic Energy programme, like the British, also suffers from the fact that development work has been partly carried out in a state organ, though a good deal of technical work is carried out under contract in industry. The programme has not given industry the same chance to stretch its capabilities or to take overall development responsibilities, as in America, though the contrast between the two systems is often exaggerated. Indeed, where difficulties have occurred (as at the Chinon power station, the first to be built for Electricité de France) they have been caused by the failure of industrial equipment (for instance the heat exchangers) and not by the basic reactor core. France, in short, like Britain, has invested heavily in prestigious nuclear energy, but the results, bottled up in a state agency, have shown all too little sign of yielding a commercial

TABLE D

Spending on Nuclear Technology ($ million)

| | France | | Total | United Kingdom | | USA | | Total |
	Civil R & D	Military Spending	Nuclear Spending	Civil R & D	Military Spending	Civil R & D	Military R & D	Nuclear Spending
1962	200ᵉ	204	470	134	..	535	835	..
1964	250ᵉ	428	832	132	61	687	995	..
1966	300ᵉ	..	850ᵉ	140	78	707	890	2,347

ᵉestimates.

Source: Reports of UKAEA; *Data on Science Resources No. 10*, NSF Washington; Reports of CEA.

return. There has been no massive market for submarine reactors and aircraft carriers, as there has in the United States, to create a large-scale nuclear industry. By 1964 the French nuclear programme, burdened by Pierrelatte and bomb development, was still costing $832 mn. Although this included a substantial element of production (uranium mining and so forth), it still took a big slice of French research and development. This may seem the correct priority to the French President, but as Table D shows, a nuclear programme much larger than Britain's and one third the size of America's devoured a formidable proportion of France's brains and cash.

Computers: US Dominance

The vigour and drive of France's defence, space and nuclear programmes have stimulated a sophisticated electronics industry, at least in certain fields. In many fields of avionics, for instance, France can stand comparison with all comers. Yet French exports of electronic and telecommunications equipment in 1964 were worth only some $100 mn. compared with Britain's $278 mn. and West Germany's $236 mn. In the crucial field of computers, it has been taught a devastating lesson in the facts of scale and economic power. In 1963, the leading French firm of Machines Bull ran into grave financial difficulties. It found itself unable to raise either the financial resources or the skilled team needed to remain competitive in the new arena of computers. After an abortive attempt to preserve the company by pumping in fresh French funds, President de Gaulle was forced to accept a 50-50 marriage between Machines Bull and America's General Electric. Virtually the entire French computer industry was now dominated by the United States. The experience was made more galling when for two years the US Government forbade the sale to the French Atomic Energy Commission of a large computer.

In 1965, the French Government sought to make a fresh start. Within the framework of the Fifth National Plan, a new *plan calcul* for the development of the French computer industry was anounced. A new company (Compagnie Internationale d'Informatique) was set up by three leading electrical companies (Compagnie Générale d'Electricité, French Thompson Houston and Compagnie Sans Fil) to manufacture computers. This, together with a new software company, plus a new components group, was to be financed by the government to the tune of some 500 mn. francs ($130 mn.), to be spent over a period of five years.

The task CII has taken on is formidable. It has started by manufacturing computers made under licence from the American company, Scientific Data Systems (SDS). By 1969, however, it is expected to produce a new 'P' series of computers. The configuration will conform closely to IBM's 360 series; the trouble is that by the time this appears IBM may be moving on to further new developments. Above all, there is no sign that CII has the ability to develop the immense library of programmes for the application of computers which is essential to success. CII will have 6,000 employees by 1970 compared to ICL's 36,000 and IBM's 200,000. The *plan calcul* will succeed in training a team of computer engineers and programmers. It is most unlikely to succeed in creating a company which can compete profitably in world markets on its own.

In integrated circuits, the French market is no less dominated by American enterprises. Texas Instruments, Fairchild and Motorola lead, with Holland's Philips also strongly in the race. The only significant French rival is COSEM, a subsidiary of CSF. In defence and space the French electronic industry is the strongest on the Continent, but in the wider field of consumer products, as in such major markets as circuitry and computers, international companies, based outside France, predominate.

The steering wheel

Like Britain and the United States, France has moved through several phases in the evolution of a science policy. The Centre Nationale de la Recherche Scientifique (CNRS) was created after the war, a kind of mini-national science foundation. The CNRS gives grants to university research, runs 104 laboratories of its own, provides information, training and other services, and reports on science policy. It was not, however, a steering wheel, but an instrument of one ministry, the Ministry of Education.

In 1958, however, a steering wheel was built into the vehicle, the Délégation Générale à la Recherche Scientifique (DGRST), under the Prime Minister. This body, like America's OST, services a science advisory committee and an interministerial committee, both responsible to the Prime Minister, whose executive delegate is the Ministère de la Recherche. The two committees together work out a national science policy, which fits into the framework of France's five-year plans. President de Gaulle, keenly aware of the political implications of technology, takes a lively interest in the work of these committees and often intervenes when a key decision has to be made.

On paper France has the most logical and clear-cut machinery for science policy of any major West European country. And in practice too, it has made rapid progress in developing a group of science policy planners who combine scientific knowledge with economic and administrative skills. The days of plain lobbying by powerful professors are fading. And though the great departments are still mighty, France's centralized structure gives the DGRST, the Prime Minister and President greater authority within the French framework than federal America's OST in its vaster arena.

The Fifth Plan on research and technology (1966-71) spells out a broad strategy for research and development: the size and breakdown of the effort in education; the priorities for the many ministries —defence, agriculture, medicine; and a number of significant new themes. One is the idea of *actions concertées*, in which grants are given to a number of research centres in institutions, universities and industry, to push forward research in a particular field.

In the Fourth Plan, one of these, for instance, was in oceanography. The separate efforts of over a dozen different universities and laboratories were brought into a common 'concerted' programme. In the Fifth Plan this effort, which has gone well, is to be put under a new national agency (CNEXO). Other 'concerted actions' range from cryogenics to cancer research and molecular biology.

One new tool, used for the first time in the current Fifth Plan, is the development grant to civilian industry. 'Round tables' or committees, grouping together industrialists and officials, are being formed for a number of key sectors: metallurgy, electronics, mechanical engineering, and so on. These committees will select areas, such as advanced machine tools and air-cushion technology, where research is needed. Grants from the government to industry to back them up were expected to reach some $25 mn. in 1967.

Another preoccupation of the Fifth Plan is to shift the centre of gravity of research out of the Paris region, where 64 per cent of French research workers now work. So far the effort has had only limited success. But in aerospace a major 'centre of excellence', grouping the great schools and a large part of the industry, is being developed at Toulouse.

All Captains Together?

With characteristic logic and single-mindedness, France, in short, is setting about closing the Atlantic gap in science and technology on a national basis. It has set up a clearly defined machinery for making science policy; and it has initiated national programmes in space, computers, nuclear power and defence, where the challenge of America is strong.

There are still, however, basic weaknesses, particularly in the social and educational scene. French universities remain tightly controlled by central government; professors are isolated occupants of a multitude of status-oriented 'chairs'; the rigid system of examinations stifles research and creative thinking, and places young men and women in carefully allotted slots for life. The result, in research, is a grave absence of mobility and teamwork. The barriers between university and industry seem insurmountable. French firms, too, are still smaller in scale than their British or West German counterparts. Of the 25 largest European companies in 1966, only one was French. Family firms still predominate. Secrecy vitiates the working of the capital market and limits the effect of competition. France, in short, is still a long way short of adjusting its structures to a continental market, or achieving the mobility and dynamism of its American rivals.

Above all, a conscious blend of selfishness and enlightenment characterizes French attitudes towards cooperation in advanced technology. Where the British, taught by their costly mistakes, grope often naïvely towards a European answer, the French consciously blend the pursuit of national greatness with European ends. In space and aviation for instance, France is deliberately seeking cooperation. But it is seeking, equally deliberately, wherever possible to give France a lead in cooperative schemes. With much skill the French sometimes pre-empt the site or leadership of a joint venture by making a bold offer or going ahead themselves. On occasion, as in the Hawk missile consortium, France has won the leadership of a major joint project, and then cut down the number of production orders placed. In Euratom, France has been a wrecker on and off for many years. In the background lurks a willingness to partner anyone, including Russia, if it increases French independence and bargaining power. In colour television, for instance, France has destroyed the possibility of a single European system by partnership with Russia on the French system, SECAM. In space, Russia is to launch French Satellites, as America has done. Frenchmen involved in the partnership with Russia recognize its limitations, and its real content is obscure. When the Russians discovered that the French SECAM system depended on American components, there were doubts about the future of the entire arrangement. The French

Government itself gives broad priority, in international cooperation, to Western Europe.

All the same, the inherent contradiction in France's nationalist, yet European view of science and technology, must one day be resolved. A European team in advanced technology, all of whose members expect to be captain, is unlikely to score many goals against the vigorous American side.

CHAPTER 5

RESURGENT GERMANY

Though West Germany has re-emerged as Europe's leading industrial power, its advanced technology industries, shattered by war
and held back by allied restrictions on the arms, aircraft and
nuclear industries in the early postwar years, have not matched
this resurgence. As the market for new products like computers
and nuclear power stations grows, and the German 'miracle'
falters, West Germans have growing doubts about this weakness.
The result has been a growing interest in advanced technology.

There is a strong base to build on. In the bread and butter industries of the second industrial revolution, West Germany has the
most powerful industrial structure in Western Europe. While Britain
has the largest European chemical company, West Germany has
three in the top eight. It has the largest mechanical engineering,
vehicle and steel industries in Western Europe, and three of the eight
largest electrical firms. But in the postwar technologies of aviation,
computers, nuclear power and space technology, it is a relative new-
comer. At first, like Japan, it has sought to fill the gap mainly by
buying technology from America. The question is whether, in the
new phase of more advanced development, West Germany will seek
to go it alone, and if not, who will be its partners.

West Germany's research and development expenditure reflects
its historical position. At $1·4 bn. in 1963-64, or 1·4 per cent of
national income (a figure which has grown since), it was comparable
to France's effort but a good deal smaller than Britain's. And unlike
France, but like Britain and America, the bulk of the effort (66 per
cent) is in industry rather than government establishments. Most of
this research is for civil purposes. Indeed, if Britain's large defence

bill for R & D is lopped off, the research and development efforts of the two countries look, in quantity, remarkably alike.

But there have been qualitative differences. In West Germany industry has had the lead, with state involvement, discredited by experience under the Nazis, taking a back seat. Can West Germany, with its powerful industrial and commercial structure, find a complementary relationship with Britain and France, with their prestigious technology, developed in part for defence objectives?

Defence

In defence, after five years of total prohibition by the allies, it was only under their prodding that West Germany rearmed. Even then there was no inclination by the West Germans to rebuild their defence industries. In cabinet, Dr Erhard argued that it made political and economic sense to manufacture profitable and exportable machine tools and cars, and import West Germany's defence equipment; from outside, America and Britain pressed for the purchase of their own equipment, both to keep West Germany firmly integrated in the western system and to meet part of the costs of their armies by the Rhine. In the ten years from 1955, West Germany has therefore been the world's largest importer of defence equipment, at a cost of some $5-$8 bn. (out of purchases of equipment of some $10 bn.).[1] Its own reviving defence industries have been correspondingly limited in scale.

Defence thus took a mere 11 per cent of research and development expenditure in 1964 ($160 mn.). Some of this work is done in defence establishments, but most inside industrial firms. The major development and production projects have been cooperative in nature, like the Milan and Hot missiles developed with France, and West Germany's participation in the NATO consortia to manufacture the Raytheon Hawk ground-to-air missile.

The aircraft industry has been almost wholly tied to cooperative projects. West Germany's infant aircraft industry employs a mere 30,000 people and is still divided up into six small family airframe firms. It has produced a whole series of interesting prototypes, but, except for light aircraft, and the Hansa 320, none has actually been produced in quantity. So far the main production activity of the infant West German industry has been to lead the European consortium (Italy, Belgium, Netherlands, West Germany) which pro-

[1] C. J. E. Harlow, *The European Armaments Base, Part II*, Institute of Strategic Studies, London, 1967, p. 41.

duced 700 Lockheed F-104 Starfighters under licence in the years 1960 to 1964. The aircraft has proved notably unsuitable for West German requirements, and it is not unfair to say that it was bought for political reasons with disastrous results (some 90 have crashed). 150 Fiat G-91 fighters were also built under a licence agreement with Italy. With France, West Germany built the Bréguet Atlantique and Transall.

Of these joint projects, only the Transall and Atlantique included joint development, as well as production, and orders for these aircraft have been much fewer than expected. The Transall and Atlantique did, however, serve to build up an engine development and production capability in MAN (which produced the Rolls Royce Tyne under licence); BMW also rebuilt its capability on an even larger scale by manufacturing 700 General Electric J-79 engines for the Starfighter.

As it emerges from this period of tutelage, it is plain that the small West German aircraft industry cannot expect to be a major factor in world markets on its own. The question is whether it is to be, essentially, a subcontractor from America (as it was for the F-104) or whether it is to be a partner with its European neighbours. Whichever it chooses, it will need to concentrate its forces. The industry is still far too fragmented to share in efficient production of large and complex modern planes.

Space

West Germany's space programme, like its new defence industries, developed under pressure from a western ally. This time it was the British, whose Blue Streak rocket had proved militarily redundant. Anxious to form a European space club, they persuaded the West Germans in 1961 to join in.

At that time West Germany had no space capability. The brilliant inventors of the V1 and V2 rockets, like Wernher von Braum, had long since gone, or been taken to, America or Russia. A new space commission was, however, created. Since then the West Germans have slowly built up their capability, both in the European club and with the Americans. American rockets have put up three scientific satellites, and a joint West German-American sun-probe is planned in 1973-74. This project and the possibility of a European-American probe to Jupiter provide the occasion for really advanced work. At the new West German space centre, there is work on titanium, on hypersonic flight, and experiments in a sun-simulating chamber.

While the French polytechnicians are proving that Europe can emulate, in miniature, America's space achievements, West German space scientists, who have fewer inhibitions about partnership today, give greater priority to the problems of the future. West Germany is building up its space programme fast, but it continues to see its national effort as a base for cooperation.

TABLE E

West Germany: Spending on Space ($ million)

	1962	1963	1964	1965	1966	1967
	2·7	12·7	35·2	35·2	42	70
of which European	..	..	..	..	20e(27)p	..
National	..	..	..	..	22 (24)	..

Source: *Bundesbericht Forschung*, 1967.

eEstimate of actual spending.　　　　pPlanned programme.

Nuclear Research

Spending on nuclear research and development in West Germany is rising fast. In 1967, the Federal Government planned to spend $193 mn., and the Länder $61 mn., compared with Britain's $140 mn. Unlike Britain's effort (and France's even larger nuclear bill) the bulk of West German spending is carried out in industry. The West Germans set up an Atomic Energy Ministry which allocates federal funds to semi-autonomous research corporations at Karlsruhe and Jülich. Central guidance for these corporations has been less effective than that of the AEC and Joint Congressional Committee in the United States, but with the transformation of the Atom Ministry into a Ministry for Scientific Research it has begun to improve. Pure research is done in the corporations but development and application inside industry. Given the powerful structure of the West German industry this may well lead to formidable results.

Siemens and AEG, the two major West German groups, each began by developing Westinghouse and General Electric water reactors under licence. So far this has not led to large orders for power stations, but two 600 MW stations (one boiling water and one pressurized water) are under construction and a boom could be round the corner. A wide range of experimental reactors have been built under contract for Euratom and the West German Atomic Energy Commission while, in third markets, the West German firms have been undercutting their American foster-parents. The British, too, have experienced the capability of West Germany's new nuclear engineers. Mainly through design improvements the West German branch of Swiss Brown Boveri has tendered an AGR under licence at prices 20 per cent below the British price.

West Germany, like Britain and France, is embarking on a programme of research and development in fast-breeder reactors. The pure research is done at the Karlsruhe centre of the Atomic Energy Commission, which has a big programme in physics, testing, and fuel technology. But once the prototype stage is reached, industry will take over. The original plan was for the two major nuclear companies, AEG and Siemens, each to build a prototype under development contracts. AEG led a consortium with GHH and MAN. Siemen's partners are Inter-Atom and Babcocks. Under pressure from Karlsruhe, the two companies agreed to build different types of fast breeder: AEG a steam-cooled reactor, and Siemens a sodium-cooled one. In fact the plan to construct a steam-cooled breeder prototype is to be abandoned. The successful company, Siemens, will be obliged to license its knowhow to its rival. The fast-breeder programme, as first planned, would have cost West Germany some $380 mn.,[2] a major claim on its resources. No doubt it will succeed eventually; the question is when. The triplication of effort in the field of fast breeders between Britain, France and West Germany (at a total cost of between $1,000 and $1,500 mn.) is a strange way to employ Europe's limited wealth.

Computers

The West German computer industry, like the French, is dominated by IBM, which has some 75 per cent of the market. But a deliberate effort to build up a national-owned industry, with government support, is beginning. The West Germans, however, though fearful, like other Europeans, of seeing this key industry controlled wholly from across the ocean, have been more cautious in their response than have the French. Dr Erhard's philosophy of 'Prosperity through competition'[3] has been a guiding light for the West German economy in the postwar period, and a most effective one at that. The West Germans, too, are as anxious as the British not to upset the Americans who guard their security. Some intellectual acrobatics have therefore seemed necessary to justify a policy aimed at

[2]350 mn. DM on the work so far at Karlsruhe; 96 mn. DM on pre-prototype studies by the two companies; 750 mn. DM for the two prototypes; and 300 mn. DM for further work at Karlsruhe, making a total of 1,496 mn. DM ($380 mn.).

[3]Ludwig Erhard, *Prosperity through Competition*, Thames and Hudson, 1962.

countering IBM. The West Germans have found their justification in the valid argument that IBM and other American companies benefit from government contracts and preferential purchasing at home. The result has been a massive distortion of the market. To redress the balance, the Bonn government argues, support is needed for the local industry from European governments.

The West German Government is giving this in two forms: low-interest loans to computer manufacturers and development contracts from the Science Ministry. Together this help should total some $75 mn. over five years. The Science Ministry also sponsors a number of 'model' computer application programmes, in hospitals and in universities, for instance. A 'buy national' policy in government departments also helps the local industry. Leaving aside price and competitive considerations, which of course play a part, West German government departments buy first from nationally-owned industries, next from firms that manufacture in West Germany, such as IBM, and third, from other foreign manufacturers.

Two firms, Siemens and Telefunken, are the 'favourite sons' of this government-backed programme and indeed inspired it. Telefunken has a considerable military business and is attempting to develop large computers. Siemens, like English Electric, is a licensee of America's RCA, whose 'Spectra' range it sells and increasingly manufactures. Helped in part by government funds, Siemens is now spending some $120 mn. on the development of its own range of computers, mainly used in process-control.

On its own, Siemens might have some success in the field of process-control where it already has experience, in the control of power stations for instance. It is less certain whether it can build up the massive software library that is needed for data processing. Certainly, even Siemens has a long way to go to make its computer enterprise a viable long-term operation. In 1967 it had some 12 per cent of the West German market—a turnover less than 1 per cent of IBM's.

Seeking a Steersman

West German science and technology are not guided by centralized policies to the same degree as in France and Britain. The postwar Federal Constitution placed education, science and culture in the hands of the provinces or Länder. It made no provision for a central science policy at all.

The Constitution was, however, not allowed to prevent the creation of a Ministry for Atomic Energy in 1954. This became responsible for the Space Commission when it was set up in 1962. In 1962 the Ministry was given wider terms of reference and renamed the Ministry for Scientific Research. Gradually it is seeking to develop an overall science policy and now produces an annual report[4] or plan relating at least federal spending to a five year programme. The Science Ministry services a science council (Wissenschaftsrat) which both seeks to coordinate the efforts of Bund and Länder, and provides top scientific advice. A cabinet committee for science and research seeks to harmonize the efforts of the ministries at federal level; its chairman is either the Chancellor or the Science Minister himself.

It remains true that the Science Ministry has only limited authority and power. The industrial application of technology is not its province; thus part of the responsibility for computers lies with the Ministry of Economics; the aircraft industry is guided by the Ministries of Economics and Defence. If the real strength of West Germany's technological development lies in industry (the right place to win a commercial return), the strength of West Germany's pure research efforts lie in the remarkable series of cooperative institutions which have sprung up, not merely from the postwar constitutions, but from the federal tradition of the last 500 years.

The Forschungsgemeinschaft or Research Association is a cooperative body which brings together representatives of the scientific universities and academies, and the key scientific societies and institutions of the country. Financed by the Federal Government, the Länder and private industry, it gives grants to reseach in universities and other institutions and provides a broad range of services to the community in scientific matters. It spent some $45 mn in 1967. Of key importance are its *Schwerpunktprogramme*, or key programmes, under which the Association deliberately promotes cooperative research in a vital area between a number of institutions. There is a *Schwerpunktprogramm*, for instance, in oceanography. In computers, the Ministry of Science has only three officials (compared to 60 in Britain's Mintech); it passes on responsibility for deciding where to put West Germany's new university computer centres and 'model applications' to the capable Forschungsgemeinschaft.

A second major cooperative institution (which is represented on

[4]*Bundesbericht Forschung*, Bundesministerium für Wissenschaftliche Forschung, Bonn.

the Forschungsgemeinschaft) is the Max-Planck Gesellschaft, originally the Kaiser Wilhelm Gesellschaft, and renamed in 1945 according to the political fashions of the time. It maintains over 50 independent research institutes throughout West Germany at an annual cost of some $50 mn. in 1965. Many other independent institutions, strong industrial research associations and the technological universities (Technische Hochschule) also contribute to West Germany's sturdy infrastructure of decentralized research.

This set-up is not without its problems. While the universities benefit intellectually from the old German conception of 'free study', it plays the devil with organized research. Too often even the 'key programmes' of the Forschungsgemeinschaft are a kind of common denominator of many professorial demands, not a carefully conceived project for a joint breakthrough. Mediocre stop-gap programmes are sometimes the result. A strength of West German research is the intimate relation between universities and industry, a stark contrast with France. At the nuclear centre at Karlsruhe, for instance, many key men also teach in universities. A high turnover is encouraged, to train young men who then go out into industry. Yet the universities are still inhibited by hierarchical structures and rigid curricula. It is harder to develop a new multidisciplinary course in a West German university than in, say, Britain. The long, gruelling five to seven-year degree course ought probably to be split by an intermediate exam. West German universities face something of a crisis, both in buildings and in shortage of teachers.

All these considerations are much in the minds of a new National Education Council (Bildungsrat), which is seeking to reform education and overcome the separatism of the different Länder. Essentially the problem is to modernize a fine tradition, and remove the weaknesses of federalism while keeping its strengths.

West Germany stands on the threshold of a new era of advanced technology in which it is willing to cooperate with others; indeed, in some of the new industries described in this chapter, partners are indispensable. What is not clear is how much the major West German industrial concerns wish to free themselves from their us tutelage. How keen are they and their government to seek new European partners? In 1966 the Americans used the implicit threat of troop withdrawals to try to force the West Germans to buy $700 mn. of weapons, more than the West German forces needed; the effect of such gestures is to accelerate West Germany's quest for European partners. But in fields like aviation and nuclear power,

F

the West Germans are not going to combine with the French and British unless these countries show signs of making a powerful and permanent commitment to projects that are economically sound. The idea that West Germany can be coaxed into buying British or French aircraft or reactors to spite the Americans and in the name of a vague European sentiment is doomed to failure. Without deeper political and economic links with its neighbours, any West German reaction against America leads, not to Europe, but to nationalism; there are signs enough of this, not only in West German politics, but in, say, computer policy or even high energy physics. If, in the postwar period, West German science and technology was obliged to learn from others, growing success must encourage the wish to go it alone, above all if partners prove arrogant and short sighted.

West Germany too has still to strengthen further the central steering wheel of its science policy. Progress is being made. But the loose federal character of West German science has already made it difficult for West Germany to speak effectively in discussions in the European Community on a science policy. West German research associations can speak to their equivalents in France or Britain. But Siemens and the Atomic Energy Authority are different types of animal for whom a common language is hard to find. Uniting European efforts in science and technology requires, in short, not just a will to integrate, but a deliberate attempt to create new kinds of partnership between state, parastatal organizations, and private enterprise. Paradoxically, Europe in technology requires a degree of similarity in organization at the level of the nation state.

CHAPTER 6

PROBLEMS OF THE LESSER POWERS

None of the smaller countries of Western Europe has tried to go it alone in science and technology, as have the large powers. None has cherished comparable ambitions to produce and deck itself out with the full panoply of modern military power. Especially within the European Community, the small nations have been increasingly keen on the pooling of resources in science and technology. For them, common endeavour has not been reluctantly accepted after many painful lessons, but a sheer commonsense reaction to the facts of life.

Total research spending by Italy, the Netherlands, Belgium, Sweden, Switzerland and the other small West European countries amounted to some $1,200 mn. in 1963-64, about the same as France. In total, not one of these states spent more than a quarter as much as one of the Big Three. Italy, with its population of 50 million, has a potential comparable to the three large countries, but lower incomes per head have ruled out investment in research and development on the same scale. These states are mackerel beside the three European porpoises and the American whale.

There are striking differences, however, between them. Sweden spent more per caput on research and development than France or West Germany, and Holland a larger proportion of its national income (1·9 per cent) in 1964. Both small states contain powerful international companies, especially in electronics (Philips, Ericsson) or chemicals (Shell, Unilever), a reminder that the small size of a nation is not necessarily a bar to industrial production and innovation on a modern scale. A free trade philosophy and a high level of education and organization are important compensations for small national scale.

Small size does, however, generally require a high degree of specialization, whether in private industry or in research and development backed by public contracts. By careful specialization, some of these countries have developed and sold some remarkably successful defence products: Belgium the FN rifle, Italy the 105 mm. howitzer and Fiat's G-91 fighter; Holland much important military electronic equipment and, in civil aviation, the incredibly successful shorthaul Fokker Friendship, of which some 400 have been sold.

What these small countries cannot do is to spread public research and development expenditure over a wide range of goals. Thus in defence again, for instance, Belgium, Italy and Holland all buy much equipment from abroad. All of them have produced military aircraft only under licence or consortia arrangements (F-104, G-91). The question for these countries is not whether to work with others, but whether to buy direct, manufacture under licence, or, if they are to cooperate, with whom.

In nuclear matters, these three smaller European countries were keen on Euratom, the atomic community of the Six, and are now disappointed with it, perhaps because they expected the wrong thing (contracts), rather than research results. Belgium and Italy both spent roughly as much on European nuclear research and development in 1964 as on their national programmes; a gross contrast with France, whose national civil R & D programme was some five times its European effort. In self-defence, Italy is now seeking to strengthen its national programme, and in December 1967 vetoed Euratom's provisional research budget for 1968. Yet going it alone will solve no problems. If Italy were to try to build a prototype version of one of the new fast-breeder reactors, it would have to spend twice as much on this each year as its entire nuclear research budget today.

In space, there is a tiny but successful Italian national programme. From a sea platform off the Kenya coast, the 130 kg San Marco scientific satellite was fired into equatorial orbit in 1967, bringing useful experience for equatorial launchings which will be necessary for a European communications satellite. This and two other satellites were fired by American Scout missiles. But even in a peak year (1968) Italy's national spending on space ($3·3 mn.) will be little more than a sixth of what it spends on European space endeavours ($18 mn. in 1968), and it regards its national programme purely as a support for these. Holland began a small national space programme in 1967. But it and all the other small countries of Europe appreciate that participation in a successful space programme of some scale means working together.

In the computer industry, the two leading companies in Italy and Holland, Olivetti and Philips, have both experienced the bitter facts of scale and the tremendous difficulty of getting into the race late. Olivetti first set up its own data-processing division, then, after making heavy losses, went into partnership on a 25-75 per cent basis with General Electric. GE-Olivetti has not prospered any more than Bull-GE. By 1967 many of Olivetti's best people had returned to the parent company; Olivetti has wisely decided to stay out of the manufacture of central computer processors. Instead, however, it has cleverly embarked on the manufacture of peripheral equipment (teleprinters, on-line cash registers, and other kinds of terminal equipment) which make admirable use of its prowess in development and production of typewriters and the like.

Philips at first hung back altogether in the computer race, hoping to be able to stay out. But by 1967 it was investing heavily, if belatedly, on an attempt to get in—a somewhat dubious prospect even for Europe's second largest electrical concern.

The small countries and their companies can plainly succeed when they make a deliberate effort to specialize, and rely on the international division of labour. So why should they worry? One source of disquiet can be political. They, like others, do not want to see the control of all key industries in foreign hands. But plainly they cannot control them all themselves. Here is one of the many reasons why the small countries in the Common Market want the European programmes, which they ardently desire, to come within a community system, in which policies and control are exercised in common, for the good of all. They have no desire whatever to exchange an American hegemony for a French or British.

The small countries, in general, welcome American investment. The Belgians, for instance, recognize the part it can play in revitalizing their old industrial structure and have done much to encourage it. Italy's state holding company, IRI, has had no inhibitions about setting up joint companies with Raytheon, Westinghouse, General Electric, Armco, and others, in a judicious attempt to increase productivity and implant American knowhow in the Italian economy. The small countries of the European Community would like to see Community policy work. But they will not slam the door on other external sources of knowhow and investment capital. They would like to improve the terms on which they acquire licences and knowhow from America. But the slower Europe integrates, in technology, the more they must turn to America and the worse the terms.

The Swedish Paradox

One European country is a remarkable exception to this picture of dependence, imposed by small size. Sweden, with a population of under eight million, has, somehow, contrived to maintain a national capability in many advanced technology industries, as part of its determined policy of armed neutrality.

Sweden, with the highest living standard in Europe, spends some 5 per cent of its national income on defence and buys 85 per cent of its defence equipment at home. Its one aircraft company, Saab, which employs a total of some 15,000 people, has succeeded in developing a successful series of strike interceptor aircraft culminating in the Viggen supersonic strike interceptor aircraft, a poor man's TSR2. Advanced aeroengines are built under licence from the United States and Britain.

Sweden's leading electrical company, Ericsson, is a world technical leader in telephone equipment, and there is an astonishingly strong nuclear industry. AB Atomenergi, a parastate agency, was formed in 1947 and has promoted development of at least three types of reactor, two using heavy water as moderator, and one light water based on work with GE. ASEA is the major private company in the field and favours other types of reactor. By 1980, Sweden expects to have 4,000 MW of nuclear power in operation, compared with 30,000 MW in Britain. It is already competing for contracts in export markets in Rumania, West Germany, Finland and elsewhere.

Yet even Sweden feels the need for partnership. In computers, where Saab is developing certain applications, it is working increasingly with ICL. In fast-breeder reactors, Sweden is anxious to work with Britain. In space, Sweden already works within the European organizations. Even in aviation, Saab's success has been based on a skilful combination of licensing, plus a concentration of local development skills on a carefully selected end. In missiles there is much production under licence or purchase from abroad.

Like Japan, Sweden has also systematically pursued a policy of retaining control of key industries in the hands of Swedes, at least where the ownership of existing Swedish companies is concerned.

The Swedish model shows that given free trade policies, careful selection of fields for action, a continuous history of industrial development, the highest level of education in Europe, and a high social status for engineers, the minimum threshold size for national autonomy in advanced technology can be reduced considerably. But rising costs are pushing even Sweden more and more towards cooperation.

A Variety of Steersmen

The machinery of science policy in the smaller European states has reached a variety of stages of evolution. In Belgium, for instance, the National Council for Scientific Policy, guided by a small but able secretariat, has, since 1961, conducted an inventory of national scientific resources and sought, increasingly, to promote research selectively, according to carefully devised criteria. Though the universities, in particular, have not proved easy to guide, Belgium thus has one of the best machines in Europe for making scientific choices. The Prime Minister takes clear ultimate responsibility. The Belgian Government has also been most articulate in formulating the small state's need for a balance between selective national endeavour, European integration and import of technology from the United States.

In Italy, by contrast, a national organ for guiding science policy is only in the making. There is an atomic energy authority, Ministries for Industry and Education, and a National Council for Research strongly manned by professors with responsibility for presenting an annual report on science policy and objectives. But so far, especially in applied technology, it is Italian industry, not government, that has led the way.

Then there is Norway, for instance, where a single man, Mr Robert Major, has had a notable influence on the development of a highly successful policy for applied research. The Council for Industrial Research, of which he is director, has skilfully developed research in areas relevant to Norway's needs (like automatic shipplate cutting); success has won him the ear of those who count.

Structure for the guidance of science and techology policy may vary immensely from country to country and this goes for large states as well as small. This is revealed in a series of reports from OECD,[1] as well as in the composition of the OECD meeting of ministers

[1]Country Reports on the Organization of Scientific Research, OECD, Paris.

on science policy which took place in May 1965. At this meeting, some delegations were led by ministers for education and ecclesiastical affairs, others by ministers for science. The West German delegation included representatives of the provinces of Niedersachsen and Baden Wurtemburg; the British, as ever, were led by their tandem team, the Ministers of Technology, and Education and Science.

The states of Western Europe need each other to pursue effective research and development. They also need to develop common features in the national organizations of science and technology, if they are to work together.

PART THREE

FUMBLING TOWARDS UNITY

CHAPTER 7

EUROPE HUNTS THE QUARK

The necessities of scale, which today oblige European statesmen to debate a technological community, were first effective in postwar Europe in the field of basic nuclear physics; the scientific key to our knowledge of the material universe and the key to one of the main technological revolutions of the last 50 years.

In 1919 Rutherford split the atom in his laboratory by shooting natural alpha particles, with energies around 5M electron volts, at nitrogen atoms. His previous experiments had unveiled the basic structure of the atom and the molecule, showing how these consisted of electrons moving round a small but heavy nucleus. This led around 1925 to the discovery of quantum mechanics which explains how the electrons interact with the nucleus and how they bind the nuclei to each other to form molecules or solid bodies. The foundation was laid for our modern understanding and use of chemistry, solid-state physics and electronics.

Probing deeper, in the 1930s and early 1940s, the scientists went on to explore the nature of the nucleus, and discovered that it consisted of protons and neutrons arranged in dense configurations. They guessed that fusion of light nuclei liberated the nuclear energy of sun and stars; they discovered how fission of heavy nuclei could be made to release nuclear energy on earth.

By the late 1940s physicists were probing even more deeply into the nature of elementary particles and asking what the neutron and the proton are themselves. Yet by a law of nature the smaller the object investigated, the higher the energies required to do so. Rutherford's natural alpha particles moved with an energy of a mere 5M electron volts. To investigate the particles which make up the neutron and the proton requires energies a thousand or more times as large. In nature, particles moving at very high energies (up to 100 bn. electron volts) can be found in the form of cosmic rays. These can be studied, particularly at high altitudes. But vastly more information can be collected, far more rapidly, by building powerful machines which accelerate the particles artificially and give the scientist the chance to observe great numbers of experimental collisions in his laboratory under conditions over which he has a close control.

Europe's most successful joint scientific enterprise has been the construction, at Geneva, of—at the time—the largest particle accelerator in the world.

The first large successful synchrocyclotron accelerator began to bring results at Berkeley, California in 1947. A much larger 6 giga electron volt Bevatron came into operation in the United States in 1953. At Harwell, a first small European accelerator (a 180 MEV synchrocyclotron) was built. But on the Continent experiments in the postwar years were limited to a study of cosmic rays in the Alps and Pyrenees. Not surprisingly a first dramatic draining of Europe's younger physicists to America began.

Yet at this time no individual European government was prepared to invest the large sums needed to build, alone, a large high energy accelerator. At a time when statesmen were beginning for the first time to explore the possibilities of European unity, this seemed, to some of Europe's leading nuclear scientists, an ideal field for a practical effort.

There was, nevertheless, luck as well as much drive from the top nuclear physicists of Europe behind the birth of the European Organization for Nuclear Research (CERN). In 1946 a number of physicists and diplomats (Oppenheimer, Auger, de Rose, Kramers and others) were thrown together at the United Nations in an abortive search for a world inspection system against nuclear weapons. They began to search together for ways of developing imaginative international cooperation, with perhaps a base in Europe.

The building of European endeavour in basic physics soon won the backing of the United States, as did so many schemes for European unity in the 1950s. In June 1950, Professor Rabi of Columbia, the official American delegate, proposed a European regional laboratory at the General Conference of UNESCO in Florence. Professor Auger of France, UNESCO's director of natural science, was given the authority to act. Very small sums of money were soon after granted by the French, Italian and Belgian governments, which gave Professor Auger the room for manoeuvre he needed. The movement gathered way, with distinguished Italian scientists, such as Bernardini and Amaldi, playing a key role. They were soon joined by other distinguished European scientists, including Heisenberg, Cockcroft and Niels Bohr.

Unlike so many European joint enterprises which have begun with political acts, Auger began by getting his brilliant scientific pressure group to work out a project. He invited a team of distinguished scientists to form a board of consultants. They proposed, as a central objective, to construct the largest accelerator in the world and to prepare the way by building a small conventional machine. Politically, too, they proposed to advance step by step, beginning at once by the establishment of a 'provisional organization', which, at a cost of some $200-$250,000, would draw up detailed plans over a period of 18 months or so. In December 1951, eleven European governments signed an agreement setting up a provisional organization with Professor Amaldi as Secretary-General.[1]

This provisional CERN was remarkably free from the legalism which has dogged so many subsequent European enterprises. Instead of waiting for the signature of a convention, for ratification, and so on, this team of creative individuals took the risk of pushing ahead with planning, and even the placing of contracts, before the formal ritual was over. Indeed, 125 contracts were signed before CERN had a proper legal basis. CERN's creators believed that their baby would develop a life and momentum of its own.

In June 1953, a permanent convention was signed, and a proper 'interim organization' came into effect. At once work began on the establishment of a provisional laboratory in Geneva, preparation of a site, detailed architectural drawings, and training of staff. By September 1954, when the CERN convention, signed and ratified, came into force, it was possible to push straight ahead with the construction of a giant accelerator; three years had been saved and the Big Machine was complete and in operation by November 1959.

The bold decision to aim for the largest accelerator in the world paid off. To make the new high energy laboratory attractive to the best brains of Europe, it needed, Auger believed, a bold and precise aim. Though at first many European physicists were sceptical

[1]For an account of these years see L. Kowarski, *An account of the origin and beginning of Cern*, CERN paper 61–10, Geneva, 1961. See also J. B. Adams, The European Organization for Nuclear Research, in Sir John Cockcroft, (Ed.) *The Organization of Research Establishments*, Cambridge University Press, 1965.

of the wisdom or possibility of doing this, they were infected by the arguments, success and drive of the CERN team. The brain drain to America was reversed and able European physicists who had gone west came back to work on the Big Machine.

The British played a characteristic role in the early phases of the enterprise. From the start they were benevolent, but were at first reluctant to accept a full commitment. They were merely 'observers' in the 'provisional CERN'. But as it became clear that CERN might come off, their enthusiasm grew. When the convention came to be negotiated, Sir Ben Lockspeiser, the Director of the Department of Scientific and Industrial Research, played an active and constructive part; the British became full members and were indeed the first to ratify the Convention. J. B. Adams, a young engineer who two years before had doubted whether such a large accelerator could be built, led the team which designed and built the Big Machine, using the new principle of alternating-gradient focusing. He became CERN's Director-General in 1960.

Why has CERN become a model for other efforts of European scientific cooperation? What are the secrets of its success?

First the sheer size of the machine. It would have been hard for an individual member state to muster the resources for an accelerator of this scale, and impossible for one state to make effective use of it, considering the limited number of high quality high energy physicists in Europe. CERN works because its Big Machine is a 'big science' project in which the nation makes no sense.

It also worked, in part, because it was concerned with pure research. No sharp conflict of commercial and industrial interest between members has emerged to pull CERN apart and place real strain on it. Some governments, it is true, probably agreed to support it initially in splendid ignorance of the abstract character of CERN's research. Nuclear physics, they may have thought, might turn up something relevant to the bomb. But in practice there has been no such application to bring politics and conflict into CERN.

The high quality of both administrators and scientists who led CERN from the start also played a part. CERN is guided by a council, with two representatives from each member state, and usually one scientist and one administrator were sent. A council containing men of the stature of Heisenberg, Niels Bohr, Perrin, Valeur, Cockcroft and Lockspeiser could be expected to produce remarkable results.

From the start, however, CERN's imaginative creators firmly placed managerial authority in the hands of the chief executive, the Director-

General. Until 1967, when it met three times, the Council met only twice a year; the budget is settled in a mere three days discussion. The Council has two key subcommittees, for science policy and finance, but the scientific committee is appointed according to scientific merit, and the formulation of policy remains in the hands of the powerful Director-General (first Professor Block of Switzerland, followed by Professor Bakker of Holland, Dr J. B. Adams of Britain, the Austrian born American, Professor Weisskopf, and now Professor Gregory of France). Under him is a directorate of seven departmental directors, each responsible for a major area of activity: research, applied physics, technical coordination, and administration and so on.

The Director-General has the task of feeding the Council and its two committees with proposals for the budget and the long-term programme. Initially, as CERN embarked on its unprecedented task, some forecasts were underestimated (the 'Big Machine' by 20 per cent). Costs of operating experiments were underestimated even more. Then came a period when another kind of damage was done, as governments tried to impose rigid ceilings on spending and cut down the productivity of the new machine through lack of funds for the necessary experimental equipment. But a judicious balance has since been struck. CERN's directors have learnt to estimate their budgets extremely accurately and have thus earned in the Council a fund of trust. Their carefully thought out proposals leave little room for political bickering, so Council decisions get taken fast. Voting in the Council is usually on the basis of a simple majority, with a two thirds vote required for establishing the scale of contributions every three years, adopting supplementary programmes, and so on.

CERN has also developed and applied a number of techniques which could usefully be applied to other laboratories, European and national. From the start contracts for equipment and construction were placed on a competitive basis, with the condition that there must be at least three tendering firms. Staff has also been appointed on the basis of merit; the criteria have not been particular qualifications but the ability and temperament to do the kind of research work CERN involves. In both cases the possible pressure from member states to choose staff according to nationality has been successfully held off.

The lack of legalism, the boldness and determination of the group of European scientists who created and led CERN, their skill in harnessing European idealism to a precise practical objective, the sturdy independence of CERN's permanent management and its ability to keeping the politicians away, the fact that the organs of management are in the same place as the installations; all these factors have contributed to CERN's success and contrast favourably with other European scientific institutions.

What of CERN's scientific achievements? The elation was tremendous when CERN, racing the Brookhaven laboratory in the construction of its Big Machine, beat it and for six months in 1960 indeed possessed the largest accelerator in the world. CERN soon found, however, that despite its successful 'small machine', the synchrocyclotron, European physicists were badly handicapped by the absence in Europe of intermediate sized proton accelerators of the kind that had been built at Brookhaven and Berkeley in the United States. Work on the Big Machine involved a whole new range of techniques. European physicists were like pilots learning to fly supersonic aircraft with hardly any experience of jet flight. For two or three years therefore the American machines continued to produce the most exciting results.

The Europeans, however, led by CERN, have since rapidly caught up and produced a flow of experimental results comparable with those in the United States and Russia. These combined efforts have in the last seven years opened up a new world of understanding in our knowledge of the physical universe. It has been discovered that the familiar elementary particles, protons, neutrons, electrons, can be transformed into a much larger number of short-lived particles of higher energy. Behind this multiplicity of particles a novel, mathematically ordered symmetry has been unveiled. Many physicists believe that this symmetry may reflect the existence of even more fundamental objects within, say, the proton. The hunt is on to identify these tiny objects, known as 'quarks'. The search hardly sounds romantic to the layman, but it has an obsessive fascination to those involved and could at any time produce results which would have dramatic effects on the world around us.

The size of the Big Machine at CERN, far larger than any national or university accelerator in Europe, plus the high quality of its management, has enabled CERN to become the instrument and guide of European high energy physics as a whole. The CERN laboratory has not been an international ghetto, like some other international scientific enterprises. The Big Machine was constructed, above all, as an instrument for the use and education of nuclear physicists throughout Europe. But it was realized early that if outside physicists from the universities or national laboratories were to use the machine they must be helped by permanent staff who know how to use it. Mixed teams therefore perform the experiments. Of the 800 high-level physicists working on it at any one time, about 100 are staff members, maintaining and operating the machine and helping with experiments. One hundred are fellows or visiting physicists paid for by CERN, performing experiments, and the remaining 600 are physicists from universities and national laboratories throughout Europe, performing experiments on this giant common facility and paying for themselves. A number of major scientific subcommittees, each with an outside president, vet proposed experiments, of which there is a large waiting list, and select on grounds of quality, with the need to maintain a balance of nationalities amongst experimenters as a very secondary consideration. These committees are thus in a position to exert strong guidance in the direction of rationalizing the European high energy physics effort as a whole.

The experience and skills of CERN have been used to help national efforts directly. For instance, CERN experts helped the British team who built the Nimrod accelerator at the Rutherford laboratory. CERN has thus provided both a common service and a source of guidance of the highest scientific calibre for European high energy physics. Its example, indeed, set off a wave of construction of smaller accelerators at Hamburg, Frascati in Italy, at Chiltern and Daresbury in Britain. In just over ten years this great enterprise has thus ended the imbalance in high energy physics in the Atlantic world, reversing the brain drain in this field, and placing Europe on a par with America and Russia.

CERN's relationship with the other two giants is indeed intriguing. There was both friendly rivalry between the CERN 28 BEV machine and the new 33 BEV machine developed at Brookhaven over the same period of time (1954-60), and a close working relationship between the two. The Russians, on the other hand, built only a 10 BEV machine in the 1950s and thus were unable to perform experiments at the highest energies. Since the early 1960s, however, CERN has worked hard for a close relationship with the Russians. The result was that, since 1963, a growing number of Russians have come to work on the CERN machine on the understanding that Europeans would be able to work on the Russians' new 70 GEV machine from around 1969. Later, when and if CERN builds an even larger machine, the flow will be reversed once more. Ever since 1962

regular annual conferences of high energy physicists from the three
great continents have been an exciting feature of the scientific scene.
Thus CERN has typified, in its scientific field, the classic 'European'
doctrine that once Europe unites, it will be able to play the part both
of equal partner with Russia and America, and of a bridge between
them.

Yet even CERN cannot stand still, and its success in the future will
depend on whether both member states and executives take the
right decisions to keep it in front in the high energy research race.
The formulation of such policies is the work of the European Committee for Future Accelerators, set up in 1963 under Professor
Amaldi's chairmanship and containing 54 of the most eminent high
energy physicists in the member states. One key decision recommended by them has already been taken. In June 1965, the Council
approved a five-year budget of $100 mn. to construct 'intersecting
storage rings' which will greatly increase the power of the existing
accelerator. Instead of merely being accelerated in a huge circle
until they hit a fixed target, particles will be accelerated round a
further loop so that they collide. This means an immense increase
in energies; the smack when two cars moving in opposite directions
collide is a great deal more violent than when a moving vehicle
hits a standing one with the brakes off. Unfortunately, the density
of the beams is lower than with a conventional accelerator, diminishing the number of experiments which can be performed. Nevertheless, the new storage rings which will be completed by 1970—and
which will involve extending CERN's international territory across the
Swiss frontier into France—will give CERN exciting work and enable
it to remain on the frontiers of the science for a few more years.

It will not remain there, however, unless a decision is taken for
a far bolder leap ahead. As the physicists explore smaller and smaller
particles and their relationships, even higher energies are needed.
By 1969 Russia's 70 GEV machine at Serbhukov will be in operation. The United States, as we have seen, has decided to leap further
ahead and build a 200-400 GEV machine. CERN's committee for
future accelerators proposes to go even further and construct a 300
GEV machine, to be built under an eight and a half-year programme,
with construction starting in 1969 and to be completed in 1976.

This truly Giant Machine, with a diameter of 2·4 kilometres, will
enable physicists to probe far more deeply into the structure and
nature of elementary particles; it will employ some 4,000 people
(twice as many as CERN today), and of these more than half will be

experimenting or working on the machine; it will also soak up some pretty heavy spending. Over the eight-year period construction is expected to cost some $316 mn., reaching a peak of over $50 mn. in each of the years from 1971 to 1974. Operating costs will rise, year by year, reaching some $93 mn. per year in 1981. When these sums are split between the CERN members, they look less formidable, as the table below shows. Nonetheless, CERN's new Giant Machine will take a major chunk of science budgets. It is a large decision for Europe to take.

TABLE F

National Contributions to CERN

Country	% Contributions	1966 Costs ($ mn.)	1981 Estimate ($ mn.)	
			300–GEV	CERN–MEYRIN
Austria	1·9	0·8	1·8	1·7
Belgium	3·8	1·4	3·5	3·2
Denmark	2·1	0·8	1·9	1·8
France	18·6	7·6	17·4	15·7
Germany	22·8	9·3	21·3	19·4
Greece	0·6	0·2	0·6	0·5
Italy	11·2	4·5	10·5	9·5
Netherlands	3·9	1·6	3·5	3·2
Norway	1·4	0·6	1·4	1·3
Spain	1·7	1·3	1·7	1·5
Sweden	4·2	1·6	3·9	3·5
Switzerland	3·2	1·2	3·0	2·7
United Kingdom	24·6	8·8	22·9	20·6
	100·0	39·7	93·0	84·0

177·0

Sources: European Committee for Future Accelerators, Report 1967, (CERN/ECFA 67/13/Rev. 2) CERN, Annual Reports.

The thought naturally occurs whether some cheaper, more ingenious way, might not be found of accelerating particles to high energy. The trouble is that no one has yet discovered it.

Opponents of the 300 GEV accelerator also argue that the life sciences, for instance, have a better claim on such big money. Fifty years ago, they say, pure nuclear physics led to a breakthrough in our understanding of the universe which is still being exploited.

G

Today, they hold, it is the new science of molecular biology, the study of the physical nature of cells, in which chemistry, physics and biology blend to provide clues to life itself, which offers the hope of revolutionary change. Understanding and control of genetic change, biological control of our environment, medicine, agriculture; in all these immensely practical fields, the life sciences pioneer the way. To choose physics before such an exciting prospect is a large decision for Europe to take.

The answer to this is that technology today is indivisible. Work on the frontiers of the life sciences cannot advance fast without comparable progress in nuclear physics, and chemistry too. Progress in the exciting field of integrated circuits and computer logic depends on progress in physics, chemistry and mathematics. Thanks to CERN, high energy physics is one of the major fields of basic science where there is no 'scientific' gap between Europe and America. But unless Europe stays in the front rank of the accelerator race, CERN will slowly die. European universities and national centres will become once again satellites and suppliers of physicists to the big machines in Russia and America where the advanced work is done. The 300 GEV machine is thus a necessity for Europe.

Its heavy costs can be sustained only if national and university high energy facilities are kept within proper bounds. Since CERN's Big Machine was built, smaller national accelerators have blossomed. Britain has the Nina electron accelerator at the Daresbury laboratory, and the new Nimrod proton accelerator at the Rutherford laboratory; France the older 3 GEV Saturn machine at Saclay; West Germany a very good 6 GEV electron accelerator; and Italy a new 1·5 GEV machine at Frascati. There are eleven other large accelerators in different countries. These smaller machines and the laboratories round them provide a valuable local base for experiments. CERN's Big Machine can benefit from the support of scientists trained on other less ambitious types of facility; they in turn must have the chance to work at the 'summit' at CERN. The danger is that growing national ambitions may devour the resources necessary for the Giant Machine, and thus force Europe's effort back into the second rank. For, as when CERN was born, no single European state could possibly sustain an effort on the scale of the 300 GEV machine on its own.

The Amaldi committee's plan for the future would not give high energy physics a larger share of research and development resources than it gets today, but Europe's spending would grow by 8 per cent per year; the expected growth rate for Europe's total research effort.

These resources would pay for the CERN giant, provided national programmes do not expand but are limited to modernization and replacement. Quite apart from the strategic significance of the 300 GEV machine for European science, its advocates can show, with some convincing figures, that CERN machines are more productive. In 1966, for instance, CERN's operations, including those of outside physicists, cost $40 mn., and national programmes some $50 mn. But CERN, working intensively to make full use of its facilities, keeps some 800 physicists busy, compared with 600 on the national programmes; and CERN on the whole gets the most advanced results.

The difficulty is that there is almost always one of the four larger countries with a national programme whose scientists are pressing for a new national machine. France, with its two ageing accelerators, has firmly said that it now backs the 300 GEV machine. But if the decision is postponed, it will almost certainly replace them with a new one and then resources will not be available for CERN. The West Germans, who also have a lobby for a new national accelerator, will probably back CERN only if led by France and Britain. Smaller countries will follow large ones. Here, then, as in so many European technological decisions, Britain could tip the scales, deciding whether CERN is to flourish or decay. The British decision, announced in July 1968, not to support the 300 GEV accelerator was therefore a cruel blow.

If a positive decision is taken, a further major choice has to be made. Where is the giant facility, covering several square miles of country and employing some 4,000 people, to be? Naturally enough, almost every member country would like to play host to the Mecca of European physics, with its interesting construction contracts and its jobs for local labour. Modern financial techniques of burden-sharing can, however, much reduce the unfair advantages of the host country. The choice is certainly no more difficult than the choice made in America over the 200 GEV machine, and once again CERN provides a model of how such choices should be made.

The site committee received 22 offers of sites from ten member states. All of them were awarded points by special subcommittees which each had to consider a group of factors: geology and other vital technical factors; data from other institutions and laboratories; physical communications; and so on. Many sites were eliminated on technical grounds straight away; the remainder were then given points by each expert group, with nationals forbidden to vote for their own country. The list is gradually being whittled down, until, it is hoped, the points system will throw up a very short list, and then a final choice—if, that is, a choice is ever made.

The method would probably succeed, but only because the men who have made CERN have an overriding loyalty to the great aim of their enterprise: to enable Europe to compete on the far frontiers of science. Once politics begin to dominate a scientific enterprise of this kind, no points system will ensure a firm decision. The result will be a crude political choice, like the rather badly chosen site of the American 200 GEV machine.

Such a choice, for a single great project, taken in isolation, quickly sticks in the gullet of less lucky members, and sets up tensions which threaten the whole enterprise. A more sophisticated method is needed for making such decisions. After all, big scientific projects—a laboratory, a launching site—are a major source of jobs and economic activity, a legitimate topic of political interest and lobbying, as well as of scientific concern. In Europe, as in America, the scientific estate cannot indefinitely expect to succeed by insulating itself from politics, as we shall see all too forcefully in later chapters.

The choice of sites, however, invidious when focused on a single project, becomes in a sense far easier when many projects are in the game. Technical considerations, like geology in CERN's case, have to be answered with technical solutions. But a political and economic balance can be struck by distributing installations between the major countries: the Giant Machine in one country; a common molecular biology laboratory in another; a major space installation in a third. Just as the real answer to the choice for or against CERN's Giant Machine is to look, together, at Europe's overall science budget and choose, deliberately, between this and other fields, so the real answer on the site question can be found only within a broader strategy, in which the siting of giant projects is shared out amongst members with regional economic considerations fairly weighed.

CERN, in short, has so far skilfully stayed out of politics, helped by the abstract nature of its work. But it cannot expect an indefinite virginity. As we turn to other fields of European scientific and technological endeavour we find political choices and considerations that must be faced head-on.

CHAPTER 8

NUCLEAR RIVALRIES[1]

The years before 1939 were the golden age of European nuclear physics, when men like Rutherford, Joliot-Curie, Heisenberg and Fermi, made the discoveries which led to the atomic bomb. The war transformed this situation, making America the unchallenged capital of nuclear technology. Europe's first postwar endeavours to get into the application of nuclear technology, in a sense sprang from the common allied programme. They were the work of Britons and Frenchmen who had worked in Europe and America on the atomic bomb. And from the start they were conditioned by the ambivalent and shifting relationship between the Europeans and the United States.

The British, in particular, were the first to develop a strong national nuclear programme based on their wartime experience. Twenty key British scientists had worked at Los Alamos on the most intimate secrets of the bomb, making a disproportionate contribution to it. But for two wartime years intermittent and sometimes acrimonious negotiations between the British and Americans failed to give the British the assurance they sought that there would be a full and free exchange of knowledge between the partners. At last the Quebec Agreement, signed in August 1943 between the British and Americans, appeared to sanctify and make permanent the Anglo-Saxon partnership. It set up an organization which was to share the available uranium resources in the western world between the two countries. It provided for complete freedom of ex-

[1]For a full and fascinating account of the development of the French, British and American nuclear diplomacy, see Bertrand Goldschmidt, *Les Rivalités Atomiques*, Fayard, Paris, 1967.

change of information between the two countries during the war and for a mutual right of veto on the use of the bomb. It left the question of how much information Britain could obtain and exploit for industrial purposes till after the war. Britain agreed not to pass on information to third countries without American approval, even if that information sprang from its own scientists' discoveries.

In the postwar years, Britain's high hopes of a complete partnership with the United States were disappointed. In the immediate postwar months when Mr Attlee sought to persuade President Truman to accept a free flow of industrial information, hopes of agreement with the Russians on a world system of control held the Americans back. Later Congress and, after 1948, key members of the new US Atomic Energy Commission, took a dim view of nuclear sharing. In the end, the British got a pretty free exchange of scientific information and some information on limited industrial fields. But while they continued to benefit from the joint fuel arrangement and kept their promise not to tell secrets to outsiders, they never got a full and free exchange of industrial information. When the war ended the British scientists knew how to make the bomb, but they were obliged to push ahead with a national programme to develop, first the bomb, and then peaceful nuclear power.

Late in 1945 the Attlee Government decided to develop its own military programme. Three years later in May 1948 Parliament was told. In 1952, plutonium was first produced from reactors at Windscale. Meanwhile, a plant was built at Capenhurst to produce enriched uranium. In 1954 the programme was transfered from the Ministry of Supply to the newly created Atomic Energy Authority. In 1956 the world's first peaceful nuclear power station, at Calder Hall, went on stream.

The French did not share as fully as the British did in the American wartime programme. In the spring of 1940, Halben and Kowarski (Austrian and Russian physicists of French nationality who had worked with Joliot-Curie in the laboratories of the College de France), came to England and joined the team at Cambridge in the Cavendish Laboratories. They brought with them precious heavy water and soon completed the first experiments which led to a nuclear chain reaction. They were followed by other French scientists, notably Guéron and Goldschmidt, from the same centre. Because of American reluctance, the French group were never integrated fully into the Anglo-Saxon bomb programme. Instead, their main contribution was the development at Chalk River in

Canada of a heavy-water reactor which was later to form the basis of Canada's heavy-water reactor programme. In 1942, Halben concluded a personal agreement with the British that they would help France with scientific knowedge from their own programme after the war in return for an exclusive licence on the French discoveries in the British Empire. The agreement had no official backing on the French side, since the Free French Government knew nothing of these nuclear activities. It was, in any case, killed by the Americans who were not prepared to acknowledge any French contribution and claimed forcefully that it contravened the Quebec Agreement.

France, therefore, even more than Britain, was obliged to go it alone in the postwar pursuit of nuclear power. Guided in part by those who were aware of developments in America, President de Gaulle, then head of the French provisional government, set up the Commissariat à l'Energie Atomique in January 1946, with the 'ex-Canadians' in key positions. ZOE, the first very simple reactor, with heavy water as moderator, was completed in 1948. At first, thanks to the Anglo-Saxon monopoly of fuel supply, the CEA had to rely for its uranium on ten tons bought in 1939 and hidden in North Africa during the war, and on other scrapings. But in 1948, exploration led to the first major discovery on French soil. In 1952, France's first five-year nuclear plan, to cost $140 mn., finally shifted the emphasis from scientific exploration to industrial and potentially military application. A plutonium extraction plant was to be built, and two reactors, graphite moderated and gas-cooled, in the same stream of development as Britain. The French were about three years behind.

During these years, the French showed themselves no wiser than the British in their attitude towards European cooperation. An overture from Norway, whose heavy-water plant was supplying the French programme, was snubbed. By the time the French line had changed, Norway had turned to Holland; the two sought advice from the Americans on the wisdom of further collaboration with France and got a dusty answer. Norway and Holland eventually got a limited arrangement with Britain.

In 1954 the plan for a European army rose into the diplomatic sky, and fell, shot down by the abiding nationalism of both Britain and France. That year, in the vacuum left by its collapse, the idea of a French military programme matured. As far back as 1951, the decision to build a third natural uranium reactor producing plutonium has implied a possible military programme. Britain had exploded its first A-bomb in October 1952 and was to explode its first H-bomb in May 1957; in December 1954, a first positive decision of principle was taken by the cabinet of M. Mendès-France; a study programme on a bomb and a nuclear submarine was secretly begun. In May 1955, an able Minister, Gaston Palewski, who was also an intimate friend of General de Gaulle, persuaded the French cabinet to take a more decisive plunge and enlarge the plan from $140 mn. to $350 mn. This was partly to allow for increased costs, but also to provide for increased plutonium production, an extension of the Marcoule Research Centre, the construction of a nuclear submarine, and the construction of new installations to develop a French bomb. The fourth nuclear power was on the way.

In the last months of 1954 and early 1955 an episode, potent with political significance, occurred in the field of fuel supply. Though France, like Britain, had embarked on a stream of natural uranium reactors, it was clear that reactors using enriched uranium would play a big part in the future. A plant to enrich the fuel was needed.

Such a plant was a necessity if France was to develop its own bomb. The French 'Canadians' turned to their old wartime colleagues, the British. In his book, Bertrand Goldschmidt explains how he approached Sir John Cockcroft and Sir Edwin Plowden, who led the Atomic Energy Authority at the time, and asked them whether they would sell to and build for France a plant similar to Capenhurst. The first response was positive: an invitation to come and discuss details. But when the meeting took place the two Britons put a list of specifications on the table and explained regretfully 'that the choice they had intended to offer us, was purely theoretical, for the United States, consulted under the Anglo-American agreements on atomic secrecy, had formally opposed this project, whose importance for British industry would have been considerable'.[2]

The French then turned to their European partners and began to push the idea of a common European nuclear fuel enrichment plant to supply these future needs. The United States, however, anxious to maintain its monopoly of both fuel and knowhow in a field crucial to the development of the bomb, put strong pressure on the other governments in 1956 to turn the idea down. They did so, forcing the French to consider building their own plant.

In 1967 France's own nuclear enrichment plant at last went on

[2]Bertrand Goldschmidt, op. cit., p. 227.

stream after 12 years of immense expenditure and effort, relearning the lessons the Anglo-Saxons knew.

Birth of Euratom

It is a relief to turn from this story of competing nationalisms, American, British and French, to a more constructive endeavour. Nineteen fifty-four was a year of atomic euphoria; at the Geneva conference on the peaceful use of nuclear energy, the United States shifted position and offered to lift the veil of secrecy for a wide range of peaceful applications of nuclear power. Europe was beginning to appreciate that nuclear power would have to fulfil a growing proportion of its fuel needs. It was natural that when the Six met in Messina to consider next steps towards European unity, they should consider, side by side with the common market, the creation of an atomic community for the peaceful exploitation of nuclear power.

In 1955 the atomic budgets of France's five partners were, together, no more than a quarter of the French nuclear budget. To some Frenchmen the creation of a nuclear community seemed an ideal way of containing any possible German nuclear revival. To 'Europeans' the pooling of resources in this hideously expensive and politically explosive matter seemed both economically and politically wise.

The new Community followed a pattern since made familiar by the European Economic Community. The Council of Ministers was to take decisions, sometimes by unanimity, sometimes by a qualified majority vote. A commission of five was to formulate policy.

The main objective of the Treaty was to develop a joint research programme, financed by a common budget, fixed at some $215 mn. for a first five-year period. The Community was empowered to place development contracts in member countries to back up an overall policy of coordination. In theory, knowledge was to be pooled between the member countries, and complex patent provisions were devised to make this happen. Finally, teeth were given to the new Community by the establishment of a new agency with a monopoly of import and distribution of nuclear fuels. An inspection system was established, with the right to inspect plants in the Community, to ensure that they were operated for the purposes declared.

These bold purposes were inevitably weakened from the start by the national postures of France and Britain. At the very moment when the Euratom Treaty was being negotiated, France was embarking on her own national military programme. For a brief moment, in 1956, Premier Mollet appeared to retreat. Europe, he declared, had to decide whether the new Community would develop the atom for peaceful or military purposes. He opted for peace, which meant that no member could embark on a military programme. It was not long before pressures inside France shifted him from this pacific stand. And when the Community emerged, it allowed member countries, other than West Germany, which had promised not to manufacture nuclear weapons in 1954, to develop separate national military programmes if they wished. Nuclear knowledge and fuel supply for military purposes could be kept separate. A flaw was built into the very foundations of Euratom.

Britain stood aloof from the new atomic venture, as it did from the economic community of the Six. At that time the British Government, though unwilling to join the Common Market, was seeking association with it through a free trade area. In July 1957 the question of joining Euratom, or seeking close association, was seriously considered by the Atomic Energy Authority, and by the government. 'Europeans' who argued that Britain, with its nuclear lead, could lead the new Community and give it a massive send-off, were defeated by islanders who argued that, since Britain was ahead, it was better to keep our knowhow to ourselves, and hope to gain a commercial lead by going it alone. Instead of joining Euratom, the British encouraged the development of the looser European Nuclear Energy Agency, an agency of the 17-nation OEEC (now OECD).

This body, unlike Euratom, has no general powers to develop a European policy and no overall research budget; decisions of the Council of Ministers have to be taken by unanimous vote. But, judged by results, ENEA has done well on far smaller resources than Euratom has enjoyed. Norway's development of a heavy-water reactor was extended by bringing in other OEEC countries to operate and finance it. A new company, Eurochemic, was set up to build and operate a plant for reprocessing nuclear fuel at Mol, in Belgium. It was completed in 1966. Most successful of all was a new experimental reactor, the Dragon high temperature gas-cooled reactor, built at Winfrith, Dorset, with Britain as the major partner, together with Euratom and some smaller European countries. We shall return later to the Dragon, for it occupies a key position on the European nuclear chessboard today (see page 122). The ENEA working principle of allowing those members who wished to set up projects to do so, and leaving others out, has worked. The Euratom

Commission made an important contribution by its policy of vigorous participation in joint projects with the European countries outside.

These specific efforts, however, were not enough to compensate for Britain's self-exclusion from Euratom and the Common Market. After the signature of the Treaty, 'three wise men', Louis Armand, Franz Etzel, and Francesco Giordani visited the United States and Britain to explore possibilities of collaboration and lay down objectives for Euratom. In Britain they were received in a friendly way, but nothing emerged from the encounter except a modest arrangement to exchange information on some areas of basic research.

The United States, by contrast, seized the opportunity with both hands. At the time (1957), nuclear plants were not yet economic in the United States, but the water reactors, developed in the submarine programme, plainly had potential. Europe seemed an ideal testing ground, a new arena where American reactors and technology could be tried out, and a commercial influence established.

Politically, the new European Community seemed an ideal partner for the kind of peaceful arrangement the United States had been willing to negotiate since the Geneva conference of 1955. The fuel agency and the inspection system provided effective means of controlling peaceful nuclear development. The United States agreed to supply Euratom with enriched uranium supplies and the two partners agreed on a joint reactor research and development programme in Europe. So far some $60 mn., divided between America and Euratom roughly in equal parts, have been spent on industrial development contracts for water reactors.

For four years, the Euratom Community developed in a hopeful atmosphere. The first five-year programme of research got under way. The decision was taken to concentrate applied research in one main centre (Ispra in Italy). The Italians, however, took a long time to ratify the arrangement and the Community was forced to revise its plans and distribute research to four centres each specializing in a different field. Two of them, Geel in Belgium and Ispra in Italy, were opened. At Ispra work began on the development of a new reactor prototype, the Orgel, a variant of heavy-water technology. This, together with the Dragon project, provided a possible second generation reactor type. An important new technique was also developed, which has proved a highly effective means of extending the Community's influence and effect. Under 'contracts of association', the Community finances only a part of a particular development and sends representatives to share in the management and work. Industry or governments provide the remaining funds and men; contracts of association have multiplied the effect of Euratom's limited budget, and increased its influence on national policies generally. The second President of the Commission,[3] Etienne Hirsch, an ardent 'European', provided effective political leadership and drive.

But in 1961 President de Gaulle, now in office, struck Euratom a political body blow. When the time came to renew the mandate of the first Commissioners, the French Government insisted on removing the pro-European President, M. Hirsch, and replacing him by the Gaullist, M. Châtenet. His treatment for a somewhat ailing patient has been to administer, not medicine, but euthanasia.

As Euratom's second programme got moving, its research budget increased to $425 mn., nearly double the first. The four research centres built up to a full strength of 2,500, absorbing about half the budget. Work on Dragon and Orgel continued. But by 1963, difficulties were closing in on the Community.

The second five-year plan had been cut by the Council in June 1962. By 1963 it was becoming clear that the cuts were playing havoc with the programme. Inflation provided a good reason to restore them in part. But by this time differences about the programme were emerging. France was pushing ahead with its national programme. The omens for the Orgel reactor, the main project operating in Italy, were not good; the Italians were beginning to resent the downgrading of community projects and hoping for more Euratom expenditure in Italy. It took a year and a half of often acrimonious debate for the Council to agree to a revised second programme.

The strength of resurgent national interests was most apparent in plans for the vital third generation of reactors, the fast breeders. In this field the British were ahead and in 1962, during Britain's first common market negotiations, the British proposed to make Dounreay a common research centre. The British authorities, however, always insisted that construction of a fast-breeder prototype must remain an independent commercial matter, and when the first Common Market negotiations collapsed, the proposal on Dounreay collapsed too.

Inside the Community, the Commission had little more luck. Both France and Germany resolved to go ahead with their own fast-breeder programmes; the French Commissariat à l'Energie Atomique

3Louis Armand, the first President, retired through ill health after a year.

is to build a sodium-cooled prototype (Phoenix), starting in 1969, and in West Germany Siemens, the largest industrial nuclear concern, is to do the same. In all, Europe expects to spend some $1,500 mn. on fast reactor prototypes and research, three of them of the same kind. Until the end of 1967 the Euratom Commission had 'contracts of association' with the French and West German programmes, but the flow back of information has been less than it should be; the attempt to develop a rational common programme has plainly failed.

By the end of 1966, when Euratom's third programme should have been prepared, the Community was deep in crisis. The Italians were bitterly declaring that, since others had turned nationalist, they would too, unless, in the next programme, the Community financed a major test reactor in Italy. The Belgians were proposing that the next programme be drastically cut. In press interviews, M. Châtenet publicly washed his hands of all this. Euratom staff were beginning to look for other jobs. By 1968 Euratom was struggling on with a stop-gap one-year budget far below the previous rate of spending. The main contracts of association on reactor prototypes and development were carried on with national funds; only the work on fusion and the bulk of biology survived intact. At this turning point in Euratom's fortunes, let us draw up a balance sheet of its failings and achievements.

About half of Euratom's research budget has been spent in its four research centres, where 2,500 people are employed. These centres have done useful common research on a wide range of programmes, from radiobiology to metallurgy and fuel studies. The four centres have had varying degrees of success: good in Karlsruhe and Geel (nuclear measurements), more problematical at Petten and Ispra, where much energy has gone into the Orgel heavy-water reactor. The Orgel reactor, imposed as it was by governments, has been criticized as a poor choice and there are still problems to overcome. But it has been unexpectedly successful, and we shall see later that it could play a part in a European development strategy. Certainly all this work has undoubtedly helped to disseminate nuclear know-how and build up a trained body of nuclear scientists and technologists in the Community, one of the first objectives of Euratom.

In many fields, Euratom's contracts of association have also proved successful, both in reactor development, and pure research.

The programme with the United States certainly helped to transfer America's new technology rapidly. And there have been valuable developments in Europe itself. In reactor development, to take only one small, recent, but interesting example, AEG and SNECMA have recently developed an idea of SNECMA'S to improve the performance of the water reactors developed in the United States. A spiral metal coil surrounds the fuel cores, guiding the flow of steam and thus doubling the thermal efficiency of the reactor.

In pure research, association contracts have had certain striking successes, particularly in the field of nuclear fusion, a way-out field involving relatively expensive equipment, which could bring a dramatic breakthrough in energy production sometime in the future. In fusion, the six contracts of association with different research institutions have been welded by a permanent scientific liaison committee into an effective common programme, which was allocated some $34 mn. in the second five-year programme.

Britain's work in fusion, at the Culham laboratories, has been at least kept in contact with the programme of the Six. In the early 1960s, when CERN, having built the Big Machine, was looking about for fresh fields of endeavour, J. B. Adams, then its Director, instigated the creation of a new European fusion committee. It has since evolved into a rather looser seminar-type gathering of scientists engaged on fusion research. It nonetheless still helps to avoid duplication of work, even though it has not integrated the Culham effort into a single European programme.

Euratom has also provided a number of valuable common services. Detailed technical papers on Community research and development are available to Community industries. The Documentation and Information Centre provides a large library of nuclear information from all parts of the world, with a computerized system of coding, storage and retrieval. With 600,000 publications already recorded and a growth of 10,000 per month, such a system is becoming essential. The Centre has developed a thesaurus or code which has been adopted by the United States, Russia and East Germany as well. As many as 4,000 of the 10,000 monthly publications come from the US Atomic Energy Commission, with which Euratom has a close working relationship, and about the same proportion of requests for information come from America. Europeans, except the West Germans and Dutch, make less use of it than they could. The Centre proves its value by the fact that it could, if necessary, become a profitable commercial operation. At a cost of $2·5 mn. it is one of the Community's most valuable investments.

Euratom thus follows a pattern, which we shall find repeated in many European endeavours. Despite the discouragements some governments have placed in the way of top men working for it, Euratom's own programmes of pure research and services have worked well. In 20 years Europe has developed, from nearly nothing, a fairly wide range of nuclear skills. But there has been an almost total failure to blend the main streams of national atomic policies or to develop an integrated optimal industrial structure. Once the stakes rise, and national interests and the hopes of gain from commercial exploitation come into the game, separate interests begin to triumph over the common good, and this tendency is getting worse, not better.

It is true that some industrial companies, especially in West Germany, are showing a growing talent for applying the basic research and development done elsewhere. Siemens now offers a highly competitive light-water reactor, based on licences from Westinghouse. AEG does the same with GE-based boiling-water reactors. Both these companies perhaps have the strength to loss-lead in order to gain a foothold in the market. Brown Boveri, the Swiss company which has highly independent subsidiaries in France and West Germany, has been one of the first companies to get in a position to assess the comparative virtues of the main different types of reactor. Its West German subsidiary is working with Atomic Power Construction, one of the British consortia, as a licensee of advanced gas-cooled reactors; and the Swiss parent is working up designs for a Dragon-type high temperature reactor, as well as doing designs for a boiling-water and light-water reactors. Belgo-Nucléaire, the main Belgian nuclear enterprise is working with AEG (Germany) and SNECMA (France) on General Electric boiling-water reactors, and with the British Nuclear Power Group on advanced gas-cooled reactors. In Sweden ASEA are developing an American-type boiling-water reactor of their own design. The technology of existing reactor systems, in other words, is being rapidly diffused.

The European licensors of American companies, however, have their problems. While Westinghouse and General Electric get knowledge from the Atomic Energy Commission free, they license to Europe at whatever terms the market will stand.

Westinghouse, for instance, has given exclusive licences to different companies in different countries (Siemens in West Germany; Ansaldo in Italy). The anti-trust laws, it is claimed, do not permit the licensor to allow the two to work together, a further deterrent to an integrated European effort.

Fuel is also a critical question. The American water reactors depend on imported enriched uranium; so even reactors built in Europe imply a large flow of dollars for the fuel imports. Exports from Europe pose even larger problems. Can the United States be expected to provide fuel, indefinitely, for exported reactors built by its competitors?

The test of Euratom's first ten years of work and of European industry will come with the next two generations of reactors. Much money has gone into the development of 'intermediate converters' (Orgel, Dragon etc.), a generation of reactors between the present British-French gas or US water-cooled reactors, and the fast breeders of the future. Will any of these European ventures be needed and will any come off as competitive industrial efforts?

Even more vital for Europe will be the success or failure of the fast-breeder development programme, where resources are being squandered by development in triplicate. At a total cost of some $1,500 mn., the three main European countries are each trying to go it alone, each believing that it may get a marginal lead on its competitors. Meanwhile the American giant, in the person of the AEC, bides its time, systematically building up a capability in industry, by placing contracts for components, tutoring, monitoring, exploring crucial weak spots (like fuel testing) which will ensure that once the programme takes off, it will succeed. Big American companies, however, are beginning to put on the pressure. And once the AEC and the companies both decide that a possibility of commercial exploitation is in sight, a massive financial shove will no doubt be given to the programme. Once more Europe might find that any lead it has in fast breeders will vanish when the time comes for commercial exploitation.

Thus continental Europe finds itself in similar plight to Britain, with a growing nuclear capability, but badly organized to exploit it. In the next vital phase two factors will decide whether Europe's potential is realized or not: the skill and resources which the European Community puts into a refurbished nuclear policy now that the executives are merged in one; and the role of Britain.

Lessons from Euratom

A skilful and more effective common policy by the European Community will depend on learning from the lessons of the past. Why did Euratom have such limited success?

Plain politics and resurgent nationalism of course played a part.

France has pursued a national nuclear policy, and others have begun to echo it. France has pursued a line of reactor development designed to maximize independence from America. Others have, until lately, been prepared to accept an American-based technology, even at the price of political dependence and industrial penetration by American firms.

Bad organization and poor leadership also played a part. The Commission of Euratom has not been led by men of comparable stature to those of the EEC Commission.

There have been no distinguished scientists on the Commission. And the scientific advisory committee has been ineffective. Certainly politics, sometimes of a pretty provincial character, have mixed in with Euratom's technical decision-making, with unfortunate effect.

Such shortcomings, however, do not explain why Euratom failed to enter the fast-breeder race, at a time, at the beginning of the second programme, when it might have developed a truly European policy. First the French and then the West Germans fought a common policy and instead stuck out for two; the Italians in turn demanded a third, and when they failed to get it, became wreckers too.

The inadequacies of the Euratom organization owe something to the original terms of the Treaty, and something to subsequent events. Much of the prolonged wrangling over the research programme would have been avoided if it had had to be decided by qualified majority vote, as are many other key decisions in the Euratom Community. Then members would have been under pressure to agree, and the Commission would have been better placed to exert a creative influence. Etienne Hirsch, the Commission's European-minded second President, lost his job precisely because he sought to establish a majority vote over changes in the programme —the same kind of issue which brought Professor Hallstein into conflict with President de Gaulle.

In retrospect, the decision to make the Euratom research programme essentially a supplement to national programmes (a balancing wheel like the National Science Foundation in the US) appears to have been a mistake. The national programmes have burgeoned, consuming the bulk of resources and bringing growing waste and duplication. There is an increasingly urgent need for a real harmonization of Europe's entire research and development effort in atomic energy: a steering wheel. The sacrifice of some of Euratom's own research effort, in return for a real willingness by European countries

H

to thrash out a common nuclear policy fitting national policies to-gether, would be a price well worth paying. Europe now has an abundance, perhaps a superfluity, of good nuclear research es-tablishments. The need is to make better use of them.

Some of the original, good conceptions of the Euratom Treaty have not been fully implemented. One is the idea of an open pool of information. On the whole, Euratom has received back most of the information due to it from companies with contracts of association. There is provision for the grant of automatic non-exclusive licences to other firms. Yet the Italians complain that they have not received much useful information on fast-breeder develop-ment, acquired by Euratom under the contract of association with France. Some observers of Euratom believe that they could in part get this if they took the trouble to pack the Euratom staff of the association operations with their men. They still complain of in-sufficient information and resented France getting the lion's share of Community funds in this field. The Commission has not even made use of all the powers provided in the Treaty. For instance, Chapter V of the Treaty provides for the setting up of 'joint enter-prises', which could be backed by private and public shareholders from different countries, and which might, say, build a prototype reactor on a power grid, leading on later to larger scale production. This would be an ideal way of bringing industrial concerns together. Chapter V has hardly ever been used.

All this means that the main research or prototype reactors de-veloping in the Community do not form part of a common market of information as in certain state-backed sectors in the United States.

An Industrial Strategy

The merger of the three Community executives in July 1967 pro-vided a chance for a new approach. What tasks, policies, and im-provements in organization are needed to make the most of the opportunity?

It must be faced that part of the task is simply to make the Treaty work. The system of contracts of association, for instance, must be revised. One major proposal comes from M. Gueron, the French director of research at Euratom. He proposes a 'community of prototypes': to carry forward research into the crucial industrial phase, a range of prototype reactors should be built in Europe within a common market in knowledge, and backed partly by Euratom. Such prototypes might be built by 'joint enterprises' under

Chapter V. They would include reactor types as diverse as Dragon, Orgel, and other intermediate types already being developed in Community countries as well as a varied range of fast reactors. Industry throughout Europe would be free to pick from the pool and produce and market whichever reactor won the race.

This interesting idea has shortcomings. It takes too little account of the stake particular companies and governments already have in certain types of reactor. It is logical enough, but does not really show how separate national interests can be prevented from clashing, diverging and spoiling the harmony of the 'community of prototypes'. It says nothing of the need to develop in Europe powerful transnational groups which can not only develop prototypes, but go on to produce and sell, forming effective competitors to the American giants. The idea of a community of prototypes is only valid if it leads on to something more.

What is needed is a European industrial strategy, which seeks to form two or three major transnational European groups each developing and eventually producing and marketing a group of reactors, forming a natural stream of developments. Such groups might also act as operating enterprises for fuel processing plants and enrichment plants. Euratom would play a part in such a development. However, it would depend on the will and skill of industry as well as government and would have to evolve out of existing interests.

Europeanizing Capenhurst

The first major common interest is in fuel supply, where Britain could help fill a European need.

By 1980, the Euratom Commission expects the Community to have installed at least 40,000 MW of nuclear power, and the figure could be as high as 60,000 MW. The bulk of this capacity is likely to take the form of reactors using partially enriched uranium: water reactors, AGRs, or some kind of more advanced converters. Europe will therefore need a massive increase in supplies of both natural and enriched uranium. On the basis of these estimates, continental Western Europe should need between 11,000 and 16,500 tons of natural uranium of which between 8,000 and 16,000 would be absorbed by isotopic separation plants which partially enrich the fuel. After 1980, fast-breeder reactors, which produce more fissile material than they consume, will be playing a growing part in power installations. But though the growth of demand for enriched uranium will slow down it is not expected to start falling till about 1995.

Natural uranium is no longer as scarce as it was after the war and raises few problems. France, for instance, has now concluded arrangements with the African territory of Niger, which, together with its home supplies, will provide more than its needs up to 1980. Other European countries now find it much easier to buy natural uranium in many parts of the world. The fuel monopoly of the Anglo-Saxon powers is long since broken. Natural uranium, though still channelled by Euratom through its fuel agency, is a fairly abundant marketable commodity, like other minerals.

Enriched uranium, on the other hand (containing more of the fissile material, U_{235}) is a far more sensitive commodity, for it is only produced on a large scale in isotopic separation plants of advanced technology, of a kind originally developed to provide fissile material for bombs. Outside China there are only seven in existence today: three in America, two in Russia, one in Britain, and one in France. It was this kind of plant which the French asked the British to build for them in 1956—and were refused. Of the plants in the western world, only the three American plants are of an optimum size; each consumes some 2,000 MW of electricity, enough to feed a large city. These giant plants were developed to provide fissile material for America's enormous stockpile of nuclear bombs. But their scale and the availability of cheap electricity has meant that at present America is the main supplier, and the cheapest, of enriched uranium for nuclear power reactors throughout the world.

As Europe's requirements grow it must inevitably ask whether it can continue to depend on imported fuel to this extent. There is, first, the effect on the balance of payments. The fuel consumed during the lifetime of one of today's American-type water reactors is worth about twice as much as the original power station. It is the major part of the business. By 1980, if the six Euratom countries were importing enriched fuel for, say, 40,000 MW of electricity, this might cost them some $150 mn.[4] for fuel enrichment, in addition to the basic cost of the natural uranium involved. Compared with Europe's bill for oil imports, this sum is not enormous. But two other factors add to fears of dependence on outside supplies. One is the prospect of a shortage of supply. It is not only continental Europe's requirements that will have expanded meteorically by 1980. In the OECD countries there may be some 300 mn. MW of nuclear

[4]Internal Document of European Community, EUR/C/1800/2/67.

power installed by 1980. America's existing enrichment plants will cover only about half to two thirds of this need. Will a shortage of enrichment capacity actually slow down the development of nuclear power, or raise the price of fuel? Europeans naturally ask whether new capacity should be built in Europe.

Europeans also worry about security of supply. At present the American enrichment plants provide fuel on equal terms to foreigners and Americans. From 1969, all will be able to benefit from a new facility; users will be able to arrange for their own fuel to be processed in the plants on payment of a processing charge. Long-term contracts might safeguard such facilities for Europeans, continuing and expanding America's relatively helpful role of fuel supplier to Euratom.

Yet there are dangers. Some financial facilities for purchase are already available to American users and not to Europeans. US long-term contracts abroad must respect quantitative limitations laid down by Congress within the overall allocation of fissile material for civilian use decided by the President. These might be tightened up. Some Continental Europeans already feel that the US has gently but firmly made use of its fuel monopoly to obtain other advantages; plutonium has been sold to the French and West German fast-breeder programmes on condition there is exchange of information on the programme at the same time. In the future, when European manufacturers of nuclear reactors are competing with the United States in third markets, will America never make commercial use of its monopoly of the indispensable fuel supplies? In 1967 European fears were set alight by the proposed non-proliferation treaty, which embodied tighter controls on the distribution of nuclear fuel to non-nuclear powers, and threatened to replace the Euratom inspection system, under which the six members inspect each other, by a system of inspection from outside. As if to rub it in, when Euratom sought, in March 1967, to double the quota for plutonium imports from America to 1,000 kg per year, the United States replied by making agreement conditional on a tighter inspection system, a further exchange of information and a much higher price.

It is hardly surprising that Europeans have been asking whether the time has come to build, after all, Europe's own fuel enrichment plant to fill the soaring needs of the late 1970s and 1980s. A scheme drawn up by the Euratom Commission envisages the construction of a plant, comparable in size to the three existing American plants, and costing some $1·3 bn., to be spent mainly in the second half of the decade before 1980. It would consume some 2,000 MW of electricity, and process some 7·5 mn. units per year.

The snag is that no one in Europe, outside Britain and France, at present has the knowhow to build and operate such a plant efficiently. Hence the importance of the British contribution.

At Capenhurst, the Atomic Energy Authority completed Europe's first nuclear enrichment plant for the production of bomb material in 1955. Britain now has, in addition to the plutonium from the reactors at Calder and Chapel Cross, an ample stockpile of enriched uranium for bombs, but, with the switch in its nuclear power programme from natural to enriched fuel, it is converting Capenhurst for this purpose. A first stage, costing £13-14 mn. ($32 mn.) will be completed by 1970; during the 1970s a further £50 mn. ($120 mn.) will be spent to expand the plant sufficiently to provide enough fuel for Britain's needs in 1980. Yet even then the plant will still be consuming only some 1,000 MW of electricity and will have about half the capacity of an optimum-sized American plant. Because of its small size, fuel from such a plant will probably still be uncompetitive with American fuel, and might need a protective tariff of some 15 per cent. The idea of expanding the plant further, to satisfy wider European needs, springs to mind. Foratom, the organization of the European nuclear industry, has done a useful study of the need and how to satisfy it.

With this in mind British representatives embarked on a series of carefully muffled talks in European capitals during 1967, and made definite proposals, especially in Bonn. Capenhurst, they suggested, could supply other European countries with a guaranteed fuel supply, if these countries would be prepared to share in the investment in the plant.

Unfortunately the initial proposal, like so many British European proposals since the war, was shrouded in ambivalence. The British offered to make use of Continental money to expand the plant, but not to share the knowhow. Naturally, some Continental Europeans reacted with asperity. On those terms, why not just buy from the Americans, instead of lending money to the British?

The French, the possessors of Europe's second nuclear enrichment plant, were no more forthcoming. Forced by the Anglo-Saxon powers to evolve their own technology, they had considerable difficulties in bringing their plant at Pierrelatte on stream; 5.500 mn. francs ($1,100 mn.) were spent on construction of the plant between

1960, when it began, and 1967, when production of 90 per cent enriched fuel for military purposes began. It will no doubt take some further time before all the bugs are out of the plant. The cost of expanding production of low enriched uranium for civilian purposes to up to a million units per year, or one third of the Capenhurst target for 1980, has been put as high as a further 2 bn. francs ($400 mn.). When, in December 1967, the British offer spurred the French to make a similar proposal to the Six, they were just as unwilling as the British to share the technology of the plant.

The potentialities of a bolder British initiative are plain. If the British Government was prepared to make Capenhurst a European enterprise, with other Europeans sharing, not merely in financing, but in running the plant and in the technology, the second phase of expansion in the 1970s could be doubled, bringing it up to an optimum capacity of say 7 mn. units by 1980, and supplying part of the needs, not only of Britain, but of continental Europe.

At the same time, British knowhow could help the French to cut costs and speed the expansion of Pierrelatte for commercial purposes, provided, that is, they too were prepared to make the enterprise a 'European' plant. As demand continued to grow in the early 1980s a second major European enrichment plant could be brought up to optimum capacity.

Why has a sensible but nonetheless dramatic overture on these lines not been made by the British? One reason, given to the West Germans, for instance, is that 'ties with the United States' inhibit any sharing of the knowhow. Yet leading French journalists were told, unequivocally, by the Prime Minister's chief scientific advisor and by members of the Atomic Energy Authority that no agreement now exists with the United States which would prevent Britain sharing the knowhow. The truth is that, while no formal agreement exists on the technology, which was mainly developed by Britain on its own, the US and British governments still consult together on what is 'classified' information, and the British—above all the Ministry of Defence—have been as reluctant to offend the Americans in a major matter as mice to give up eating cheese.

More to the point is the proliferation problem. Fuel enrichment is one of the remaining secrets of the bomb. Are the West Germans, Italians, and other Europeans, to be let in on the secret? There is one vital qualification here. The enrichment process is carried out in stages: a low-enrichment plant enriching the fuel up to, say, 3 per cent, and three further stages enriching the fuel up to 90 per cent or more. It is in the last stages that the French encountered their main problems and where the most tricky technology is involved. A European plant for low enrichment could thus easily be developed without involving nationals of non-nuclear countries in the more sophisticated branches of the art.

Paradoxically, too, a non-proliferation treaty might actually help to solve the problem. If an international system of inspection were agreed, which satisfied the Russians, they could feel more confident than ever that the West Germans, say, would not make use of new knowledge, acquired at Capenhurst and Pierrelatte, to sneak off into the woods of Bavaria and construct, secretly, a multimillion dollar bomb enrichment plant. The thought is far-fetched, to say the least.

In such circumstances, the United States might, in fact, not react unfavourably to a move, if it were made decisively and skilfully. When asked, US spokesmen usually reply that their reaction would depend on what question was put. If a proposal to 'Europeanize' Capenhurst were agreed amongst the Europeans, and then sold to the Americans as a contribution to the broad strategy of European unity—with peaceful aims, and technology clearly separated from the more advanced warlike part—the American administration would probably accept it. It is up to the British to take the plunge.

A new shadow fell across the idea of a 'European' Capenhurst when the Dutch announced, late in 1967, that they were well on the way to developing an economic form of the alternative gas-centrifuge process. The odds are, however, that while this process can provide an efficient and cheap form of small-scale production, it will not be as cheap as the diffusion process on a large scale. The Dutch Joker could provide small would-be nuclear powers with bomb fuel on the cheap, but it may not take the British and French aces when it comes to satisfying Europe's huge needs for commercial fuel.

How would joint European plants at Capenhurst and Pierrelatte be organized? There is a strong case for introducing major industrial companies into the management of such an enterprise, as in the United States, as part of a broader policy to overcome the separation between Europe's governmental research establishments and industry. The 'mixed company' formula provided in the Euratom Treaty (and open to third countries) might well be suitable. In Britain suitable participants could be the Atomic Energy Authority, Rolls Royce (with its fuel experience for submarines), ICI, and Rio

Tinto Zinc, the three companies which have, for years, pressed the government for the right to share in fuel production in Britain. In France the Société pour l'Usine de Séparation Isotopique, the Société des Usines Chimiques de Pierrelatte and the Société de Fabrication d'Éléments Catalytiques already group the major companies with an interest in this field. In West Germany Siemens and AEG, in Belgium Belgo-Nucléaire, in Holland Neratoom, in Italy Ansaldo and Fiat, in Sweden ASEA provide potential industrial participants for an enrichment plant. The best formula for industrial participation in running such a plant would probably be to invite tenders from joint management companies, set up for the purpose, on the condition that they include representatives from, say, at least three countries. But a definitive picture of an industrial structure of the future cannot be reached until we have looked more widely at the industrial structure of the European nuclear industry. Can two or three effective European industrial groupings be developed which can match the United States in development, production and marketing of reactors as well?

Ideally, a new efficient industrial group should bring together companies with experience in a related family of reactors which might lead logically on to a more advanced reactor. The merger or combination must also lead to a real increase in industrial strength, perhaps a marketing presence in a wider range of major markets, a real, not paper, strengthening of research and development resources. To put it in another way, companies should combine when they like each other and it looks commercially profitable; they should be encouraged, but not pushed around by governments.

Finally, there has to be a sensible balance of national interests, both between and within the groups. What areas or streams of common interest can be discerned?

One obvious stream of common interest is that of gas reactors. France is still stuck with the obsolete natural uranium Magnox reactor for its power stations, years after Britain has gone over to the partially enriched fuel AGR. Electricité de France is pressing openly for a jump over to American-type water reactors. The French Government is hardly likely to agree. Could not a close working partnership with Britain be developed on the advanced gas-cooled reactor, and further developments of it?

It could be argued that it is getting late for such a partnership to concentrate on AGRs. In that case why not push further ahead, and develop, jointly, a more advanced gas-cooled reactor, to fill

the gap before fast breeders come in. The Dragon reactor fits the
need. Let us turn briefly to look at one of the few bright stars in
the sombre European nuclear sky.

Dragon; rationalizing fast-breeder programmes

The Dragon project was originally a British conception; and
Britain is the leading partner. Its high temperature gas reactor has
been built at Winfrith, Dorset, next to the Atomic Energy Authority's reactor division. It is nonetheless a highly effective European enterprise. Formally, it comes under ENEA (OECD's nuclear
agency) with the Euratom countries participating as a group; it has
some of the highly effective managerial characteristics of CERN.

There is a single executive director in charge, a board of management which meets three times a year (for no more than a day) and
a steering committee which meets four times a year. Staff are re-
cruited under a curious arrangement; they must be seconded from
some national company or organization. This means that Dragon
could not recruit bright European scientists directly in the market-
place, but it has the supreme advantage that staff know they have
secure jobs waiting on their return, and that the results flow back
automatically to European industry.

Dragon has also achieved its goals within its initial budget—a
rare achievement. Contracts to industry have been placed competi-
tively, and its management has succeeded in keeping the cost of the
research and development work in check. When Dragon tenders for
scientific work were put out to large bodies like the AEA, counter
proposals almost invariably came back suggesting wider scientific
investigations in the interests of science. The Dragon management
firmly kept the work down to its own limited needs.

The Dragon team's skill was also rewarded with an element of
technical luck. Helium as a coolant, the major innovation of the
reactor, proved far easier to handle than most people expected. And
the new ceramic fuel, small particles of uranium coated with
graphite, has proved simple and cheap to fabricate, and very reliable
in operation. Finally, helium, an American strategic material when
Dragon began, turns out to be plentiful in North Sea gas. The
Dragon experimental reactor works, and looks like being highly
competitive. The next step is to construct a prototype, or several,
on a grid. Why not push ahead with construction of prototypes with
companies from Britain, France, and other countries developing an
industrial partnership around them?

A group of private European companies have in fact taken an initiative; Britain's Nuclear Power Group, Italy's SNAM-Projetti, Belgium's Belgo-Nucléaire, West Germany's Gutehoffnungs-hütte, France's GAAA and others have formed an association to develop and market Dragon-type reactors throughout the world. The group might thus exploit both first and second generation gas reactors.

It is in the third generation—fast-breeder reactors—that we find the biggest potential of all, for both waste and savings through collaboration. Sodium-cooled reactors are the fashion for this next great phase and these the three largest European countries are systematically preparing to undertake in triplicate. This is a decisive area in which Britain could take a lead, because it is three years ahead of France and West Germany in the construction of a 250 MW reactor. A British offer to invest the Dounreay knowhow in a strong European industrial group or enterprise, in return for welding French and West German (in this case Siemens) efforts into a common programme, would have a real chance of bringing results. First, it would save money. West Germany and France could abandon construction of their prototypes and invest part of the resources in developing alternative prototypes (say, steam or gas-cooled) or in development work complementary to, or carrying on from, the British effort— work which in turn would benefit Britain. In such a joint company or enterprise the main initial contribution in technology would come from Britain. Britain would therefore get a commensurate shareholding in the enterprise, with other countries getting shares equivalent to the cash or knowhow they put in. For such a scheme to work effectively, government, or public electricity authorities, would of course have to replace their present Buy National policies by Buy European policies for such types of reactor. It would be worth doing, for precious time would be gained in the world competitive race. Today research on fuel performance, and the development of components, and indeed the whole fast-breeder programme is all being repeated, at great cost, in the three main European countries; in the United States, it forms part of a common programme. And at any time a massive US effort could devour the lead of Britain or other separate European countries, with the result that once again American companies and knowhow acquire a hold on large parts of the European market. The British with their prototype are taking certain risks. The West Germans, with Euratom, and the Americans, through General Electric, are together building a fuel test reactor (the SEFOR project) which will provide vital information on one of the key problems of fast breeders, namely, containing the reactor so that it does not overheat and get out of control. The Atomic Energy Authority has been in negotiation with the West German Karlsruhe research centre to get access to information from the SEFOR project; it has not proved easy to reach agreement, for no one knows in advance what such information is worth.

This single illustration is a reminder of the difficulties of limited ad hoc cooperative arrangements. In theory it might be possible to bring about a more effective pooling of effort in fast breeders in Europe by cross licensing and a systematic attempt to rationalize the production of components; one company to develop a line in sodium pumps, another, say, in heat exchangers. The difficulty is that Britain has already pre-empted such a division of labour by putting out all the components for Dounreay to British companies. In any case cross licensing arrangements and a division of labour on components will always tend to fall apart unless there is a much wider agreed strategy for the nuclear industry.

Much greater gains for all could be achieved if a systematic attempt were made to integrate the fast-breeder development programmes of the major countries in a number of Europe-wide industrial groupings. Because of their lead, the British would have to make the main move here. It would not be worth their while to do so unless they got, in return, a full industrial integration between British and other Continental firms, so that all benefited from joint exploitation and marketing in the future. Mere sharing of research must inevitably break down, when the different partners seek commercial benefits.

A common strategy would also help Europe as a whole to foster the development of more than one stream of fast-breeder reactor development, as the West Germans are already doing. In addition to the sodium and steam-cooled breeders, what about using gas as the transmitter of heat to the boilers? If the British, by sharing Dounreay knowhow with the West Germans, would save West German industry two or three years of expensive work, the British in turn would get an insurance policy if they shared in a European project for a gas-cooled fast breeder. We must look again at the idea of evolving two or three European industrial groups, each pursuing a line of reactor development culminating in a particular branch of breeder technology.

Three European Reactor Companies

Some of the ingredients are apparent. Why not bring together Britain's English Electric and Babcock and Wilcox who have almost all the work on the Dounreay sodium fast breeder, with Siemens, Neratoom, and perhaps a French group that has done studies for the French Phoenix fast breeder?

A second European group is, as we have seen, already taking shape with the purpose of developing and marketing the Dragon-type high temperature reactor; they might logically move on to a gas-cooled fast breeder; governments, saving money in sodium breeding, could afford to place joint development contracts for such a project.

A third group might conceivably develop a stream of heavy-water reactors, culminating in a steam-cooled fast breeder.

Europe's experiments in heavy-water reactors are ridiculously scattered. As an inheritance of wartime Canadian experience, the French Atomic Energy Commission has developed a 70 MW gas-cooled, heavy-water moderated reactor (EL4) and has a continuing relation with the Canadians. No less than four different types of heavy-water reactors have been developed in West Germany. Britain has one national project; and of course there is Orgel, Euratom's own white elephant, or white hope. Perhaps the Orgel reactor should not be underestimated. Three hard-headed companies, GAAA, Montecatini, and Interatom have together volunteered to submit proposals for a prototype. The reactor has one interesting quality; it produces twice as much plutonium per unit of natural uranium as proven light-water reactors, a significant contribution to future fast-breeder programmes, which will at first require large quantities of plutonium. The doubts are about its engineering.

Somewhere in the groups we have sketched, a place will have to be found for the interesting thorium high temperature reactor being developed by Krupp-Brown Boveri at Jülich.

The experts are divided on whether an intermediate generation of reactors is needed between the proven reactors of today and fast breeders. In our ideal European industrial groupings, it seems necessary to keep the options open, giving the embryonic European industrial groups the chance to develop an intermediate reactor, but moving on rapidly to fast breeders, if this is necessary or possible. AEG, which is expected to build West Germany's steam-cooled fast breeder, if this comes off, plus the other companies mentioned above might thus form a third group—from heavy-water to steam-cooled fast breeders.

Such a strategy, to develop say three strong European industrial groups each pursuing a stream of development, has certain preconditions. There has to be a prior arrangement, as there is already in West Germany, for example, that the group whose fast-breeder system proves least economic will have the right to get licences from its more successful rival.

There also has to be some reform of local domestic structures. Britain's Atomic Energy Authority will have, deliberately, to use its knowhow to build up the capabilities of the two main British industrial groups, by deliberately devolving development work into industry. In the past the West Germans found it impossible to communicate with Britain's atomic industry because no one had overall authority. As the AEA pumps its skills into two major industrial groups it could do so in a way which promotes the emergence of powerful European transnational enterprises. It could, for instance, transfer the Dounreay fast-breeder team to English Electric-GEC on condition it makes an effort to develop sodium breeders with Siemens. A real common market in nuclear equipment, in the background, would in such a situation soon promote the emergence of a few strong specialist component firms.

In addition to the main work on reactor development and the special field of fuel enrichment already described, there is a wide range of other businesses which emergent European industrial groups could exploit more effectively than they do today. The British firm of Weir Westgarth had, until recently, more than half the world market for desalination equipment; today, as the market explodes, the American Government is making a massive financial effort to boost the performance of American industry and help developing countries at the same time. For the British, industrial partnership with European countries in the Mediterranean, such as Italy, could be of immense value to both.

Fuel processing is another area where Europe has embarked on a wasteful multiplication of facilities. Again, it is only through integrated industrial operations in a company or consortia that rationalization can take place.

Creating European industrial groups does not merely mean consortia, though this could be the first stage. Ultimately, if the whole pattern of industrial effort is to hold together, and common interests are to overcome centrifugal tendencies, common companies must emerge, which can really exploit common development together.

What instruments do governments need to develop such a pattern? Industrial companies are talking together. But obviously it would be a help if the major governments, who are spending the money, would agree on a strategy backed, it must be hoped, by a revived Euratom.

In the past ten years Europe has built up an effective research capability in the nuclear field, in part by common efforts. It now has to move on to the next phase: the creation of a viable European industrial structure.

CHAPTER 9

TOWARDS A EUROPEAN
AIRCRAFT INDUSTRY

The Bristol Aeroplane Company was originally founded by Sir George White, who saw a French Zodiac aeroplane flying in 1910, built it under licence, and set up a flying training school in Bristol. After the first world war an aero-engine Department was founded and this manufactured Fedden's Jupiter engine. This engine was built under licence in many countries, including France at the Gnome-Rhone company. Two Bristol engineers, Rowbotham and Ninnes, went over to France, to help with the manufacture of the Jupiter and became the French company's chief engineer and chief designer. Both lived in France until the early 'thirties. Around them grew a network of personal ties between the two companies and countries: intermarriages, friendships, an ability to speak each other's languages and get on. The French firm of SNECMA, set up after the war, with government participation, as France's main aero-engine producer, was based, essentially, on the Gnome-Rhone company, and several of its key men were engineers taken on by Ninnes and Rowbotham. SNECMA took out a licence on the Bristol Hercules engine and the prewar partnership revived. In 1956, when Sud Aviation first began to show interest in developing a supersonic airliner, the Bristol Company (later Bristol Siddeley Engines and now the Bristol engine division of Rolls Royce) began to offer SNECMA the Olympus engine. When, in 1961, Bristol Siddeley Engines and SNECMA became partners in the development and production of the Olympus for the Concorde, it was thus the outcome of a long and fruitful partnership.

Almost inevitably there have been equally long histories of rivalry within European aviation, within nations, and across frontiers. In the aero-engine field, for instance, Rolls Royce and Bristol Siddeley have been, until their merger in 1967, major rivals in the postwar years, both for British Government contracts and for commercial markets in Europe and elsewhere. Rolls Royce's past relationship with SNECMA was less happy than Bristol Siddeley's. Both Rolls Royce and Bristol Siddeley had sought to supply engines for the supersonic Mirage IV, the arm of the French *force de frappe*. Instead they were beaten to it by their rival, Pratt & Whitney. To SNECMA Pratt & Whitney, the world's largest producer of aero-engines seemed a conveniently distant friend, whose power and technology might help SNECMA to build up to a position nearer equality with the British. The French Government was already having difficulties in financing the soaring cost of the *force de frappe*. It seemed a godsend to the Finance Minister, when Pratt & Whitney offered technical collaboration in return for an 11 per cent holding in SNECMA. Later the Mirage IV was scaled down to take Atar engines; the Pratt & Whitney engines were not needed and the US sold France Boeing tankers to refuel the aircraft instead, but Pratt & Whitney got its holding in SNECMA and its seat on the board just the same.

In the end the connection has probably proved valuable to SNECMA. SNECMA services many Pratt & Whitney engines based in Europe and elsewhere, a useful bread and butter business, and has introduced a stream of Pratt & Whitney engines modified by its own ideas, in parallel with the stream from Bristol. But to those who are seeking to organize a European aircraft industry, the Pratt & Whitney link certainly raised new complications. It rubs home the fact that the smaller, weaker partners in every European cooperative pattern tend inevitably to look to America for means to buttress their strength.

These stories show that both friendly collaboration and competitive struggle have a long history in the European aircraft in-dustry. If this industry is sometimes an arena for chauvinism and tribal loyalties, in which memories of the Battle of Britain, France's resurgent national pride, and the proud traditions of Germany's family aircraft firms all play a part, there is also a unique spirit of comradeship and friendly rivalry in the great adventure of flight. In this industry, more than most, politics and the excitement of the technical challenge often dominate the economics. Characteristically, the aircraft industry both leads the way in developing tangible European joint industrial projects, and comes under constant fire from

I

economists who ask whether its expensive adventures are really necessary.

TSR2 and HS681, the scaled-down Mirage IV, and the West German shop-window full of prototypes that have never gone into production, remind us that it is in the aircraft industry that the European countries have been forced, most brutally, to realize that the small European nation-state cannot afford to go it alone.

In this industry, joint projects, cooperation and proposals for common European efforts have become a commonplace. The Plowden Report on the British aircraft industry in 1965 pointed out that America's vast home market, which accounts for some 75 per cent of world military and space purchases and half civil aviation purchases, automatically gave a great advantage to its aircraft industry. The average production run for American military aircraft between 1955 and 1961 was 530, compared with 177 in Britain; for transport aircraft the average American production run was 4·5 times larger. Yet development costs of a modern aircraft have soared to some $150-$300 mn. for a modern subsonic airliner, and $1,400 mn. for the Concorde. A large market spreads development costs and so brings down the price. Large-scale production also brings down production costs, both as the producer learns from his

TABLE G

The European Aircraft Industry 1966

	Numbers Employed (a)	Turnover (b) $ million	Turnover per man (b) over (a) $
United Kingdom	247,000	1,650	6,680
France	103,000	1,100	10,680
W. Germany	43,000	250	5,814
Italy	22,000	150	6,818
Sweden	17,000	190	11,180
Benelux	10,000	100	10,000
Spain	8,000 ⎱		
Others	7,000 ⎰	100	6,666
Total W. Europe	457,000	3,540	7,740
USA	1,400,000	23,800	17,000

Source: F. J. L. Diepen, in paper submitted at Symposium held by *Association Internationale de Constructeurs de Matérial Aeronautique*, London, 1967.

experience and through fuller use of tooling. Table G[1], above suggests the lower productivity of the European aircraft industry compared with its American competitors. Plowden concluded that Britain should not try in the future to develop any large and advanced civil or military aircraft, but should promote 'whole-hearted collaboration on a comprehensive range of civil and military aircraft projects with European countries, with the aim of evolving a European industry to produce aircraft fully competitive with the United States'.

The real question about European aviation is how this laudable objective is to be achieved. By cooperation and integration inspired by governments? By commercial processes? Or by history's traditional means, the technological hegemony of an outside power?

In the early postwar years the British industry played a significant part in reviving a European industry. Meteors and Vampires, and later Hawker Hunters were made under licence in several European countries. The British engine industry, as we shall see in more detail later, established a powerful hold on markets through sales and manufacture under licence. Through offshore orders and licensed production, the United States also played a part in building up a European aircraft industry. F-86 jets were built in Italy, for instance. But none of this set a new pattern for the future.

During the 1950s, a more sophisticated pattern of cooperation began to emerge. Following the creation of NATO, the collapse of the plan for a European Defence Community, the survival of its shadow, Western European Union, and the emergence of the EEC, the idea of common production and procurement policies became more fashionable. Militarily as well as economically common weapons and ammunition obviously made sense. In Western European Union, the Armaments Committee constantly pleaded for common buying policies. These proposals had little effect on the Americans, to whom standardization usually meant buying American, or the British and French, who had still not fully grasped the diseconomies of their small national markets. But they did carry more weight with other countries, in particular West Germany and Italy, and the small Benelux countries, as their far smaller

[1]These figures should be used with great caution, when making comparisons between countries; for a high degree of vertical integration (e.g. in UK) reduces turnover figures, and apparent productivity. Much subcontracting (as in France) raises the turnover figures, for what may, in fact, be similar levels of output and productivity.

armaments industries revived. West Germany, in particular, had been forbidden to manufacture arms for a decade, and then showed no enthusiasm for doing so. For both the West German Government, to whom NATO and Europe were cornerstones of policy, and its allies, it seemed axiomatic to integrate any reviving West German arms production with allied countries. Under NATO auspices, a series of joint aircraft projects took shape. These projects already reflected the two opposing currents of politics and economics which are the subject of this book: American leadership and European partnership.

By the late 1950s, as America's balance of payments swung into deficit and the massive build up of the US space and defence programmes got under way, pressure was growing on the Europeans to buy American equipment in some form or other and thus help 'pay for the alliance'. An expression of this emergent American interest was found in the F-104G programme, under which West Germany, Italy, Belgium and Holland built the Lockheed Starfighter under licence. By 1958-59[2] new West German forces were taking shape and Germany was re-emerging as Europe's leading industrial power.

Both Herr Strauss, West Germany's Defence Minister, and an element in West German industry, realised that in advanced technology, the place of the defence industries in Britain and France gave them a special position of influence and power. Construction of an advanced aircraft under licence seemed a rapid way of re-building West Germany's aeronautical capability. Pushed on by West Germany, and by vigorous American salesmen, the Starfighter was adopted as a NATO basic military requirement for an advanced strike fighter. The NATO Starfighter Manufacturing Organization (NASMO) was set up by Belgium, Holland, Italy and Germany to manufacture the aircraft. Nearly a thousand were built over a period of five years, at a cost of about $2 mn. per aircraft.

The Starfighter programme for the first time involved development of a weapons system of the most advanced kind. It gave the West Germans, in particular, the capability to push forward development plans of their own. It taught all concerned how to plan an integrated production programme involving four countries and many manufacturers.

But it also set a pattern of cooperation, which established close links between the infant aircraft industries of these countries and

[2]John Calmann, *Co-operation in Arms Procurement in Western Europe*, Institute for Strategic Studies, London, 1967.

the American giants. Estimates suggest that, out of a total cost of some $2 bn., between $500 mn. and $1·150 mn. consisted of payments to the United States in the form of licence fees, payments for parts, etc.

A number of other joint projects, in the missile field, followed the same pattern of joint European production under American licence and guidance: the Bull-pup (begun in 1962), Sidewinder (1959) and Hawk (1959). And direct arrangements between companies led to a whole series of bilateral links between the infant West German aircraft companies and American firms. VFW, the largest German group, based at Bremen, short of working capital and keen to acquire technology, now has a 26 per cent holding from United Aircraft, Bölkow, the missile group, has a 25 per cent Boeing holding, balanced by a 25 per cent holding from the French company, Nord, acquired during its joint effort with Nord to develop missiles.

During the 1960s the strong American position in the European arms market was pressed even harder, with the appointment of Mr Henry Kuss as chief arms salesman in the Pentagon. Because of the US balance of payments problem, a ten-year programme was drawn up for the years 1961 to 1971, designed to increase direct arms sales, mainly to Europe, to $15 bn. from the $5 bn. of the previous decade. Gifts of arms, $17 bn. in the previous decade, were expected to fall sharply to compensate. US salesmanship, political and commercial, was at first pretty successful in the civil as well as military markets, especially in West Germany. In the ten years 1955-64, between $5 bn. and $8 bn. of West Germany's total defence procurement of $10·4 bn. was spent abroad, mainly in the United States. But by 1966, the US Government had begun to overplay its hand. It was flatly demanding arms purchases worth $675 mn. per year, the equivalent of the total 'support costs' for US forces in West Germany, just when West Germany's actual needs for new weapons were declining, and when its own infant industry, after the completion of the F-104 programme, was running short of work. At the same time the young West German aircraft companies were beginning to grow restless with their US partners. They had learnt much from them, but there was no sign that any of the advanced development they were participating in (like a vertical take-off project which came to an end in 1967) was likely to reach the production stage, or that the West Germans would be anything but very junior partners. It is time to turn to the second stream of cooperative projects, which began under NATO auspices in the 1950s: the European.

Transall and Atlantique: Britain Out

The first deliberate joint European projects were the Transall[3] transport aircraft, and the Bréguet Atlantique, both built round a Franco-German nucleus at a time when the EEC was being brought enthusiastically to life. The Transall, a Franco-German transport aircraft, was first conceived in 1957; and agreement was reached on development in 1959. In 1964 agreement was reached on production of 110 aircraft in West Germany and 50 in France.

Costs of development were shared equally between the countries, and of production on the same basis as orders (110/50). The project was managed by a joint working committee of the firms involved [Nord-Atlas, VFW (Weser) and HFB]. In the production stage VFW were appointed project leaders. Transall aircraft are now coming into service.

The aircraft is not particularly adventurous. None has been exported outside the two countries. And in 1967, with Herr Strauss employing his energies in finance instead of defence, the West German production programme narrowly escaped a cut. Nonetheless, a common requirement for a workman-like aircraft was agreed and satisfied. Because of the larger market, spreading costs, unit price per aircraft is judged by M. Ziegler to be 25 per cent lower than the cost of the aircraft on a shorter national production run.

The Bréguet Atlantique sprang from a joint NATO requirement for a naval reconnaissance and anti-submarine aircraft based on a Franco-British-American assessment. A common aircraft, it was thought, would not only be cheaper, because of the large quantity, but facilitate operations of NATO's integrated fleets. There was a large market for the aircraft, which was to replace the American Neptune, of which 2,000 were in service throughout the world. In December 1958, Breguet's design was unanimously accepted by the NATO Armaments Committee, after a hotly contested international competition.

The United States and Britain, however, still the major maritime powers and the main countries interested in aircraft to 'watch and keep the sea-lanes open' immediately announced that they would each continue to use their own aircraft after all; striking evidence

[3]For a more detailed description of these and other joint projects, see M. Ziegler, Paper No. 3, in AICMA Symposium, 13 September 1967.

that, at this period, the leading aviation countries were all for standard production, provided the firms were theirs. The Americans immediately set about developing the Orion, which has been a fierce competitor for the Atlantique and even succeeded in ousting it from the Dutch market, though Holland shared in producing the Atlantique. As for the British, they declared they had no need for a replacement for their existing Shackletons. 'This', to quote one bitter Frenchman 'was a lie', for, soon after, they replaced the Shackleton with the maritime version of the Comet, which was, the British claimed, a cheaper and better way to do the job. Despite the fact that Britain was beginning to knock at the door of the Common Market, the British Government had not yet recognized the implications of scale for aviation.

A consortium of Bréguet, the Avro subsidiary of Hawker Siddeley, the Dutch firm Fokker, Dornier, and Sud Aviation was set up to manufacture the aircraft. Avro soon withdrew, but was replaced by the Belgian group, ABAP. In the end no more than 60 aircraft have actually been produced, 40 for France, and 20 for West Germany. Sixteen to 20 may still possibly be ordered by the Dutch. The project was led, from the start, by Bréguet, who managed the common company SECBAT, set up by the partners, and was responsible for technical leadership and final assembly.

Like Transall, the Bréguet Atlantique was not a dramatic technical departure. It was an ingenious workman-like job. The project was on time. Unlike many national, as well as international projects, it kept within the budget, mainly by the large scale use of fixed-price contracts. Because other NATO countries, and notably Britain, did not buy or build the aircraft, sales were smaller than expected. All the same the cost per unit to France, for instance, is estimated by M. Ziegler to be 25 per cent lower than the cost of a nationally built aircraft, even though total investment expenditure was 10 per cent higher, and production expenditure 2 per cent higher than would have been necessary in one country alone. Thus the Bréguet Atlantique and the Transall taught what was to become a standard lesson about European projects: cooperation has a cost, but this is outweighed by the savings of a larger market. The trouble is that the Transall did not in fact fulfil a real requirement, and some of those who drew up the requirements for the Atlantique did not buy the plane.

Though Britain bought no Atlantiques or Transalls, it got a major part of the market through the engine industry. The Rolls Royce

Tyne (developed initially for the relatively unsuccessful Vanguard, used by BEA and Air Canada) was used in both aircraft, and was manufactured under licence by the French firm Hispano-Suiza (44 per cent of the work), MAN Turbo (20 per cent) in West Germany, and the Belgian arms manufacturer Fabrique Nationale (8 per cent). Rolls Royce (20 per cent) was responsible for development. Orders for 677 Tyne engines have been placed with the consortium. Engines are produced on two production lines, one at MAN for the Transall, and one at Hispano-Suiza for the Atlantique.

The Tyne programme worked out reasonably for Rolls Royce, but Hispano-Suiza made a loss. At best it can be said that the programme created a pattern of subcontracting and joint operations between many European companies which provides a foundation for the future.

It was not until the early 1960s that the British who had Europe's largest aircraft industry, and who for a decade had sought to dominate markets by going it alone, began to reverse this policy, as they too learnt the hard realities of scale. A new pattern of Anglo-French cooperation began to emerge.

The Concorde Gamble

Concorde, somewhat perilously, was the first giant step in this direction. When, in the late 1950s, both Sud Aviation and BAC began to consider a supersonic airliner, it was quite clear that neither government could afford its huge development cost alone. At the time Mr Macmillan was teetering on the brink of the Common Market. His 'European' Ministers of Defence and Aviation, Mr Thorneycroft and Mr Amery, keen to back the negotiations with joint activities with France, succeeded in clinching an agreement in November 1962.

The agreement divided the work on a 60-40 basis for the airframe, with Sud Aviation given the lead over BAC. For the engine, work was to be divided on a 60-40 basis, with Bristol Siddeley Engines, which had already developed another version of the Olympus, given the lead over SNECMA. The net effect of all this was supposed to be a 50-50 division of work between the two countries, with Sud leading the airframe development and BSE the engines. The pattern reflected the technical supremacy of the British engine industry, and the political need to give the French a compensating field of leadership (the airframe) in return.

Originally two aircraft were considered for development, a

medium-range aircraft (Sud's conception) and a long-range one (BAC's)—specifically for London-New York. The shorter-range aircraft would have carried fewer than a hundred passengers, involving high costs per seat-mile. Market studies make it clear from an early stage that it was in transoceanic transport that the main market lay and this pushed up the size and specification. Instead of a 280,000 lb. medium-range airliner, Concorde will be a 370,000 lb. transatlantic plane. This increase, plus inflation, largely explains the increase in development costs from an original estimate of $400 mn. to a $1,400 mn.-plus estimate today.

At government level Concorde is supervised by a standing committee of officials (Concorde Directing Committee) which meets at about two-monthly intervals generally in a two-day session; the second day is usually devoted to a joint meeting with the two Contractors' Committees of Directors, which have been set up for engines and airframe. A full-time Concorde Management Board consisting of three British and three French officials reports to the Concorde Directing Committee, and working groups are set up from time to time on particular subjects.

These bodies are designed only to take such decisions as require Anglo-French agreement. The execution of the governments' relations with the companies is carried out in a national framework. The financing of Concorde is also very much a national affair. The original agreement did not provide for a common budget, contributed on a 50-50 basis, to be split afterwards between the contractors. It merely laid down a division of work between the two countries to be financed by the national governments. The breakdown, it was hoped, would land each of them with a roughly equal bill. Not surprisingly, when the House of Commons Public Accounts Committee discovered that $78 mn. are being spent in government-owned laboratories, on top of the bill from the companies, it asked whether the French are paying their fair share. Not surprisingly, the French retort, indignantly, that it is no part of the agreement that France shall pay for escalating costs in Britain.

At industrial level, the organization of Concorde is a development of the traditional pattern of relations between independent companies. No new joint company or companies have been set up to run the project; instead there are two joint committees of directors (for airframe and engines) and a constant movement of people at many levels working together on practical problems. A common sales organization has been set up, and a customer liaison committee which is working well on the task of incorporating customers' needs into the aircraft.

The sharing of work at the construction phase is less inefficient than some critics suggest. The engine is a BSE development; SNECMA have been given the job of developing and manufacturing the detachable exhaust part of the engine. In the airframe, nose and tail are being built by BAC, wing and the centre fuselage by Sud. There will be two final assembly lines, at Bristol and Toulouse. This duplication, and the toing and froing of parts which it involves, plainly means extra cost. But many modern aircraft, including some highly successful ones, are partly built in different places. Neither Sud nor BAC would have had the capacity to assemble Concorde on the scale envisaged, in one place, on their own.

So far, indeed, the industrial work on Concorde has made good progress. Technical difficulties have been overcome; good working relationships have been established. For a first giant experiment it has gone remarkably well.

The weaknesses lie less in the execution than in the nature of the original agreement and the conception of the project itself. In the design phase (as opposed to construction) the carve-up of the work and the vague definition of 'design leadership' have left much to be desired—in the airframe, at any rate. BAC, for instance, is responsible for one of the most critical features of the aircraft, the fuel system. This is critical because, as fuel is used, a complex pumping system is necessary to maintain the equilibrium of the aircraft. But much of the fuel system is in the wings—to be designed and made by Sud. In all aircraft, a multitude of bits and pieces of equipment are bought out from subcontractors who have a clear relationship with the manufacturer. In a relationship of delicately balanced equals clear decisions are far harder to attain.

There is no doubt that the top-heavy decision-making machinery (two governments and four companies) also makes for inefficiency. In the purchase of equipment, from electronic navigation systems to toilet mechanisms, the companies put work out to tender; but they then have to put their recommendations to the governments for approval, except for equipment worth less than $56,000. Usually the officials, who are in close touch, agree, but there are tricky discussions when American equipment is recommended. And airlines of course have their own views. The involvement of government plainly adds to the complexity of an already complex job.

The biggest doubts of all about Concorde concern its commercial viability. And here comparisons must be made with its US competitor, the Boeing Supersonic Transport. Concorde's main advantages are earlier delivery (in service by 1971-72(?), compared with 1977-78(?) and lower initial price (some $21 mn. compared with $40 mn.). Because of its greater size, speed and weight, the SST plainly provides Boeing with bigger technical problems to overcome which could even lead to the complete abandonment of the project.

The main advantages of the US SST are size (250 seats compared with 136-140), speed (1,750 mph compared with 1,450 mph), and lower costs per seat-mile. These are contested by BAC and Sud, which believe that costs per seat-mile should work out at about the same for the two aircrafts: Boeing disagrees. If both aircraft do eventually come into service the SST's better economics should give it a lead on dense routes. As a commercial proposition, Concorde would then depend on two hypotheses: earlier delivery and the airlines' need for a small aircraft on less dense routes in addition to the large supersonic machines. A small airline, for instance, may not be able to afford more than one SST; it cannot run a service on one aircraft of a type. A smaller aircraft may also continue to be needed to feed the main trunk routes, like those across the Atlantic. The airlines, at any rate, have already provided evidence of their will to buy both aircraft. Twenty-five airlines have reserved 113 delivery positions with the Federal Aviation Agency for the SST; 16 airlines have reserved 72 delivery positions for Concorde. More to the point, a deposit of $700,000 has been placed on each Concorde and the airlines are devoting much staff time to planning its introduction. At today's fares and prices Concorde would pay. It would bring an 11 per cent return to airlines with a 60 per cent pay load. If there were no fare differential there would be a 100 per cent load in Concorde, for who would cross the Atlantic in six hours when he can do it in three for the same price? To protect conventional aircraft, fares would no doubt be increased by a surcharge; whichever way, Concorde wins. Lockheed, a relatively impartial observer, puts the market for Concordes at some 320 aircraft. The Russians have paid it the compliment of designing a strikingly similar machine.

The uncertainty surrounding the commercial future of both Concorde and the SST is increased by the question of supersonic boom. Will governments ban the aircraft over land, and should they? The thorough tests conducted by the US administration over

Oklahoma City showed violent public hostility; damage to structures—from York Minster to the plates of seagoing ships—could occur. The strong case for banning supersonic aircraft over land would be even stronger if opinion, and governments, showed more concern for the everyday din, from pneumatic drills to transistor radios, which already fills the atmosphere. A land ban for supersonic passenger planes would not remove the principal market, which is for travel across the seas; but it would worsen the economics of these aircraft, compelling them to go slow at both ends of their flights, and reduce the total market.

A commercial gamble, sales of Concordes are unlikely to cover total development costs; these could amount to $1,400 mn., even though production costs (of some $6 bn., if 300 are built), would easily be covered. It must be justified on other grounds. If 300 Concordes are sold during the ten years 1971-81, sales outside Britain and France should bring in some $5,000 mn. of foreign currency, or an average $240 mn. per year to Britain, about 2·5 per cent of Britain's exports. Is it a sensible employment of limited resources to spend them on indirectly subsidising a particular export on this scale?

The crucial argument for Concorde is that here, at least, for all the doubts about the original conception, is a major advanced project where Europe is, for the time being, ahead of the United States, where advanced technology is being stimulated on a massive scale, and where the project symbolizes and draws with it a whole phase of European technological cooperation. The real question to ask is whether, if Concorde were cancelled, ways could be found, not only of investing in more commercial propositions, but of achieving these other aims as well.

First, the facts about a cancellation. The badly drawn up treaty makes no provision for cancellation; so if one government decided to do so there might be a long drawn legal wrangle involving compensation costs as well. Nor is there any particular natural breakpoint in the development programme. By the time this book is published, more than half the $1,400 development cost of the aircraft will have been spent, and there will have been a build-up of spending on jigs, tools and equipment for production. The question to be decided is whether the remaining, say, $600 mn. of government development money to be spent by the two countries together could be better spent on other things—on a programme, for instance, which promoted technology and industrial development in more effective commercial ways, patched up the damage to European integration and, indeed, drove it forward at the same time.

Such a programme is conceivable. Later in this study we look at ways of organizing European technological cooperation—and consider a common development fund (see page 226). If the resources for Concorde were put into such a fund, and devoted to a broad programme of joint technological development ($30 mn. for a common Franco-British programme on fast ground transport, $75 mn. for the establishment of a European system of information storage and retrieval in advanced technology, $150 mn. for the development of a more modest and commercially attractive medium-range aircraft to succeed the Boeing 727-200, and other projects), as well as to a massive programme of management training and technical education, the money would be better spent. Unfortunately there is no immediate prospect that such a programme may emerge. If Concorde were axed there might be a few token gestures to European technology; otherwise the distribution of the funds between ministries, taxpayers and industrial firms will depend, in Britain at any rate, on who can grab most zealously from the pork barrel in the pre-election years. There is no more likelihood that the savings will be spent on European technology, or on education, than there was after the cancellation of TSR2. Concorde is not an ideal project, or an ideal first priority for the spending of such vast sums, but there is small hope of better ones replacing it, and the certainty of complete waste of the effort made so far and of a sharp setback to European integration. Concorde has become the symbol of the whole strategy of promoting a common European technology and much damage would be done if it was axed. In an imperfect world, and until Europe has proper machinery for deciding its scientific and technical priorities together, this gigantic and costly symbol of the hopes and problems of collaboration in European aviation must go on.

When Concorde was first conceived, it was a solitary harbinger of a European policy for aviation. The British industry, at that time, was still busily producing the British VC10, the Trident, the BAC-111, and developing TSR2, HS1154 and the HS681. Since then there has been a far more fundamental shift in British aviation strategy. Urged forward by a 'European'-minded Minister of Aviation, Mr Jenkins, and by the Plowden Report, Britain's Labour Government has accepted the doctrine that in future all large aircraft shall be developed on a European basis, instead of nationally. In France, no such doctrine has been officially enunciated, but despite some setbacks there have been real signs of a government trend to move the same way. On both sides of the channel a strong group of civil servants, and large parts of the aircraft industry, have become committed to the policy of developing a permanent and viable European industrial partnership which will give to the European plane makers some of the American advantages of scale. There have been some successes, and much has been learnt. When this book was written the entire endeavour still trembled on a razor's edge, poised between success and failure.

In defence, joint bilateral research and development committees exist at government level between a number of European countries, of which the most important are Britain and France, Britain and West Germany, and West Germany and France. These meet regularly to explore whether a common operational requirement can be found as a basis for a joint development project. If it is, the exploration leads to a flow between government research establishments and industry in both countries to try to develop either a common research programme or a common project. A common industrial application is then developed and both sides sign a 'memorandum of understanding'. This is not a treaty for, after the experience of Concorde, Britain at any rate is not anxious to enter into a commitment which cannot be undone.

Two important, practical joint Anglo-French projects have emerged from this process and are now near the production phase: the Martel missile and the Jaguar strike trainer. Let us look at how they are organized, and at the lessons learnt from Concorde.

Martel and Jaguar: Possible Successes

Martel is an air-launched guided missile, jointly developed by Hawker Siddeley Dynamics and Engins Matra; it has two versions, one with a television head that sees its way to the target. Development is now coming to an end and production has begun. As with the Bréguet Atlantique programme, development costs have been split equally between the two countries ($140 mn. each) and exports are shared equally. Otherwise production is split according to orders in the two countries. Production orders have been of the relative order of eight in Britain to one in France. Budgetary savings are put at some $47 mn. in Britain.

The organization of Martel is conventional and based on co-operation between companies, as with Concorde.

Jaguar is more advanced in organization and may be the most

successful of current joint projects. Jaguar was originally a Bréguet conception, but its performance has been raised in cooperation with BAC. It is the kind of competent, practical aircraft, well within the reach of current technology, typical of French industry, but sharpened up by the sophistication of the British industry. Jaguar is expected to cost rather less than $250 mn. to develop, to be shared between the parties. A production agreement for 400 of the aircraft has been signed; with a fair prospect for exports, especially to West Germany, total production and sales could exceed 1,000 aircraft, at perhaps $1·5 mn. a piece.

Concorde teaches that divided authority and committees are not the best way to manage an aircraft. So Jaguar has a management committee, with four British and four French members on it; below it, two government executive bodies have been set up on each side of the channel, to manage, in each case, a part of the project. The French are responsible for the airframe and the British for the engine. At industrial level, two joint companies have been set up: SEPECAT (Bréguet and BAC) for the airframe, and a Rolls Royce Turbomeca company for the engine. The pattern followed closely that of the Bréguet Atlantique.

The decision-making process and management of Jaguar have been a notable advance on Concorde. Speed has been helped by the adoption of France's common sense system for airframe development suitable for a relatively unsophisticated aircraft of this kind. In Britain it has been the practice—at least in complex aircraft—to work out the design, at length and in detail, with much wind tunnel testing before constructing prototypes. The French have tended to draw up a loose technical specification quickly, construct a number of varying prototypes at fixed-price contracts and test fly on a cost plus basis. Any modifications then necessary are made at the firm's expense, if it is its fault, and at the customers', if they are responsible. Losses in the development phase tend to get made up in the production cost. The first aircraft was due to fly in 1968, with first deliveries in 1970.

Jaguar has gone well, and may turn out to be a profitable and economic operation. But the experience has once more shown that the main problems in building an integrated European industry lie in politics, feelings and power factors, not in technicalities. The French and British Air Forces had difficulty in agreeing on a specification for Jaguar, with the British generally pressing for more advanced, and therefore more expensive performance. Yet they did agree—and fast. The engine partnership has been troubled by the overwhelming predominance of Rolls Royce over Turbomeca. It has not been easy to put into effect the 50-50 sharing of work that was officially agreed. Typical of the kind of suspicions which arise in such partnerships was the French impression, based on figures like those in Table G, that productivity was higher in their own industry. Careful investigation, when contracts have been placed, has shown a remarkable equivalence in cost levels in similar work.

Concorde, Martel and Jaguar provide beginnings, which will become important if all three move on from development to the production phase. Can other projects extend the partnership so that it becomes permanent, viable, and brings in other European countries too?

An Anglo-French partnership provides the technical basis for a viable European aircraft industry. But it does not in itself provide a large enough market, in the public buying sector, to bring the full benefits of scale to compare with the United States. In the late 1950s and early 1960s, the F-104 programme and strong American salesmanship gave the Americans a powerful hold over other markets in Europe and especially in West Germany. To be viable a European aircraft industry must regain the major part of those markets. The West Germans and Italians, however, cannot be expected to buy European rather than American, unless the aircraft are either cheaper and more competitive, or provide their industries with work and a share in development and technical advance. Forced to choose between two equivalent commercial aircraft, the West Germans and Italians are bound to attach weight to political considerations too. Only if Britain and France regard cooperation in aviation as part of a wider political design will European cooperation be given priority by these countries over ties with the United States.

Variable Geometry: France Out

In the abortive Variable Geometry (VG) military aircraft and the Airbus, an attempt has been made to broaden the bilateral partnership.

When Britain's TSR2 was cancelled, it left a hole in the development of British military aviation. No advanced military plane was available to fill the need for a high performance strike and interceptor aircraft in the late 1960s and 1970s. The gap was plugged, as an immediate measure, by buying F-111s (later cancelled) and

Phantoms from the United States. But this was plainly unsatisfactory if the long-term strategy was to build a competitive European aircraft industry, commanding the most advanced technology. So Mr Dennis Healey, once a lukewarm 'European', became the champion of an Anglo-French Variable Geometry aircraft, which would supplement and succeed the F-111, and fill the RAF's variegated needs.

On the French side, it was thought, an advanced Variable Geometry aircraft would also be required, sometime in the 1970s. It seemed logical to combine these needs. If, it was thought, the West Germans could be brought in as well, the replacement market for the F-104—for over 1,000 aircraft—might be filled by an advanced European aircraft produced on a large and economic scale.

The intention of developing a joint VG aircraft was mentioned by British and French ministers as early as May 1965, but talks on the aircraft soon ran into difficulties over the different requirements of the partners. The French wanted, above all, an interceptor for metropolitan France, with a high rate of climb, to come into service from 1976 onwards, after the present Mirage series go out of service. The British, on the other hand wanted a strike reconnaissance aircraft, a shorter-range complement to F-111, with the range to operate in the Indian Ocean and Pacific and as part of NATO's European strategy. The difficulties of reconciling these requirements pushed up the estimated development costs, from $560 mn. (estimated in 1966) to $840 mn. (the estimate in spring 1967) to be spent over a period of fifteen years, to 1980. At one stage the British specification seemed to imply a more complex and powerful aircraft; at a later stage the French did.

In late 1966, Mr Healey made considerable adjustments in British arrangements to facilitate agreement by agreeing to take the first deliveries of the VG up to 1976 in order to relieve the strain on the French budget imposed by the *force de frappe*. In January 1967, a preliminary agreement was reached to go ahead with studies on the aircraft in preparation for work on prototypes starting in 1968. An immediate effort was to be made to bring in the West Germans before the final technical specification was defined.

In all the projects so far described, the British had leadership on the engine, and France on the airframe. This time an attempt was made to reverse the roles. BAC had accepted Bréguet's leadership on Jaguar on the understanding that it would get leadership on the VG aircraft. Its TSR2 team, based at Warton, Lancashire, was to lead an airframe partnership with Dassault;

K

SNECMA was to have leadership on the M45 engine, which it had been developing in partnership with Bristol Siddeley Engines. In the next six months two airframe design teams began to pool their knowledge, and a design for the Anglo-French VG began to emerge.

There were, however, imps in its industrial cradle, at least on the airframe side. Bristol Siddeley and SNECMA, it is true, with their experience of cooperation, worked well on the M45 engine and have already sold versions for civil use. As Bristol Siddeley's technical director has put it, 'To make cooperation work, you must treat your partner as an equal, even if you feel he isn't. Then you usually find he is'. The mutual respect of the Bristol-Paris engine partnership continued to work.

For the airframe, however, the auguries were bad. M. Dassault, now 72, has never liked wasting time on cooperation, especially under others' leadership. His philosophy is to design saleable, effective aircraft, quickly, and get them into the air. Shortly after the British and French governments announced the intention of working together on a prototype in May 1965, the Dassault Company began work, on its own initiative, on a variable geometry aircraft prototype. By November 1967, when the Anglo-French VG was still an uncertain paper plan, Dassault's Mirage G was in the air, the most effective possible demonstration to the French Government that the way to get quick results was to buy national. The Anglo-French project would have brought problems for the Dassault firm. In the early years, development teams would have been kept busy, but the long time-scale would have left a gap in work on production aircraft, if output of Mirage III's soon came to an end. M. Dassault believes that his aircraft fills French needs for an interceptor better and sooner than the AFVG, and may eventually, like Bréguet's Jaguar, develop into a larger aircraft satisfying British needs as well. He declares that he can develop it for a mere $90 mn., compared with $700 mn. for the Anglo-French VG. The small figure, it is true, may well ignore much of the development cost of equipment needed in a more advanced aircraft. The fact is that the joint project broke, both on the exorbitantly complex requirements of the Air Forces and on Dassault's dislike of indecision, committees, and the constant changes made in the cooperative project.

Dassault's strong position was clinched by the reorganization of the French aircraft industry, pushed through by the French Government in the first half of 1967, in which it grouped several of France's smaller companies into larger units. Sud Aviation absorbed Nord's civil transport capacity and is in future to be the sole contractor for large civil aircraft; Nord became the spearhead of efforts in rocketry and missiles. Dassault was persuaded to take over the ailing Bréguet company and expand its dominant role in the military field. What was not publicly explained was that M. Dassault agreed to take over Bréguet only in return for a promise from M. Messmer, the French Minister of Defence, that the French Government would place orders for the Mirage F1.

Mr Healey repeatedly told the House of Commons in the first half of 1967 that the French Government had no intention of developing the Mirage G. This may indeed have been their intention, but the French Minister, M. Messmer was committed to backing the production of the fixed-wing Mirage F1, which was bound to compete with the VG, as well as with Jaguar

Perhaps M.Messmer hoped that he would be able to get money for both aircraft. By the high summer of 1967, however, the *force de frappe* and the rising deficit in France's social services were bursting the French budget at the seams. In July, the French Government announced that it could not go ahead with the Variable Geometry aircraft. What Mr Healey called the 'hard core' of the RAF's programme for the 1970s was in pieces. Five months later it was clear that the French Government had at least financed development of the Dassault VG even if there are no plans to put it in production. This time it was the British who felt bitterly that the French had deceived them.

A third military joint arrangement between Britain and France is for helicopters, in recent years the fastest growing form of low priced military transport. Here Sud Aviation has a clear European lead. Westlands, the major British company, has been profitable, but less successful as an innovator, depending to a high degree on licensing designs from Sikorsky of the United States.

In April 1967 the British and French governments agreed on joint requirements and development of three types of helicopter: an air transport helicopter, which would be the Sud Aviation 330, already developed, and designed by the French to be carried in the Transall; France will need 130 and Britain 48; a light observation helicopter, the SA340, will also be developed by Sud, though there will be some production in Britain; finally Westlands will develop a multipurpose helicopter capable of anti-tank and anti-submarine warfare. Two thirds of production will be in Britain and a third in France.

The helicopter scheme does not involve an integration of the companies or new organization. Contracts for the first two helicopters will be placed with Sud and, for the third development, with Westlands. But there will be close cooperation between the companies. If scale is wanted in the helicopter field, these two are natural partners.

The lessons of the VG story will be drawn later on page 153. But first let us turn to an almost equally depressing tale, the airbus.

Missing the Bus

The airbus, like the VG aircraft, was first proposed in June 1965 by that energetic European-minded Minister for Aviation, Mr Roy Jenkins. Then for two years, during the reign (in Britain) of less imaginative ministers, discussions bumbled on, until, in September 1967, a Memorandum of Understanding was agreed in an atmosphere of considerable doubt and disillusion.

Behind Mr Jenkins' original proposal lay the level-headed thought that a viable European aircraft industry, competitive with America, ought to be built not round aerial prima donnas, like Concorde or TSR2, which thrilled the technicians at the taxpayer's expense, but round bread and butter aircraft, designed to serve the vast, expanding market for medium-range travel in Europe; aircraft which might actually pay. Market surveys, conducted by the Ministry of Aviation and the ITA (for France), on a rather conservative basis, showed that by 1980 there should be a market for some 600 medium-range aircraft seating between 200 and 300 people (400 in the US and 200 in the rest of the world). Such aircraft would succeed today's short-haul aircraft, the BAC-111, Caravelle, Trident or Boeing 727.

The size of the aircraft was significant. Increased size is a powerful factor keeping down costs per seat mile. And the Ministry of Aviation's target for the airbus is a 30 per cent reduction on the costs per seat-mile of the 727-200, the best short-haul aircraft available today. But airlines tend to like to replace their aircraft with new ones some 50 per cent larger than their predecessors. The older and smaller aircraft are then shunted onto feeder routes. Aircraft like the Trident, stretched Caravelle, or 727-200 have a capacity of between 110 and 170 people. By November 1965, the British and French had agreed on the specifications for a twin-engined 200-225 seater aircraft suitable for the European replacement market for these planes.

Meanwhile the West German industry, under government guidance, had, in parallel, been discussing the possibility of a similar airbus and had formed a consortium (Arbeitsgemeinschaft Airbus) for the purpose. Rightly, the British and French governments realize the decisive political importance of bringing in the West Germans. If a common assessment of the market could be agreed, which incidentally made it attractive to the three national airlines, and if the West German industry could share in production and development, a crucial step might be taken to break Boeing's hold on Lufthansa's buying policy, and develop a European industry with a strong chance of selling to Europe as a whole.

Unfortunately, the West Germans had been thinking on rather different lines from the French and the British. A sharp rise in internal West German air traffic, since damped down, led them to expect explosive growth in the 1970s. They proposed a 300-seater aircraft, with perhaps four engines.

Throughout the spring and summer of 1966 the three governments and authorities struggled to reconcile their differences, and eventually agreed on a 250-seater aircraft. Meanwhile, the West German firms were getting to know their French and British partners; an agreed specification was at last reached by February 1967.

Meanwhile, however, further complications and delays were being caused by the differing requirements of the airlines and by changes in industrial structure in Britain and France.

As time dragged on and the aircraft's size was increased to fit West German estimates, BEA became increasingly unhappy with the airbus. In 1964, it had called for tenders for a short-haul jet. Boeing proposed the 110 seater 737 and the 160 seater 727-200, which Air France and Lufthansa are both buying. But BEA was told by the British Government that it must buy British. Part of its requirements were filled by stretching the BAC-111. But if the airbus was to fill the rest of the gap, it would have to be early and small. As it became clear that the airbus would not be ready till 1973, and would be a 250 seater, BEA's interest in getting an alternative, smaller British or European aircraft increased. 'After many trials and tribulations', to use Sir Anthony Milward's phrase, BAC came up with a proposal for a much larger version of the successful 111, the 180 seater BAC-211. It seemed to fit BEA's needs like a glove.

Its future, and that of the airbus were, however, entangled with the competitive struggle in the world engine markets and with changes in the structure of airframe and engine industries in Britain and France.

In France, the takeover of Bréguet by Dassault and the transfer of responsibilities for civil aircraft to Sud meant more time wasted, as the Hawker Siddeley designers got to know their new partners. In Britain the change was on the engine side. In the early phases of the negotiation, when Hawker Siddeley and Bréguet had produced their first design, the assumption was that SNECMA and Bristol Siddeley Engines would extend their well-tried partnership by producing the Pratt & Whitney JTD9D engine under licence. This would have given SNECMA a chance to assume leadership; a British company, in this case Hawker Siddeley, could have been given leadership on the airframe.

At this period Rolls Royce was fighting hard to widen its foothold in the American market, first by selling a more advanced engine to Douglas, for the DC-8, next by getting its new fan-jet engine, the RB207, into Boeing's jumbo-jet, the 747, which promised massive business in 1970s. It failed to get both contracts. A new American opportunity for Rolls Royce appeared, when Lockheed called for tenders for its own 300-seat airbus, a new competitor for the European plane. The struggle for world engine markets in the 1970s remains touch and go. As some American opportunities slipped away, it became crucial for Rolls Royce to ensure that its chief rival, Pratt & Whitney, did not carve out a major place for itself in Europe with its JT9D.

For some time Rolls Royce had been watching the fate of its rival, Bristol Siddeley Engines, considering a takeover. When the JT9D threatened to create an alarming Pratt & Whitney bridgehead in the European market, Rolls Royce struck. It was given hefty encouragement by the Ministry of Technology, which believed that a larger company, combining the research and development resources and technology of the two, would be more competitive abroad. And ministers and civil servants would of course be freed from the awkward problem of choosing between them when contracts had to be placed. No one seemed worried by the fact that a monopoly engine manufacturer would now be created in Britain and perhaps Europe, unless customers bought American. Rolls Royce took over Bristol Siddeley Engines, and Rolls Royce soon began to lobby vigorously for the adoption of the RB207 engine for the European airbus. The Ministry of Technology supported it; indeed, in the early months of 1967 the British suddenly appeared to their partners to be making the RB207 engine, a 'European engine' as they put it, a condition of going ahead.

On the face of it it seemed odd that the French Government, so hot against American techno-colonialism, should hesitate about developing jointly a British engine, instead of one by Pratt & Whitney. But the Rolls Royce-Bristol Siddeley merger had shifted the balance of the well tried Bristol-Paris engine partnership. Before, it had at least been possible to maintain Mr Guy Smith's 'spirit of equality', even though Bristol Siddeley employed 30,000 workers to SNECMA's 12,000. One could at least imagine the partnership one day evolving naturally into a single European company. After Bristol's merger with Rolls, even a semblance of equality was gone. For SNECMA the partnership appears to mean a choice between cooperation at a certain distance, or being swallowed by Europe's aeroengine giant. Not surprisingly SNECMA felt more inclined than ever to seek countervailing support, in relations with its powerful neighbour, from Pratt & Whitney across the sea.

To add to French uneasiness about Rolls Royce and the European airbus, Rolls Royce set about developing a smaller version of its fan-jet engine, the RB211, as its tender for the rival airbuses Lockheed and Douglas are developing. In March 1968 Rolls Royce won the Lockheed order—which could be worth as much as $2,000 mn. over the next ten years. This vigorous competitive effort to seize a place in the American, as well as European market, is a model of how the European aircraft industry should behave. But the French naturally feared that Rolls Royce's main efforts would be diverted to competitors of the European airbus; fears which were confirmed by an order for fifty of the Lockheed aircraft from the British group Air-Holdings; on their side the British began to complain about French 'leadership' on yet a third European airframe (Concorde and Jaguar being the first and second), which the choice of a Rolls Royce engine politically implied.

For all the doubts, an agreement to go into the project definition stage was reached in September 1967. Rolls Royce got its way and is to get the master contract and 75 per cent of the development work on the engine. 12·5 per cent each are to go to SNECMA and MAN, Rolls Royce's longstanding German partner. On the airframe Britain and France were each to get 37·5 per cent of the work and the West Germans 25 per cent. Sud Aviation was to have 'leadership' on the airframe. To accelerate decision-making, the main contractor, Sud, is to place contracts with Hawker Siddeley and the West German group on the airframe and equipment. Rolls Royce will lead the engine in the same way. The three governments will merely monitor, to ensure that the work is divided in the proportions agreed. The main principles of the carve-up have to be agreed by all the industrial partners; Sud and Rolls Royce will decide the details.

Seen as a political deed, the agreement was a fair balance of the interests involved. In execution it should be more efficient than Concorde. But in structure the airbus partnership looks a step back from the Jaguar set-up. There is to be a common sales company, but not a common company for production as well. The carve-up, under the leadership of one company, Sud, presents more possibilities of strain and less of permanent team-work, even though Sud is handling the situation well. Other shadows still cloud the future of the airbus. If the first Bréguet-Hawker-Siddeley project, agreed in autumn 1965, had gone straight into development, and then production, the European airbus might actually have had a lead over a year over its Lockheed competitor; even if this time had been lost by slower European development, the two aircraft would still have entered the market at the same time. Two years of European debate have presented Lockheed with the lead. Its 227-300 seater airbus, with three engines, should be in service by early 1972. A vigorous sales drive is already under way. When the European airbus gets into service in 1973, it can no longer expect the lion's share of the market for 800 aircraft expected in 1980. It must take what it can on grounds of its different specification (shorter range, but shorter airfield run, two engines which means cheaper maintenance but more risk of disruption of services; no long flights over sea). The price, it was hoped, would be some 20 per cent less, but escalating costs place this in doubt.

Great uncertainties still surround the buying policies of the airlines, too. The initial airbus agreement provides that development and production will go ahead only if the three flag airlines, Air France, Lufthansa, and BEA, commit themselves to buy seventy-five. So far only Air France shows a clear determination to take its share. Lufthansa, a possible customer for fifteen, may have to be pressed by the West German Government. BEA may not take more than fifteen, and still regrets the BAC-211.

The conception of the BAC-211 was, in fact, a good one. There is a market for a 200-seater short and medium-haul airliner not filled, at present, by any American design. In particular, the smaller US airlines may be interested. The subsequent proposal to develop such an aircraft jointly between six European countries, as a supplement to the larger airliner, makes sense. But before any further European projects are considered, the lessons of the appalling cautionary tales of the airbus and VG aircraft must be well and truly learnt. Let us list the problems.

1 *No common requirements*

In the case of the airbus precious time was lost through the effort to reconcile the conflicting market predictions and specifications of three governments, three companies and three airlines. The VG suffered even more from the different requirements generated by different defence policies.

2 *A national industrial structure*

Cross-channel industrial partnerships have been disrupted by the French and British governments' policies of reshaping the aircraft industries on a national basis with no regard to a European strategy.

3 *Unbalanced or rogue partners*

In the British case this reshaping has given one firm, Rolls Royce, such a dominant position in one field, engines, that it is more difficult than ever to achieve balanced partnerships. Yet this company is the most dynamic and competitive in Europe, and a real match for its American competitors.

In airframes, Dassault is the most dynamic company in its field; but it has been an even more disruptive influence on cooperation on its side of the channel. The more ruthless entrepreneurial companies have thrown their weight about so that the pattern of cooperation fits their own needs. The question has to be posed how much the entrepreneurial spirit, with its essential quality of decisiveness, is compatible with the mutual give and take essential to 'cooperative' projects on present lines.

4 *No government strategy*

Despite much progress no government has been sufficiently consistent or effective in its support for the development of a European strategy. By giving in to Dassault's pressure, the French Government struck a blow at the VG aircraft, Mr Healey's 'cornerstone' of joint European production of military aircraft.

Again, how could the governments allow estimated development costs for a joint VG aircraft to escalate to $700 mn., when the two companies indignantly claim that they can produce aircraft, of comparable specifications, at a mere $240 mn. in one case and $80 mn. in the other? Who is fooling whom? Evidently, on an international as well as national basis, development costs must be far more rigorously estimated and controlled. Before embarking on further joint projects, much hard thinking is needed about procedures and it must be followed by action to put such weaknesses right.

Building European Aircraft Companies

Behind the VG breakdown were tensions with wider implications. Parts of the British airframe industry are convinced that the French manoeuvres over it were designed merely to secure leadership on Jaguar and the helicopter deal without paying a price. They believe the French aim is to secure such predominance in airframes that they can in turn set the pattern for the engine industry. As a result there is a deep suspicion in the British airframe industry of any further deals which give France 'leadership'. The French, on the other hand, ask how a balance is to be struck if Britain always dominates in engines, as it does today. Such problems cannot be resolved without a more far-reaching industrial integration.

There is a clear need for an industrial strategy to promote the emergence of viable transnational companies which can develop common interests and a spirit of enterprise of their own. The European plane makers cannot hope to compete effectively with their American rivals if the design of aircraft is the work of a dragged out diplomatic conference, and companies are stuck together on an ad hoc basis for every separate project. Time is wasted as people get to know each other and common working methods are learnt. So long as joint projects are ephemeral alliances, development teams in the separate companies will spend time dreaming up their own pet projects, which may then emerge as private or national projects (like the BAC-211 or the Dassault G) competing with European ones for money and attention. Time and energies will be wasted sorting the muddle out. There is a permanent invitation to American competitors to come and grab one of the partners the moment it has got out of bed with its European mate. Only if the skills and brains of development and production teams are organized and managed as in a single efficient firm against the background of a wider market will the Europeans stand a chance of competing effectively with Boeing, Douglas, Lockheed and the rest.

As far as possible each major airframe, or engine group, should be built round the development of a family or class of aircraft or engines in which one development leads, logically and inexpensively, to the next. Skills in marketing as well as in production and research in a particular field would be built up in the group.

The legal obstacles in the way of creating multinational European companies are real, but not insuperable, as we shall see in detail in Chapter 14. The real problems are more difficult: which groups to bring together, for what and how to organize them efficiently? In view of the failure to exploit mergers already made on a national basis, like BAC, it is vital to get the answers right in Europe.

In the airframe business, certain natural teams are apparent: Sud and BAC Filton or Weybridge plus a West German group should produce a civil family of aircraft; indeed there is a good case for a bold proposal to merge BAC's main civil interests with Sud in a first joint, partly state-owned European company.

BAC (Warton) and Dassault (when its present highly individualist chief retires) form the nucleus of an advanced military team. Westlands and Sud's helicopter division form a third potential company: Nord and perhaps BAC's guided weapon division and Bolkow; Hawk-Siddeley Dynamics and Engins Matra and other possible companies or groups. BAC has missed some opportunities in recent years to develop a joint range of civil aircraft—111, 211, airbus with Sud. Yet how much more sensible it would be for one production line to be producing the airbus in Toulouse say, and another, the European equivalent of the 211, say in Bristol. It is not too late to start.

Just how Hawker Siddeley, on the British side of the channel, fits into all this will be clear only when it is decided whether BAC is to be merged with Hawker Siddeley, or not. If this merger takes place, the Hawker Siddeley airbus team, merged into BAC, will presumably become a major British contributor to the Sud-BAC civil team. If the merger does not happen, Hawker Siddeley might combine with other European concerns (Fokker, Saab and FW in West Germany) in a group working on short-haul aircraft.

If the European airframe industry were to develop in this way, there would be only limited possibilities of domestic competition. But such a reshaping of the structure will not take shape overnight and in the advanced field competition with America will be the main spur. In the meantime, loners like Dassault, Saab, Fokker and Handley-Page will continue to play a part, and there will always be room for independents at the vast smaller end of the market where there is no need for large scale concentration.

In the engine industry, Rolls Royce's predominance is a fact of life which will have to be accepted. But if other Europeans are to accept this, they may have to be given the lead on other things. Here, as elsewhere, the way to develop a rational division of labour in the

European industry is to build on strength, not to try to give every company in every country a bit of capability all round. The SNECMA-Bristol Siddeley group might continue to develop their skills in supersonic low-compression engines. It would be better for Turbomeca to be built up as the main producer of small engines (with Rolls Royce continuing to market for it) and for Rolls Royce to remain the sole main producer of large fan-jets, than to continue the kind of wasteful, expensive effort made, in the case of Jaguar, to teach the little Turbomeca company a fan-jet capability. It is a waste of time and talent on both sides.

Why not, it may be asked, let the market rationalize the structure? The answer is that the United States of Europe does not yet exist, and that there are interests at stake which must be weighed and agreed, and which governments will not leave to the mere operation of the market. The aircraft industry means the capacity to make key defence and transport equipment; it is a spearhead of techno-logical progress. If specialization means concentrating one key industry in one country, it would unacceptably shift the balance of political power in the community of Europe. If the structure of the industry is to be reshaped the reshaping must be based on a balancing of interests. But instead of the present crude attempts to balance each project on a basis of pseudo-equality, the balance must be combined, as far as possible, with an increasing rational division of labour in pursuit of well-defined goals.

In aircraft equipment, where there are so many companies, it should be easier to let the market operate. Indeed in the electronic field the British and French governments can and are sensibly beginning to rationalize their defence development contracts so as not to duplicate. The process ought, of course, to be extended to West Germany as well.

Other elements in the defence industries can also be brought into the planning and the bargaining. If Britain dominates in aero-engines, France leads in some branches of rocket technology. One specialization can increasingly be weighed against another.

In airframes and engines companies can and must play a part in the restructuring of the industry, but they cannot move effectively without governments as well. Indeed it is the governments, and particularly, of course, the French, British and West German governments, which must devise the strategy, and maintain a long-term supervision over its execution and achievements.

A European Planning Agency

They could make a start by holding the European Conference of Ministers of Aviation proposed in the Plowden Report but never carried out. There they could discuss and agree on the broad outlines of their aims. From the start the British and French governments might decide to merge the civil interests of Sud and BAC, in a single company. As soon as possible they should then set up a small but high-powered European aviation planning agency, on the lines of the French Direction Technique de Constructions Aéronautiques, staffed in part by technical men of the highest quality. This group would have four major tasks, closely interrelated. The first would be a subsidiary, technical one, to work out common standards, and harmonize administrative procedures in the complex field of defence contracting, spreading the best and toughest contracting practices to all member countries. The development of a viable industry of course also implies a common market. Ludicrously, parts for Jaguar or Concorde still have to pay customs duties when they cross the channel.

The second and far more positive task would be to plan and guide the industrial strategy—the formation of common companies and so on, described above. This does not mean that the planning agency would tell every company what to do. There should be room for commercial initiative and an optimum degree of competition as well. But the group will have to steer the industry through the immediate critical phase of restructuring to a European pattern and will have to keep a watching brief, especially over the major companies, in the years ahead.

The third major task of the planning group would be to formulate development objectives for European aviation; after all it is European governments, collectively, who are going to contribute most of the money. These objectives are of three kinds, commercial, defence, and scientific. In the commercial field, strategic decisions must be made as to the field or fields in which governments are prepared to back development of a family of aircraft—high density routes, supersonic flight, the short-haul? Plainly, deciding on a 'family' is more complex than it sounds; the problem is to develop the right individual plane at the right time. Obviously the major initiative in development and market assessment ought to come from the companies. But the governments, if asked to back development, must have a competent instrument of assessment too, and, in the present unenterprising state of the European aircraft industry, a means of promoting commercial policies as well.

The European planning group must also decide on certain long-range scientific and technological objectives for the European aircraft industry: A common programme to develop vertical lift, swing-wing development, supersonic travel in the Mach 5 range? Of these vertical lift, where Rolls Royce has a strong position, and Fiat, Dornier and others have experience, could be the most attractive. But a conscious choice of priorities has to be made. A policy is also needed to make proper use of state-owned research facilities, at present often appallingly underemployed. Large wind tunnels, for instance, (of which there are at least ten in Europe) are underused and partly duplicated. Future investment in such major facilities ought to be collectively planned to fit estimated needs over the next ten years. To use a wind tunnel properly means having expensive computer installations, a further reason for optimum use. Perhaps some existing facilities should be transferred to the emerging European aircraft manufacturing companies. That is where they are most likely to be properly used.

In defence, the experiences of Jaguar and the swing-wing aircraft have shown that there must be further striking progress towards common requirements, if joint projects are to succeed. Here there is a role for our joint technical planning agency, but it cannot work effectively without an integration of European defence strategies as a whole. Today the separate air or naval staffs evolve their own requirements and then try, painfully, to combine them. The resulting compromise is obviously more expensive, and less efficient, than a common requirement emerging from a common strategic conception.

Such a common view should be far easier to find, now that Britain has taken the great strategic decision to phase out its defence commitments east of Suez. France's defence philosophy, which has replaced the conception of a NATO strategy for Western Europe by the idea of a national defence system centred round the nuclear deterrent, is a new disturbing factor. But the other European NATO countries which believe in collective defence of Europe ought to be able to agree now on common weapons to serve a common need. And in practice, French needs are not very different. The main source of differences remains the basic fact that separate national administrative machines continue to develop requirements within a national structure and with a national defence policy as the ultimate goal. This means, in Britain for instance, that defence requirements are ultimately settled in a body such as the Defence Research Committee or Weapons Development Committee[4] of the Ministry of Defence. These draw on advice and pressure from intelligence, research estimates, the aerospace industry, government weapons establishments and so on, and match them against national staff requirements and defence strategy generally. The French, West Germans and others are of course busy doing the same thing in a national context and in each case a pinch of chauvinism gets thrown in; no wonder joint projects end up as an uncomfortable compromise.

Efficient collective use of the resources of the European aircraft and defence industries requires a political decision to integrate defence policy generally, and then a systematic integration of staff planning and the requirements system. Such a decision is of course loaded with political implications; for how can common defence policies emerge without political union as well? In the world as it is, we can only expect to move step by step towards this goal. Indeed in aviation generally the European planning agency must, at first, have the task of injecting a common view into the partnership of governments who will ultimately decide, and probably the most crucial decisions will be taken by three governments, France, West Germany and Britain. Gradually the central institutions will gain authority. But the slower the process, and the more hesitant and half-hearted the system of collaboration, the more expensive and wasteful it will be.[5] A crucial test case is the search for a common replacement for the Lockheed F-104, used by the Belgian, Dutch, West German and Italian air forces. If this is another American aircraft, the chance to develop and produce economically a major European advanced military aircraft will be gone for a decade. Yet the Anglo-French VG has flopped; the West Germans and British have been struggling to agree on a project. Perhaps if there were more initiative by the companies to work out a common proposal there would be a better chance of success. This is surely one case where our proposed common agency could act as a catalyst, putting forward suggested common requirements and designs.

If, in the military field, a common market means systematic joint

[4]Martin Edmonds, International Collaboration in Weapons Procurement, *International Affairs*, No. 2, April 1967.

[5]Alistair Buchan, The Implications of a European System for Defence Technology, No. 6 in *Defence, Technology and the Western Alliance*, Institute of Strategic Studies, London, 1967.

requirements, because of the whimsical political character of demand, this is not true in civil aviation, where the needs of the customers—the travelling public—ought to be allowed the decisive say. In the United States, this need is met by over forty different airlines, competing together, and placing a variety of orders with the aircraft manufacturing companies. In a united European market there is no reason why a variety of airlines, some private, some nationally-owned, should not do the same. If European governments want to provide a degree of transitional protection to their civil industry, it would be best to do it, not by specific government instructions to airlines on what aircraft to buy, but by a limited tariff (or shadow tariff), which allows the users freedom of choice within the conditions set by the market. The aim should be to create companies of European dimensions and structure sufficiently viable and competitive to win orders themselves.

It is true that in the present painful initial stage, when airlines are sceptical about the emergence of a viable European industry—and indeed the process has barely begun—they have powerful incentives to buy American, for it seems safer. They have to be pressurized, as with the airbus, to take the risk of committing themselves to the products of an, as yet, non-existent European industry, as part of the difficult process of building up confidence in a European future. To go on indefinitely selling aircraft in this way, however, would merely mean developing an uncompetitive European civil aviation industry as well. A price can be paid once for buying out national prejudices and structures, but not over and over again. Our European technical planning agency would, like the aircraft companies, keep a close watch on market developments and encourage the companies to develop aircraft which fit future needs. But it would not go on permanently spending its time squeezing the European airlines to adopt common specifications on the lines proposed for the abortive Air Union of European civil airlines.

Instead the European governments, together, have a different task to perform in civil aviation: to promote the rapid development of the market. In 1966 US domestic routes carried eight times more passenger traffic than intra-European flights, in terms of passenger-miles per head of population.[6] In terms of total ton-miles US airlines carried, throughout the world, three times more traffic than the Europeans. In part these differences reflect greater distance, within America, and higher incomes per head. But they also spring from

6Traffic, *Digest of Statistics*, No. 120, ICAO.

the cost and complication of travelling across European frontiers—the customs and passport formality at airports for instance—and from the high fares and lack of enterprise in developing European domestic routes. Much traffic is lost through the lack of good domestic connections, or indeed of any kind of link between many major European cities. As to cost, there can be no excuse for the journey between London and Paris costing twice as much as the journey of similar length between Los Angeles and San Francisco. Any extra European costs at airports are more than compensated by lower wages and salaries than in America. The truth is that high overheads and inefficient operation of European airlines are cosily protected by state licensing and by IATA, the international fare-fixing cartel. If intra-European civil aviation is to develop as it should, providing everyone with the chance to travel by air when it is convenient, and opening up a massive market for short-haul aircraft and medium-range high-density aircraft of the airbus type, competition and low-priced private operations must be allowed far greater scope. It is the private operators and charter flights, breaking the IATA price ring, which have opened up most of the new markets of the last ten years. If European airlines want to enjoy the right to buy price-competitive products, they will have to face price competition themselves.

This survey of the effort to build a viable European aircraft industry has shown that, despite great efforts, there is still a very long way to go. The present halfway house is shaky and could still tumble down. Yet enough experience has been gained and enough determination shown to make possible a new surge forward towards a more efficient and complete integration, provided governments are ready to accept the political logic of continental scale.

L

CHAPTER 10

SPACE AND COMMUNICATIONS

A gardener who decides to plant a tree, leaves it lying about un-planted for three years, and when at last it is in the ground digs it up each year to shake it, prune it and generally knock it about, should not be surprised to find that the tree ails, and shows little sign of comparing in health, let alone size, with the mighty oaks which tower beside it. Certainly he has no right to declare indignantly that this kind of tree won't grow. Yet this is an exact analogy with the treatment European politicians have given to the frail plant of a common European space endeavour.

The standing oaks are huge indeed. In 1966 the United States spent $5,152 mn., or 0·7 per cent of its national income on its space programme, more than Western Europe's entire civilian research and development effort in all industries. Russia spent a similar amount. Western Europe spent the tiny sum of $216 mn. on all space pro-grammes, national and international. In terms of manpower, NASA has some 34,000 permanent employees and some 500,000 doing work under contract in industry. There are only some 20,000 em-ployees in government and international space research centres in the whole of Western Europe. The merest common sense has en-couraged the Europeans to plant the tender tree of cooperation and to make common use of the slim resources they have.

The efforts of the political gardeners, however, have not measured up to the need or indeed to the efforts of European engineers and scientists, as the stories of the European Launcher Development Organization (ELDO) and the European Space Research Organiza-tion (ESRO) show.

ELDO, Europe's club for the development of launching rockets, sprang from a British proposal in 1960. In 1959 the Macmillan Government had discovered that its new long range (3,000 mile) ballistic missile, Blue Streak, was becoming unbearably expensive, just when it was beginning to sidle towards its first application to join the Common Market. In the summer of 1960, in the cabinet shuffle which put Mr Heath at the Foreign Office, the European-minded Mr Thorneycroft was moved to the Ministry of Defence. In January 1961 he proposed to an ad hoc conference convened in the buildings of the Council of Europe at Strasbourg that Blue Streak should be made the basis of a joint European rocket programme, which would give Europe some stake in the new world America and Russia were pioneering. The French, also going nuclear by then, could provide a second stage rocket. After much arm-twisting the West Germans were persuaded to provide and pay for the third. ELDO's convention was strictly limited to 'peaceful purposes'. All the same it was an ironic but not unprecedented change from the time only six years earlier, when Britain and other western countries had taken pains to get West Germany to renounce use and manufacture of large rockets, in the Western European treaty of 1954.

After a series of discussions the ELDO convention was signed in April 1962 by the six Common Market countries plus Britain and Australia, which brought its invaluable Woomera launching range to the new group. The organization was to be run by a council, meeting at least twice annually, and a Secretary-General supported by technical and administrative directors. In the council unanimity was required for the admission of new members, the adoption of regulations on the placing of new contracts, and certain external questions, such as providing information to outsiders and delivery of launchers to them. Otherwise voting was to be by two thirds majority, provided member states which contributed 85 per cent of the funds

TABLE H

Original Contributions to ELDO (%)

Belgium	2·81
France	23·92
W. Germany	22·02
Italy	9·78
Netherlands	2·64
United Kingdom	38·79
Australia	Use of Woomera

concurred. This meant in practice that Britain, France and West Germany each had a veto, though other countries did not, as the basic contributions show.

An initial five-year budget of $196 mn. was agreed to finance the construction of ELDO's three-stage rocket. This, it was optimistically suggested, would be able to put a one-ton satellite in a circular polar orbit at more than 500 km distance, or put 50 kg on the moon. The work was carved up according to contribution, with the three large countries each producing their rocket stages, Italy the first satellites, Belgium down-range guidance stations and the Netherlands long-range telemetric links.

Unfortunately, the timetable slipped from the start; ratifications were slow and the organization did not come into formal being until February 1964. Then other teething troubles began to appear. West Germany and to some extent the other Continental countries had each to create a new advanced industry from scratch. Not surprisingly they found it difficult to maintain the timetable, so that costs began to slip over the original budget. Then the political gardeners began to get to work.

In January 1965 the French Government asked whether the original programme ought not to be scrapped and replaced by a more advanced one which would permit the launching of geo-stationary communication satellites, the first of which, Early Bird, had recently taken to the sky. The question was intelligent, but the first effect disastrous. It was realized, after a short while, that a more ambitious programme would have to follow from the initial one, which should therefore be continued; but it took the organization some months to settle back on course after this questioning of its objectives.

The next year, 1966, a different and even more disruptive political gardener was at ELDO's roots. The British inventors of ELDO called the whole scheme into question. The original convention had envisaged a reappraisal of work, after two years, with a view to considering future programmes. In February 1966, a British memorandum, designed with the coming consultations in view, questioned the value of the enterprise, in view of the escalation of costs, the failure to keep to schedule, and the realization that the load envisaged for ELDO's first launches had proved overoptimistic. The ministerial conference in July 1966 met in an atmosphere of acute crisis, with press reports from London suggesting that Britain wished to abandon the entire enterprise it had initiated. Only in the last 48 hours before the conference, after political reverberations from all over Europe had been painfully registered by the Foreign Office, did the British Government decide to soldier on after all.

Instead the conference sensibly agreed on a more equitable distribution of the financial burden between the large countries, which put Britain on a par with France and West Germany. The conference also adopted a complementary programme of development work which would put ELDO in a position to launch the application satellites, especially communications satellites, which were suddenly showing that space could pay. ELDO's first three stages are already capable of lifting a one-ton satellite to a height of 300 km. But Early Bird had shown that the most valuable communications satellites would be those in geo-stationary orbit launched from an equatorial base. In the new programme it was accordingly decided that, in addition to the Woomera range, a site at the French space base in Guyana should be developed as an equatorial launching site at a nominal cost of $25 mn. Two further stages would also be added to the three stage-rocket to enable a 150-200 kg satellite to be put into geo-stationary orbit. A new form of inertial guidance system would be developed for it.

The ceiling for the new programme, which began in January 1967, was fixed at $330 mn., on top of the escalated costs of the first programme (some $295 mn.); the conference thus fixed an overall ceiling of $626 mn. for the first two programmes.

The major reappraisal of ELDO's work was completed by strengthening the voting arrangements. Instead of decisions requiring the support of countries paying 85 per cent or more of the money, the votes of a mere two-thirds of the contributors were to be required in future. So one big power could no longer enforce a veto. The secretariat was also to be strengthened by the appointment of two managers in charge of the first and second programmes. Contracts, under the first programme, had mainly been placed by national governments, in accordance with the agreed division of work and finance, even though the Secretary-General had had the theoretical right to place direct contracts too. In the second programme, it was agreed that the direct placing of contracts with industry by the Secretary-General would become normal practice—a significant advance.

Thus ELDO's second crisis, that of 1966, was resolved constructively by decisions which gave the organization a badly needed second lease of life. A price was nonetheless paid, in wasted time and demoralization amongst the staff, during the months when the whole fate of the scheme hung uncertainly in the air. The uncertainty surrounding the whole venture since its conception, the failure to agree on budgets before the beginning of each year or (in 1965) till halfway through were infallible recipes for slipping timescales, escalating costs, and discouragement of the technicians on the job. The surprising thing about ELDO so far is that the team of technicians involved has worked remarkably well, with skill and a spirit of determination and *esprit de corps*. But before turning to the efforts of the political gardeners in 1967 and the doubts which still surround ELDO's future, we must consider the second European space cooperative, the European Space Research Organization (ESRO).

ESRO sprang from the fertile minds of the group of scientists who had created CERN. Men like Professor Amaldi of Italy, Professor Auger of France and Sir Harry Massey in Britain urged that the same approach which had had such success at Geneva should be applied to space research. Like ELDO, ESRO was thus a response to the challenge of the American space programme, and like ELDO it was conceived in 1960, signed in 1962, and put into operation in March, 1964. ESRO, however, had different objectives from ELDO and different principles of organization—mostly better ones, modelled on CERN. Like ELDO, ESRO is run by a council and a common secretariat or staff. But unlike ELDO, where the main work is carved up between separate nations and then stuck together at Woomera, where it is used, ESRO has built up a common research effort and some important joint installations: a sounding rocket range at Kiruna in Sweden, a computing centre in Darmstadt (West Germany), and central laboratories at Delft (Holland) where rocket nose cones, satellites and experiments are developed. This centre now has a staff of some 800. Unlike ELDO, and like CERN, contracts are farmed out to industry on a basis of competitive tendering. Decisions are taken by a simple majority in many cases, by two thirds in some others, and by unanimity in the case of three-yearly decisions on budgets, the admittance of new members and external relations.

The aims of the ESRO organization, like CERN, were originally purely scientific, and partly because of this, it includes, as members, not only the Six plus Britain, but Switzerland, Sweden, Denmark, Spain, Austria and Norway. Contributions are related to national incomes and were split, originally, as follows:

TABLE I

National Contributions to ESRO (%)

Belgium	4·2	Spain	2·5
Denmark	2·1	Sweden	4·9
France	18·2	Switzerland	3·3
West Germany	21·5	UK	25·0
Italy	10·6	Austria	2·0
Netherlands	4·0	Norway	1·6

A first eight-year budget of $300 mn. was agreed in 1962. It was supposed to pay for setting up the major installations and for the following practical achievements:

(a) Firing, at a rate building up to some 65 medium-sized rockets per year, of a variety of sounding rockets mounting mainly national experiments.

(b) Launching, annually, from about the fourth year of ESRO's existence, of two fully instrumented small satellites in near-earth orbits, again carrying mainly national experiments.

(c) Launching, from about the sixth year of ESRO's existence (i.e. 1968), of two fully instrumented large satellites or space probes (i.e. requiring large launchers of, say, the ELDO type).

As the programme has been put into practice, it has inevitably been modified in step with the state of the art. There has been pressure from the scientists for more sophisticated facilities: satellites rather than sounding rockets, stabilized rather than unstabilized rockets, and rockets instead of balloons. At the same time the governments have squeezed the resources available to ESRO.

The preparatory commission which originally drew up the plans for ESRO had proposed an initial budget of $400 mn. over eight years, so the $300 mn. agreed by the governments was, in itself, a cut of 25 per cent. Under the ESRO convention governments must agree on a three-year budget within this eight-year framework. During the first three-year period, the new organization, not surprisingly, spent less than was originally expected. Time was taken to plan future work and the main expenditure on installations had only just got under way when the period ended. Governments, however, instead of allowing the surplus ($26 mn.) to be carried forward into the second period, gaily lopped it off the budget altogether. The result was that to finance installations, more money had to be taken from the sums allocated to operations. In addition it has been found that some of the basic facilities have had to be more ambitious than originally planned. For instance, there are to be six telemetry track-ing stations instead of four.

The net effect of all this has been to pare down some of the basic installations, and in particular the central research centre, to reduce the amount of applied research contracted out to industry, and above all, reduce the number of operations and staff using the basic facili-ties. Medium satellites are fewer, though more sophisticated, and a huge question mark hangs over ESRO's plans for large space projects (stage three of the original programme). The effect of all this is that ESRO's excellent facilities are underutilized. Despite the fact that out of some 60 satellite experiments being developed in member states in 1967, some 34 were planned to go in ESRO satellites (and only 15 in NASA and ten in national satellites), ESRO's existing facili-ties could handle a fairly large increase in the number of experi-ments, a potential increase which is probably matched by the growth in numbers of space scientists in the member states. In industry, though three European consortia have shown themselves interested in space work, ESRO provides them with only sporadic contracts and has no continuous programme yet. The trouble is that when it comes to choosing the direction of further work, political differences and differences about objectives rear their heads.

The major scientific operation envisaged for ESRO in the third stage of its programme is the launching of a Large Astronomical Satellite (LAS), now expected to cost some $90-$110 mn. for the spacecraft and scientific package, plus around $40 mn. for equip-ment on the ground. This satellite would be a kind of space observa-tory which would not only contain an initial series of experiments but provide a tool for experiments by teams of European scientists for many years to come.

Despite the mounting cost, the powerful scientific community in Britain on the whole favour this project, as they do much of ESRO's work. Whereas the British representatives in ELDO meetings come from the Ministry of Technology, ESRO is the concern of the National Council for Scientific Research under the Secretary of State for Education and Science. The pure scientists thus dominate the British outlook and back such projects as the LAS which offer an imaginative scientific advance.

This is particularly the case when, as with the LAS, British scientists are likely to be the leading beneficiaries. In the competition for the scientific package to go aboard the LAS three teams were in the running: a German-Dutch combination, a Franco-Belgian-

Swiss team, and a British team from Culham. If the LAS is ever launched the British team will get the task, thanks in part to the excellence of their proposals and in part to vigorous pressure in ESRO's science committee. Yet the manner of this success left a nasty taste in Continental mouths; alone of the three big countries the British had made no effort to make their package a partnership with a 'European' character.

All this has probably reduced the likelihood of the LAS ever taking to the sky. It certainly underlines the difference of objectives for ESRO as seen by Britain and its partners. Whereas Britain saw science as ESRO's purpose, most of the other countries were more concerned with the technological application or 'fall-out' from space. Most, therefore, are more interested in developing such emerging applications as communications, meteorological and navigation satellites, than in looking at the stars. And all have shown anxiety to get the largest possible share of ESRO contracts, or at least a share commensurate with their contributions to its funds.

In practice this has not happened, as the following table shows:

TABLE J

Geographical Distribution of ESRO *Contracts*

Country	Ratio of Contracts % to contribution %	
	(end of 1965)	(end of Oct. 1966)
France	1·7	2·0
Switzerland	1·8	1·9
Belgium	2·2	1·6
Netherlands	2·8	1·5
Italy	0·5	0·8
Sweden	0·5	0·6
UK	0·6	0·6
W. Germany	0·8	0·5
Spain	0·0	0·4
Denmark	0·4	0·3

Source: Information given by ESRO to Council of Europe.

No competitive system of tendering can be expected to produce a flowback to the member countries exactly equal to their contributions in any one year and it is to the great credit of ESRO that it has stuck to this efficient method of contracting. On the other hand, the cost-plus method of contracting used is something of an invitation to the skilful bidder, adept at tendering low and escalating later on.

An ideal system of tendering would provide for both competitive tendering and incentive profits bonuses for firms which keep within the tender. ESRO has tried to spread the work by encouraging the formation of three competitive European consortia, which have tendered for its medium satellites. But thanks, in the main, to its national space programme, which has provided experience in telemetry for instance (responsible for about half France's ESRO contracts), and to the fact that its industrialists made some effort to get orders, France has certainly obtained the lion's share of contracts so far. With time the balance will probably even out, but not until Europe has a broad and continuous space programme which requires a wide range of capabilities. Thus even the question of getting money back on contracts is related to the more fundamental questions of what ELDO and ESRO are for.

The central objective of those who think that Europe's space effort should have practical applications has been, for some years, the development of a European communications satellite. In 1963 eighteen European countries established the European Conference on Satellite Communications (CETS), initially as a means of coordinating the European negotiating position in Intelsat, the new world satellite communications authority, and then, increasingly, as a means of examining what Europe ought to do itself. CETS first examined the broad technological capabilities and needs of Europe in this field and then, in November 1966, commissioned ESRO to draw up a detailed specification for two experimental communications satellites and a broad programme to back them. We have seen already that ELDO's second Programme for Applications Satellites (PAS) was designed to develop launchers to put such satellites into synchronous orbit. The CETS-ESRO plan was the complement to this.

By the end of 1966, however, several governments, and especially the British, were still uncertain about the value of a European communications satellite programme, for reasons which we shall return to. Precious time was drifting away. One of the major arguments for developing a European communications satellite potential was, from the start, to strengthen Europe's hand in bargaining with the United States in the world organization, Intelsat. The first Intelsat agreement had been based essentially on acceptance of the American Comsat company's technical proposals; Europe, with a relatively frail technology in this field, had small success in gaining contracts in the new world communications system and only the bargaining power of a user. If a new European capability was to have an impact on the balance of world bargaining, it must be effective by 1970, when the next round of discussions in Intelsat take place.

While CETS dawdled, national space planners were not idle in the communications satellite field. As far back as 1965 France developed a plan for two experimental communications satellites, Saros I and II; West Germany was studying an experimental television satellite to relay the Olympic games from Munich in 1972. In May 1967 the two countries decided to combine their projects and develop a satellite, Symphonie, which would be launched in 1970, with an ELDO-PAS rocket, in advance of the Intelsat meeting in 1970.

In one sense this French initiative was wholly justified. If Europe was to be more effectively armed in the 1969-70 world negotiations, someone had to force the pace. On the other hand, the Franco-German initiative pre-empted half the CETS proposal for two experimental communications satellites; the specifications of Symphonie were to be almost identical with the first of the two CETS proposals. The Franco-German satellite thus posed the question whether the whole of the CETS plan would have to be rethought and whether it would go ahead at all.

Towards a European Space Authority

Behind the doubts about plans for applications satellites lay a major weakness of the European space endeavours: the separation between ELDO, providing the launchers, and ESRO, the space vehicles. Sensibly, the assemblies of the Council of Europe and Western European Union, the political bodies to whom ESRO and ELDO report, have long pressed for a merger of the two organizations. It is certainly ridiculous that Europe's minute space endeavours should be divided, not only nationally, but between organizations. Some outsiders claim that up to 300 people would be saved if the two bodies were merged. In fact duplication is not serious. ELDO's first test satellites will use ESRO's tracking stations; its other main bills are for test beds, and launching facilities which ESRO does not need. All the same ESRO's computing facilities and the ESTEC facilities in Holland might be more fully used by ELDO. The two organizations together could be more effective in stimulating a viable European space industry by the judicious placing of contracts for development and equipment—provided, that is, they adopted ESRO's competitive formula, rather than ELDO's national one. Above all a common organization and a common policy should make possible better planning and more efficient management. In space, Europe plainly needs a single managerial authority with clearly defined objectives and budgets, if it is to get value for money.

Realizing this, the French Government, in December 1966, invited a first European Space Conference to seek a way forward out of the crises which had broken over both ELDO and ESRO. The conference usefully set in motion a process of inquiry; an 'inventory' was to be drawn up of both national and European programmes and the needs of the future examined, so that a further conference in July could be in a position to agree on a rational future programme of work.

Unfortunately, when the July 1967 conference met in Rome, few of the real difficulties and differences were resolved. The British had still not made up their minds whether they wanted to share in the development of a European communications satellite system or not. Instead of pressing, either for an early implementation of part or all of the original CETS programme, or for a new and more advanced programme, taking into account the Franco-German Symphonie, they diplomatically dodged the question. Lacking a lead, the small countries were ineffective. The French and the West Germans, content to go ahead with their own scheme, sat tight.

Lukewarm on communications satellites the British, on the other hand, pressed for the LAS, in which their own scientists were interested. And indeed they, and the West Germans, were prepared to restore the earlier cuts in ESRO's finances, to permit the Culham scientists' pet project to go ahead. But here the French dug in; with their own national space programme escalating, they were not prepared to restore the cuts in ESRO's budget. Earlier, it had been the Belgians who refused to agree to a restoration of the ESRO's funds until a European space policy was worked out.

As for the union of the two space organizations, the neutrals in ESRO remained reluctant to join a club with rocket capability. The only tangible results of the Rome conference were the decisions to put the ESRO and ELDO secretariats in one building, establish a permanent coordinating committee between them, and appoint an advisory committee on programmes to look, yet again, at the economic and technical requirements of Europe's future space activities.

This tortoise-like advance might be acceptable, if there were no American or Russian hares in the race. Certainly the efforts to integrate the work of the ESRO and ELDO organizations are sincere and practical. But such slow, pragmatic endeavours will remain inadequate, indeed Europe's infant space activities could fall apart, if decisive steps are not taken towards establishing a common organization, setting clear goals, and integrating national programmes sensibly into these.

An example of how not to face these problems was set by the subcommittee on Technology and Science of the Estimates Committee of the House of Commons in its report on space published in July 1967.[1]

The subcommittee took evidence from the British civil service, Post Office, and industry. It discovered that Britain had no overall space policy, pointed out the inefficiency of a division of responsibilities between different ministries, and called for a national space authority. The proposal makes good sense. But when the committee went on to consider the aims of space policy and the relations between national and European programmes, it came badly unstuck.

France, it discovered, was getting the lion's share of ESRO contracts, because of the capability developed in the French national programme. Britain, the committee therefore concluded, should also have a strong national programme, and cut back on expenditure on European efforts. ELDO's new PAS programme, it admitted, would have to carry on, since the commitment had been made in 1966. But there should be no new commitments to a European communications satellite, or to any other significant common applications. Instead Britain should concentrate on developing its own small Black Arrow launcher, and on a new programme to develop 'electric propulsion', an ingenious 'poor man's' means of giving a satellite extra height. Despite its hostility to further European joint efforts the committee evidently felt a Gaullist dislike for America's dominance of space technology, and urged that, for defence, where Britain had bought an American satellite system, it should develop its own satellite, which would have to be launched by American rockets. The committee had no faith in joint European bargaining with America in the Intelsat negotiations. Yet it disliked American predominance there too. It was, in short, a Gaullist document. European space endeavours were inefficient and to be discouraged. Instead a national programme was needed which brought orders to British industry.

The inconsistencies of this approach do not need underlining. The Estimates Committee accepted the continuation of the ELDO-PAS programme (cost to Britain $82 mn.), and designed specifically to

[1] *Space Research and Development*, Thirteenth Report from the Estimates Committee, 1966–67, HMSO, 27 July 1967.

develop launchers which could put a first geo-stationary communications satellite into orbit, yet on grounds of cost it rejected the expenditure of $28 mn. over a five-year period (say $6 mn. per year) for the satellites to go on the end of the rockets. In order to be independent it proposed to develop a national communications satellite for defence purposes (cost unspecified), yet launched by American rockets. It placed no faith in joint European bargaining in Intelsat, but called for changes in the agreement which would favour Britain and Europe. It did not even base its report on correct statistics. The Estimates Committee Report is entitled 'Space Research and Development', but the figures given (in Appendix I, p. 345) in fact cover other space spending. And in the figures given for British 'national' space programmes they include the cost of purchasing American defence communications satellites (Skynet) and of our shareholding in the American-dominated organization Intelsat—hardly 'national' programmes and certainly not R & D. The table below shows these discrepancies:

TABLE K

UK Space Expenditure in 1967–68,

£'000 ($'000 shown in brackets)*

		Estimates Committee Report	R and D only
International:	ELDO	9,690	
	ESRO	4,130	
	Intelsat Subscription	600	i.e. less intelsat
	Total	14,420 ($34,608)	13,830 ($33,168)
National:	Defence	7,460	say 1,260 (less skynet)
	Other	8,670	8,670
	Total	16,130	9,930
Total National and International		30,550 ($73,320)	23,840 ($57,216)

**$ figures are at current exchange rate (i.e. $2·4 per £).

One feature of the Report stands out. Despite its sweeping judgements on the European space organizations, the Estimates Committee took no evidence from other Europeans; it saw no representatives of the secretariat of ELDO and ESRO, despite suggestions from witnesses that they should, and met no MPs from other member countries (the scientific committee of the French chamber of deputies, has, to the credit of all concerned, interviewed British civil servants on joint air projects). The Estimates Committee do not appear to have read, or considered, proposals, like those in the Bannier Report, for improving the management of ESRO or ELDO. Despite their sweeping condemnation of the inefficiency of joint European space endeavours, they had no positive proposals to make for improving the organization or management of these European bodies, or for giving them clearer goals. The only concrete and definite proposal made to the committee—that there should be a mixed company to run a European communications satellite system which should negotiate for Europe in the world negotiations—was dismissed as Utopian, despite the fact that many members of the committee were supposed to favour British membership of the Common Market, a body with a common policy for the whole of its external trade. The effectiveness and practicability of Europe bargaining as a unit had just been triumphantly vindicated in this field in the Kennedy Round.

It is tempting to dismiss the Estimates Committee Report as unimaginative and insular. In fact there is a more practical moral. Unlike the new Science and Technology Committee of the House of Commons, the Estimates Committee is not in the habit of taking evidence from foreigners; the habit plainly needs changing. Moreover, even if they were, there must always be a tendency for national parliamentary bodies, seeking laudably to control expenditure, to prefer national programmes, which they can in some measure control, to international ones which they feel they cannot. The need to bring Europe's efforts under a strong common parliamentary control is plain.

Actually the Science Committee of the Assembly of the Council of Europe has scrutinized the space problem carefully and produced a series of cogent and positive reports, calling for a merger of the European space organizations, improvements in management, and clear decisions by governments to embark on a planned, long-term space programme, including the joint development of a series of applications satellites. But though British MPs played active and positive roles in this committee, none was on the Estimates Committee or was consulted by it, and the governments have so far failed to carry the Council of Europe's recommendations out.

Let us consider for a moment what would happen if Britain followed the recommendations of the Estimates Committee and other European countries also followed its approach. The small, national Black Arrow programme is at present designed to test and develop components for the larger and heavier European satellite systems of the future. This is eminently sensible since Black Arrow, a small rocket, can lift only 100 kg into low orbit (compared to a ton on a Europa-I launcher). The Estimates Committee propose that a further $9 mn. should be spent on developing electric propulsion; they are probably optimistic about the cost, and the possible results, and in any case this would only enable some 40-70 kg useful payload to be lifted into the synchronous orbit necessary for a communications satellite. If the same electric propulsion principle were applied to a one ton satellite lifted on an Europa-I launcher, a 500 kg satellite might be lifted into synchronous orbit. Thus while the application of this new principle to a purely British programme might put up a satellite of the same size as the original American Early Bird, with its 240 telephone lines, its application to a Europa-I system would permit the launching of a far larger and more advanced satellite with the potential to transmit television direct to small community receivers in Europe or developing continents. The Estimates Committee Report simply serves as a reminder that despite all the difficulties and teething troubles of the

ROCKETS COMPARED

68·27 metres

U.S. SATURN I B

EUROPA

BLACK ARROW

European space endeavour, this is a field where the facts of scale dictate a common effort. The diagram, showing the relative size of the Black Arrow, ELDO and largest US launchers brings the point home.

The case for a national effort can be taken a stage further by arguing for the development of a British Blue Streak-Black Arrow launching system, which would have a lifting capacity comparable, though not quite equal with, ELDO-PAS. Leaving aside the political implications of a withdrawal from ELDO, which will be judged differently by those who believe in the permanence and viability of nation states in their present form and by those who favour a united Europe, it could be argued that a British withdrawal from ELDO, followed by the expenditure of Britain's ELDO subscription on a national project, could build up a Blue Streak-Black Arrow launcher within the next five years. A price would be paid in time, for a fresh start would have to be made. And in the years after 1970 the cost (like ELDO's) would rise beyond that envisaged in ELDO's current programme. But the main objections are of a wider character. The Estimates Committee jibbed at the expenditure of $6 mn. per year for five years as the British contribution to a joint communications satellite. The development of a comparable national satellite would presumably cost some $22 mn. per year. The same considerations would apply to large scientific satellites, which the British scientific community is so interested in. Going it alone in this field (say a British instead of a European LAS) means a vast increase in expenditure; the alternative is to limit scientific experiments to a relatively small scale. Then there is a wider question concerning the future. Putting up more advanced and larger loads will again cost more both for the launchers and for the loads, a cost which will be multiplied many times in a national rather than European programme. The cheapest way of all to play a modest, subsidiary role in space is probably to buy American. But if European countries want some political say in space applications and some industrial capability of their own, the only reasonably economic way is to do it together. The only reason Britain can consider going it alone is because it inherits from its exorbitant earlier military ambitions the Blue Streak and indirectly (via Black Knight) the Black Arrow launchers, with their costs of development already written off. It cannot afford to pay the costs of future developments, in a viable space programme, on its own.

The applications of space technology also call for a joint approach.

M

So long as Britain tries to have a separate, worldwide defence capability, there is an argument for a British defence communications satellite system, perhaps bought from the Americans, on whom this worldwide strategy depends. But Britain is at last withdrawing from the last outposts of empire because it has found all this beyond its means. If a defence communications satellite system is needed in the future, it will be there to serve common European needs.

As for peaceful applications of communications satellites, transoceanic communications are already being handled by the worldwide Intelsat system. And all current economic comparisons suggest that, over short distances, perhaps up to 700 to 1,000 miles, telephone communication by cable and microwave will remain cheaper than by satellite. A telephone communications satellite would have no value for Britain alone though it might for television. There is a case, however, for a European regional satellite system, both for carrying trunk telephone communications over long distances, and for transmitting Europe-wide television programmes. There might be applications too for direct transmission television broadcasting, perhaps for educational purposes, in continents like Africa, India, and even Latin America. Gaullists in Britain and France can argue here for a national, Commonwealth, or French Community system. But leaving aside cost, it is plain, politically, that the emergent continents are not going to accept tutelage, old-style, from a former mother country. Television programmes beamed to these continents would have to be of an 'educational' character acceptable to the developing world, in short a form of 'aid', or of discrete influence at the most. In this context a 'European' system looks more in tune with the political realities of the future, quite apart from the cost question. Politically, as well as on grounds of economies of scale, a European group would probably also be better placed to sell complete communications systems (ground stations, launching service, satellites, maintenance) to developing regions (e.g. Pan Africa) or countries (e.g. divided Pakistan). Only the Americans and Russians can do this today. In terms of both applications and development costs, space is a supreme illustration of the thesis of this book—the need for European scale.

How to Improve the European Programmes

Energies must therefore be devoted to making the first infant endeavours, which are, after all, a mere four years old, more efficient, to agreeing on well-founded and clear objectives, and, to harmonizing national programmes so that they contribute to the common programme instead of duplicating efforts and wasting resources.

Ways of achieving these objectives have already been aired. Greater efforts must be made to merge ELDO and ESRO into a single space authority. The authority must be given a clear-cut forward programme, with a five-year *rolling* budget modified each year to maintain a carefully considered forward look. The space authority should be given wide managerial powers to carry out its task. The contracts system must be tightened to put both ELDO and ESRO contracts on a competitive basis with strong profit-incentive features brought in. Ways should be found of bringing private capital into applications to strengthen the incentive element. The programme planning body should be empowered to consider national space programmes as well as the common ones and make more use of development contracts from a common fund to promote a division of labour in the national programmes which will both optimize their contribution to European programmes and result in a reasonable distribution of work and capability between the different countries. For instance, it makes excellent sense for the British to develop electric propulsion, and perhaps experiment with it on a Black Arrow satellite; this would be followed, if successful, by a European development programme to apply electric propulsion to a 500 kg European satellite. Again, French telemetry, developed for the French national programme, has been a useful contributor to ESRO, and the CNES and ESRO stations work sensibly together. It would be still more economical, however, if they became part of a single system. Or again, the Italians are nationally exploring the technology of direct transmission satellites. This should be encouraged with a view to a European direct transmission satellite system to be developed later on.

But while it is not too difficult to suggest means for improving the efficiency of Europe's common space endeavours, the hardest question remains unanswered: to choose the goals. At bottom the biggest doubts about the European space efforts, like the doubts about Concorde or the airbus, concern not the methods but the aims of the projects themselves. Should Europe seek to develop applications satellites and if so, which? Should it try to put up a Large Astronomical Satellite or not? Is it necessary, after all, for Europe to try to develop a large launcher capability or was ELDO a mistake? It is easy to dismiss the silly proposals from the Estimates Committee for a national instead of a European space programme. It is harder to decide whether even Europe as a whole should devote resources to space, and if so why, and for what aims.

The basic arguments for some kind of European space activity are fourfold: the scientific knowledge to be acquired in space; the fall-out derived from this advanced activity; the political need to have a capability in technology which would have major applications, military and political; and the plain economic benefit from applications of space technology, which is likely to grow.

Of these arguments the fall-out argument is the weakest. There are plenty of forms of industrial investment and scientific enterprise which could both yield rapid development of new technologies, and bring more immediate social and economic benefits. The scientific argument is a pretty valid argument for ESRO, as originally conceived. The cheapest way for European scientists to make space experiments is probably to conduct experiments together, use common facilities and buy American launchers on the probably not very numerous occasions when they need bigger launchers and more complex equipment than they can economically maintain alone.

It is when one comes to applications, and the delicately balanced political and technological arguments for and against developing a European capability, especially in launchers, that the argument gets difficult and obscure.

First of all, it should be clear that the wisdom of developing a European capability in large launchers depends on what the launchers are supposed to launch. In this respect ELDO was a remarkable example of putting the cart before the horse. Thanks to Blue Streak, Europe embarked on developing a large rocket capability before it knew in any detail what it wanted the launchers to put up. Since that time, the practical applications of space have multiplied, proving that the original decision to develop a European capability was right. The requirements have become clearer too. It has become apparent, for instance, that communications satellites are best placed in geo-stationary orbits. It is high time to clarify the aims of the programme.

Moreover, it is hard to defend the thesis that Europe should develop large launchers merely to put up scientific satellites, like the LAS. For a modest consideration, and/or in return for access to the scientific knowledge which Europe's admirable scientific brains can gather, both the United States and Russia will be, in future, more than willing to make large launchers available to the European scientists to put up their experiments. The argument about developing large rockets must turn on the argument for or against applications satellites of some kind. It is here that both economic return and political advantage can be found.

The Pros and Cons of Applications Satellites

The immediate and most hotly contested decision concerns the development of communications satellites. Given the existing ELDO-PAS launcher programme, the additional $90 mn. required for the CETS experimental satellite programme is not large. But a decision on this cannot sensibly be made without considering future costs of more advanced satellites and launching systems which will be needed if the whole programme is to make practical sense. First of all, is there a need for Europe to develop such satellite systems?

The argument for developing a European communications satellite system is, at first sight, pretty dubious. In terms of telephone communication, cables and microwave communications are much more economic over short distances; satellites beat the cable competition only at distances longer than some 1,500 km. Satellite technology is rapidly improving, but so are cables, where the technology has raced ahead under the stimulus of this new form of competition. Today, for instance, some 26,000 circuits can operate through a single coaxial cable; this means that as far ahead as can be seen the communications satellite will have a crucial role to play in the transmission of telephone conversations and data across the oceans and across large continents, but much less of a role in congested, close-packed areas. The world satellite system run by Intelsat, which bridges the oceans, is eminently justified economically. And it is possible to make out a case for additional domestic systems in a large rich continent such as America or in vast areas of rough or mountainous country—Canada, Russia, India, Africa—where it is much cheaper to beam messages via satellite, than to struggle to lay long distance cables over desert, glacier or mountain range. But in tight-packed Europe the case for an internal regional satellite system becomes more dubious.

Except in Federal Germany, about three quarters of present international telephone traffic in West European countries is between national capitals. From London the only heavily used internal European trunk route longer than 1,000 miles is the link to Rome. There are also problems of interference in the crucial metropolises. Microwaves and man-made static electricity could interfere with satellite transmission and reception. This problem might be solved by the use of higher frequencies (which means more advanced satellites) but the limited commercial value of satellites over the short distances of most European telephone communications remains. Not surprisingly, European Post Offices have been lukewarm. Their judgement, that it is impossible to predict the relative advantage of the three or more technologies, is eminently fair.

One other vital point favours the satellite. Data transmission is now expanding in America as fast as telephone communications. For the smooth, continuous operation which will be vital, when this boom hits Europe, satellites may be more satisfactory than cables. Satellite capability could be an essential part of the exploding communications business associated with the computer age.

A more attractive application of a regional telecommunications satellite system, developed in Europe, would be in, say, Africa, where distance and terrain completely change the relative economics of cables and satellite. In a report to the conference on telecommunications organized by the British Council of the European Movement[2] in July 1967, an African system, using a satellite of the type proposed by CETS, is described and costed. The author suggests that a CETS satellite, linking ten African capitals with each other or with southern Europe, might provide links at a cost of $25,000 per channel, a relatively cheap rate.

Much the strongest prima facie case, however, for a European regional satellite system is for television, where the European Broadcasting Union, the joint organ of the European broadcasting authorities, has declared a requirement for two satellite television channels. One television channel is equivalent to some 1,000 telephone channels, so this is a demand for a major satellite capability. In the Eurovision system 21 television systems already make use of some 90,000 km of microwave relays and 12,000 km of cable. Yet the use of link stations and relays within the present system hampers real time transmission across frontiers, and makes advance notice necessary.

For sport, news and, especially, enducational programmes of various kinds, direct transmission via satellite is a facility the broadcasting companies want—though it should be noted that much can be done in education by recordings.

The giant potentialities of television satellites will emerge when it

[2]M. O'Hagan, *A Regional Telecommunications System for Africa.* Report of a conference arranged by the British Council of the European Movement on European Cooperation in Telecommunications, June 1967.

is possible to transmit so powerfully that television can be picked up, not merely by big ground station antennae, but by small, local, community receivers, or even by individual receivers in the home. The community receiver—perhaps placed on a hilltop in rough country—can be linked by cable to sets at home, or in, say, Africa or India, used as a communal installation for school and village. Given sufficient power, a direct broadcast satellite could eventually 'break in' to domestic television receivers, broadcasting, say, political propaganda from outside.

Such a development should be technologically possible within the next five to six years. It involves, essentially, a major increase in the transmitting power of satellites.

This means either new and more efficient methods of power production and new radio transmission techniques (say at superhigh frequencies), or a satellite weighing one or two tons involving more powerful launchers. The ELDO launcher could be developed in several alternative ways—by adding 'strap-on' boosters (to Blue Streak), and/or a new liquid hydrogen fuelled stage, and/or electronic propulsion to boost the final stage. Here the stakes for Europe become high. The cost of getting a place in this more advanced application of satellite technology may be big; but the political cost of staying out will be big too. In fifteen years' time possessors of direct transmission satellite technology will be powerfully placed to beam propaganda and influence to the television sets of the 'third world'. And though it would be wrong to underestimate the power of local governments to bargain or negotiate with the outsiders who control these powerful instruments, the satellite controllers will be in an even stronger bargaining position.

There are many other potential applications for satellites: satellites will almost certainly be used increasingly for navigation, surveillance and traffic control of air traffic and ships at sea, especially on ocean routes. At present transatlantic aircraft, for instance, are out of radio contact for some hours of their flight.

The World Meteorological Organization is promoting a world system of satellites known as World Weather Watch. Satellites can 'see' and report on cloud and wind movements, long before ground stations pick up the trends. Satellites are thus a crucial instrument of the exciting, indeed, forbidding power that man may acquire to control or modify the weather to serve his needs.

A third possible application is the collection of data about 'earth resources', mapping the state of crops, geological formations, forests or shallow seas, recording air pollution. Preliminary American data show immense potentialities here.

Should these needs be met by European satellites? Plainly, weather watching and navigation, like transoceanic communications, are matters ideally dealt with on a worldwide scale. Intelsat seems the body to develop a world navigation system, and the WMO the weather watch. Even in telephone systems, where we have seen that a certain case might be made out for regional arrangements, especially in large continents, the cheapest system of all, given a politically united world, would almost certainly be a totally integrated world system. The argument for a separate domestic system, say in the United States, which is still under discussion, is part political and part managerial. When the use of the world Intelsat system involves complex negotiations with other countries, and when a major and busy sector of the globe, like the United States, conveniently falls within the range of a single group of satellites (four are proposed) it may be sensible to manage this sector on its own, slotting it into the world system, but not making it an integral part.

The question for Europe is whether it, too, needs to develop an applied satellite capability, in order eventually to participate in direct television broadcasting from satellites, as a means of bargaining in Intelsat, and a way of getting business in the wider world applications. As the scale of this worldwide business grows, why should not Europe, like the Americans and Japanese, win large-scale contracts from world organizations? The decision is thus in large part political, or at any rate an economic decision based on power and bargaining considerations, as well as on commercial factors.

The economics of developing European applications satellites, as opposed to buying them, do not look attractive. Certainly, in the early stages, American firms could sell a complete launcher and satellite to a European body more cheaply than the Europeans could develop one of their own. An ELDO launcher, for instance, might cost some $10 mn. according to the price quoted by the ELDO secretariat and council, excluding development costs, and $25 mn. according to the British Post Office, if development costs are included, compared with $8 mn. for a US rocket. The entire delevopment cost of the US launcher is already written off under the US space programme. Is it worthwhile for Europeans to pay the price of developing the technology themselves, for political and bargaining reasons, and in the hope that later it will prove more competitive?

The original Intelsat and Comsat agreements in a sense invite a

European political response. When communication satellites first succeeded, there was a vigorous battle within the United States administration between those who sought to give the United Nations a role in the new world system, making it truly international, and the advocates of a more national approach. The national approach won. Comsat, an ingenious mixed private and public company, purely American in character, was set up in 1962. Other countries were invited to discuss a new world system. Intelsat, a new world organization, was set up in 1964, but Comsat became both the manager of the new world system and the representative of the United States. Votes and financial contributions to Intelsat were divided according to traffic, which gave the United States a 61 per cent quota. But there was one important reservation. Major decisions had to be taken by a qualified majority, which meant that some European and other votes are needed. Intelsat rents to all members of the International Telecommunications Union at non-discriminatory rates which are highly competitive with cables. Perhaps the main practical complaint of America's partners has been the high percentage of its $200 mn. worth of contracts which have gone to the United States; yet this is probably an inevitable consequence of America's massive lead in space technology, a lead which only Russia can match today.

So what should Europe do? In 1970 the interim Intelsat arrangement is to be given more permanent form. The French and West Germans, with their joint satellite, are already taking steps to strengthen their hands in the bargaining. Should more be done in the form of a long-term European programme to develop a whole range of advanced satellite applications, so that in this bargaining and in the coming age of direct transmission broadcasting Europe has a technological capability of its own?

It takes two to communicate; thus users of an international communications system, like the Europeans, are not without bargaining power. Moreover, in terms of industrial contracts, making money out of selling satellites does not look a particular profitable affair. Satellites can last five years—perhaps twenty. A world system may need, say, eight; an American domestic system, four. Much bigger business is in the ground stations, switching, and so on. Such arguments favour a cautious approach.

On the other hand, a much better case in terms of general technology can be made out for developing satellites, than launchers. Satellites are boxes of delicate instruments and electronics involving skills with many other applications. Large rockets are the really expensive part of the business and yield much less technical benefit all round. Developing applications satellites in Europe follows on naturally enough from the scientific satellites already being used. The biggest question, then, is whether the need for political influence and bargaining power requires Europe to stay in the large rocket business. Although launchers can be bought from America, it is not much use developing a satellite capability for bargaining purposes, if the launcher is to be bought from the rival on the other side.

A decision has to be made on the basis of a clear appreciation of its implications. It is useless, for instance, deciding to carry on with launching one or two ELDO rockets, and an experimental communications satellite, if later the growing cost of larger rockets and satellites needed for direct transmission is going to prove too high. An assessment has to be made of the cost, over the next ten years, of a balanced space programme for Europe. It has to be weighed against other priorities and, if these prove stronger, dropped.

Such a programme ought to include the following major objectives:

(i) Complete the ELDO-PAS programme and examine the cost of developing boosters, so that larger satellites (say 500 kg in geo-stationary orbit) can be put up. (Ultimate cost over five years $500 mn.?)

(ii) Accelerate work on electric propulsion to enable larger loads to be lifted. ($20 mn.?)

(iii) Formulate a programme of development on other forms of auxiliary power and radio techniques for direct transmission satellites and on development of receiving antennae.

(iv) Make a realistic project assessment of the costs of developing a practical satellite capable of transmitting to small 'communal' receivers in Africa. (Cost $25 mn.?)

(v) Examine the requirement for a European defence satellite system, to follow on Skynet.

(vi) CETS to develop a television satellite for Europe to satisfy the requirements of the European Broadcasting Union (EBU) as a compliment to the requirements of the Franco-German experimental satellite.

(vii) Put up a satellite capable of transmitting television to small communal receivers in 1975.

Such a programme would provide practical short-term objectives including a regional satellite for Africa, a television satellite for Europe, a possible defence system and work on a long-term objective

—the capability to launch direct transmission satellites from developments of ELDO launchers later on. This emphasis on applications will consume much cash. So consideration has to be given to the possibility of scaling down the LAS, now expected to consume $150 mn., into a still valuable, but less disproportionately expensive scientific project.

American firms in Europe ought not to be rigidly excluded from work on such European projects. IT & T for instance, with its experience of work for Intelsat, is a useful member of one of ESRO's consortia. This is a valuable means of transferring technology. Later, on, if a systematic European space policy develops, there is much to be said for taking up the American proposal of a joint American-European Jupiter probe, a project which may be less expensive than the LAS, and one in which the Europeans would carry out much of the most exciting satellite, guidance, and signalling work. For as far ahead as can be seen, Europe cannot expect to have a leading place in the space race comparable to America and Russia. It has infinitely more rewarding applications for its limited resources of brains and money. But it can devote a limited budget to specialized, economic applications, to making use of commonplace space techniques for scientific exploration, and to exploring particular new technological areas in which there may be profitable returns.

How much would a programme of the kind outlined cost, and would it be worthwhile? American estimates of the cost of a direct broadcast television system put the satellite in the range $50-$100 mn.; development of the US meteorological satellite Tyros and Nimbus cost $40-$50 mn. But developing launchers for a big direct broadcast satellite could cost some $500 mn. A CETS television satellite for EBU, making use of the experience of Symphonie, might cost some $50 mn. The acid test of the commercial value of such a project will be whether private capital is willing to invest in it. If European governments find they have to decide on the wisdom of such a project, they should invite private industry to make detailed proposals for a joint public-private company which would commission the development of a satellite system and run it later on. The Post Offices would of course fight this, which is one of the main reasons why private capital has been shy. A clear political decision is therefore needed to give private capital a real stake.

During the winter of 1967-68 the joint programme committee of ESRO and ELDO (under the chairmanship of M. Causse) produced an excellent study of a broad programme of the kind we have described, together with costs and alternative options. For the first time a coherent European space policy was put forward, welding together the work of ELDO and ESRO into a common strategy, and shifting the emphasis from abstract science and rockets without a clear objective, to that of the development of a series of satellites with practical applications in the next few years. The two organizations were to be fused together, and ESRO's contract procedures, which encourage competition between European consortia, adopted. The Chart (p. 189) shows the estimated costs of the new programme. The committee succeeded in putting a ceiling of $90 mn. per year on the launcher programme—even though these estimates included development of larger launchers to put up heavier satellites. It was the satellite programme—with its manifold applications—which was expected to soar in cost, to a maximum of some $137 mn. by 1973. The committee gave the governments three alternative options for the development of satellites, which varied in cost and the speed of building up the programme. The most ambitious of these would have meant an increase in total space spending of some 10 per cent per year.

Should Europe take the plunge, and embark on a space programme on this scale, which probably means a continuing programme of at least $200 mn. per year on international programmes, perhaps rising to peaks of $300 mn. or more? A first question which has to be asked is whether the national programmes, which in 1966 took almost as much as the European programmes, could be cut back to pay the bill. Certainly, the duplication of testing facilities, small launcher capability and so on means that, within a fixed space budget, less can be spent on the big international projects. But parts of the national programmes provide a necessary infrastructure for the European ones. Ideally, they could perhaps be cut by half; but in practice one doubts whether this will happen. So, if the 'European' space budget is to be bigger, this probably means putting up the total, perhaps to somewhere between $300 mn. and $400 mn. per year. The answer to this question can only be given in terms of priorities—which comes first, this space programme or other scientific needs?

The British Government quickly gave its answer in April 1968. Disconcerted by the prospect of an increase in expenditure, and with its own budget under acute pressure, it decided, not only that it would not join in a programme of applications satellites, but that it would also withdraw from the ELDO rocket programme, when the present agreements and programme expire in 1971. There was a cer-

THE CAUSSE PLAN

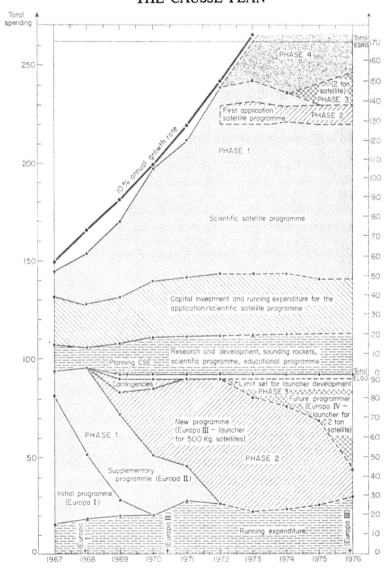

Total spending in $mn.

tain brutal logic in this posture. If the British Government was not prepared to join in a programme of applications satellites, which would at last have made practical use of ELDO's large rockets, there was little purpose in continuing to participate in the rocket programme. And since the economic calculations clearly showed that the satellites proposed for the near future (like the television satellite for the European Broadcasting Union) could not be produced and launched in Europe at a price competitive with American satellites, unless development costs were written off (like those in the USA), 'cost-effectiveness', in the words of the British Minister for Technology, suggested that the British Government should say no.

The trouble was that this rather elementary calculation left out other massive factors. What would be the impact on bargaining in Intelsat of having no European capability? What would be the effect on the European balance of payments of relying on America? The West Germans expect that by 1980 communications licensing and other fees to the Americans will cost Europe some $200 mn. to $300 mn.—or as much as the annual development costs suggested in the proposed European space programme. Communications satellites may be in the same position as computers were ten years ago—on the eve of a large and unexpected growth in applications.

Indeed the closer one looks at the British Government's decision, the curioser and curiouser it becomes. While deciding, on grounds of 'cost effectiveness', not to go into practical applications of space technology, the government accepted the persuasions of its powerful scientific lobby that it should continue to expand the scientific work of ESRO, which may have no practical application at all. And some $15 mn. continued to be spent each year on buying the Skynet defence satellite system from the US, a system originally designed to serve Britain's worldwide—including East of Suez—forces.

Most curious of all, the British Government also decided to spend an unspecified amount on a national programme to develop electric propulsion—an interesting notion, as we have seen, but one which would only become critically valuable if used as a supplement to large ELDO-type launchers as a means of getting a large direct transmission satellite into geo-stationary orbit.

Within the broad context of a European science policy in which resources are already effectively pooled, it is quite conceivable that the European nations together might agree that spending on space should have lower priority than other scientific and technological aims. We consider the broad choices before a European science and technology policy in Chapter 14.

The British Government's unilateral decision, however, was not taken in that context. The six Common Market countries, or at any rate France and West Germany, will perhaps try to go ahead even without Britain. More time and money will be lost to the European space endeavour through yet another political upheaval. But in the end it will struggle on. Britain, however, will be out of the mainstream and the chances of success for those who remain in will be less.

A Communications Policy

Discussion of a European communications satellite has been all too centred on the spectacular hardware and technology and all too little on the practical needs it might serve. America has one, so we must have one too, the argument has run. It would be more satisfactory if the choice were set in a wider framework, that of the growth and use of European communications as a whole.

Western Europe is still relatively undeveloped in terms of telephones and their use. In 1966 it still had only one telephone for every six people compared with one for every two in the United States.[3] Growth in Europe is faster than in America and telephones have more than doubled in ten years as the Post Offices struggle to catch up with demand. But the waiting lists in almost every country, the delays and mistakes, provide pretty devastating evidence that capacity and engineering capability have not kept up with needs. Anyone who has tried to telephone from Sicily to Innsbruck or Hampstead, and compares his experience with a phone call from Florida to Chicago will know this. In North America about half the growth of calls in the next ten years is expected to be the transmission of data, from computer to computer. This is not yet happening in Europe, but it will soon; the need for a rapid expansion of the system will become more acute than ever.

What are the obstacles to a more efficient European telephone system? One is simple lack of investment and capital. The Post Offices have not invested enough, even though their performance shines (at least in Britain) compared with some other public services and private industries. Here important changes in organization will help. In Britain the Post Office's telecommunications business is being separated from the postal service; this ought to mean that

[3] AT & T, *The World's Telephones*, 1966.

telephones will no longer have to subsidize the mail. More rapid growth should follow. In France, a similar change is being debated. The sooner telephone systems throughout Europe operate as commercial enterprises, investing in proportion to the tremendous growth of demand, the better.

The inheritance of nation states, however, also adds to the costs and diminishes the efficiency of European telephones. Each Post Office has its own research programme, and most have their own special requirements for telephone exchanges and equipment. The result is, not only technical complexity and inefficiency, but waste of skilled manpower and finance and sub-optimal production. AT & T, which runs the American telephone system and the Bell Laboratories, points out that Western Europe spends more on telephone research and development than the United States, despite the fact that the US has twice as many telephones as Western Europe. This is hardly surprising when, in America, one company with one central laboratory (Bell) runs almost the entire system. To fill different requirements for different European Post Offices, the largest supplier of telephone equipment was, in 1967, developing seven different types of electronic telephone exchanges and six different microwave developments. All of them were claimed by the customer to be relevant, and some interlock. The dissipation of resources was absurd, just the same. Europe's problem is not so very different from that faced by AT & T when it began the immense engineering task of integrating the multifarious telephone networks, born from many private companies, which it took over in the United States.

In looking at the rationalization of Europe's telephone system, the achievements of the existing International Telecommunications Union (ITU), the Joint Committee for International Telephone and Telegraph (CCITT) and Comité Européen des Postes et Telegraphes (CEPT) should not be underestimated. The ITU, which has been working since 1865, has reached some twenty volumes of agreements on standard accounting, engineering and user procedures: an essential precondition of the telephone and telegraph communications which we enjoy today. But the work of the ITU has been concerned, above all, with the interfaces between nations, with making it possible to talk from one country to another, not with standardizing and rationalizing the basic systems used in Europe, in order to achieve an optimum system, with equipment supplied in the cheapest and most efficient way. What is needed now is both a common public market in European telephone equipment, and a deliberate policy by the national telephone and telegraph authorities to work together towards a common European system.

Some progress is being made in the existing bodies. The CCITT have agreed on a number of common techniques for push-button telephoning and are moving towards agreement on data transmission. In this new field, indeed, the disagreements in the United States are even greater than in Europe.

On the other hand, the variety of telephone exchange equipment has got much greater in the last twenty years. Before the war the Strowger switch was normal in the Commonwealth and parts of Europe, the Bell system dominated France and Belgium, Ericsson was strong in Scandinavia and Siemens in the rest of Europe. Since then there has been a proliferation of systems, though Siemens, Ericsson and IT & T (Standard Telephones, Bell, etc.) dominate the market. Different countries still have different standards in vital matters. For instance they each require a different standard 'sending level' or minimum noise level, which then have to be raised to agreed international levels. Post Offices, in most countries, though showing polite interest in a policy of rationalization, explain that it is not possible 'just now' to agree on common telephone exchange specifications, for instance, since their buildings and existing equipment are different and new equipment must fit in.

What then should be done? First, create a common market in public purchase of telephone equipment. This in itself would start to bring a healthy change. The British cartel with the Post Office, for instance, would collapse and its members would face both competition from, say Siemens and Ericsson, and the chance to get into the market in West Germany and France. IT & T, straddling most of Europe, would be able quickly, to rationalize production and offer equipment made in one country to another.

Next the governments must decide to instruct the Post Offices to make a more determined effort to develop an integrated European system, perhaps through the existing CEPT. They could make a start by agreeing on such immediate matters as common specifications and standards for data transmission, and a common minimum 'noise level'. They could then move on to more positive common planning. For instance, why not plan ahead together some ten years and agree on an integrated numbering plan for the whole of Europe, as the United States has done? Future development of lines and exchanges would fit into this. Bit by bit agreement would have to be reached on common specifications for facilities—laying down, in the case of

N

each type of service, what is expected of the equipment involved. Then the companies would be in a position to tender as equals in a common market.

As far as telephone exchanges are concerned, the best way forward might be for companies and Post Offices to agree first of all on common standards for business exchanges and equipment, then move on to small sub-exchanges, and finally thrash out the problem of common requirements for central electronic exchanges.

The process would be much facilitated if the European Post Offices would bring the heads of their research departments together so that they could work together on designing a future common system.

Such a policy would not give Europe the same degree of uniformity, in telephone development, as the United States. It would probably be in the public interest if at least four or five major producing companies would continue to compete, providing a degree of variety in innovation and equipment. These units would be further strengthened as competitors in the world outside, by the chance to provide equipment for all Europe in a field where European industry is already strong. A common procurement system, with genuine competitive tendering, and encouragement to the formation of European consortia and mergers through a contractual system similar to ESRO's, would encourage competitive companies to emerge which had a base in several countries. As progress is made towards a common system, costs of R & D by the Post Office should fall, the results should improve, and Europeans should benefit from a cheaper, more efficient telephone system.

As the Post Offices began to operate and think in terms of a common European system, decisions about the use of communications satellites, microwaves and cables, would fall into place. Probably the growth of long-distance traffic which resulted would make regional European coaxial systems more viable. Today much international traffic is still distorted by such things as the high rates charged for transit. It pays major European countries to have their own cable or satellite transmission systems to funnel calls across the Atlantic, even though it might be cheaper to have one outlet. Common planning and integration of the system should make it possible to diminish such anomalies.

By nature communications are international. There is a prima facie case for developing a European communications policy now.

CHAPTER 11

A STAKE IN THE
COMPUTER REVOLUTION

Technology has developed through three successive phases in the course of history. For many millenia it was concerned, above all, with increasing, replacing, or applying the muscle power of man and beast. The wheel and the loom, the steam engine and the pump, the jet engine and the typewriter, were all concerned to increase and apply man's physical power to manipulate his environment. In the second phase, occupying the last hundred years, technology has increasingly replaced and augmented the power of the senses. Radio, television, radar, telephones, seismic devices, all seek to multiply the powers of sight, hearing, touch and voice, so that man's powers of communication are vastly multiplied. In a third phase, a mere 25 years old, and only a decade old in its impact on our daily lives, technology is multiplying and applying the power of the brain itself. This is the significance of the barely begun computer revolution, a revolution which could transform society, and indeed the human species itself.

The computer offers a tool by which those thought-processes which can be translated into mathematical terms can be carried out with lightning speed. A payroll calculation, which would take several hundred clerks many hours each, can be handled by a computer in a few hours. The implications of wind tunnel experiments, revealing a whole series of data on stresses and strains, metal fatigue and aerodynamic flows, can be interpreted and translated into practical conclusions in a few minutes; hence the result of six months' experiments can be compressed into a few hours.

An architect's conception of a building, which might take months to translate into detailed drawings, with the plumbing, electricity, water, etc., in the right place, can be translated in this way in a few hours. Or again, information concerning stocks in a large retailing firm with many brands can be fed continuously into a central computer which places orders, and at the same time calculates profitability of different operations, with different cost and demand factors analysed and exposed. As for the ability of the computer to help in scientific calculations, the possibilities are immense.

In a chemical or oil refinery a computer can monitor temperatures, pressures, reactions, speeds of flow and automatically make adjustments which optimize the operation. In education, banking, airline operation, the control of industrial processes, automatic flying of a supersonic aircraft, and countless other needs, the application of the computer is in its infancy. Small wonder that many Europeans ask whether Europe should not have a stake in this new industrial revolution.

Yet of all the key advanced technology industries, this one is most completely dominated by the United States. IBM has two thirds of the world and European markets. In Europe at least another 10 per cent of the market is in the control of US firms (making 75 to 80 per cent). Up and coming Honeywell has a strong base in Britain, West Germany and France. CDC is a key supplier of large computers. GE has absorbed Bull and Olivetti's computer operation. Burroughs has won a tidy share of the UK banking market; Univac and NCR have small positions too. What could and should Europe do to respond to the challenge?

The first, instinctive, response of the three largest European states has been to try to develop or protect a national industry, as we saw in Chapters 3 to 5. In Britain, the British Government invested $14 mn. in ICT's development programme, at a crucial moment, enabling the one successful European company which is virtually independent of American technology or finance to survive. ICT actually made a profit in 1966, has a soaring order book, and has a skill in putting computers into commercial operation which perhaps no other company can rival. In 1967 $21 mn. were lent by the British Government to the new English Electric-Elliott combination, and a further sum was invested in the combine by the government-backed IRC. English-Electric-Elliott is partially dependent on the technology of America's giant RCA. Despite this, the British Government for two years put systematic pressure on ICT and English Electric to merge together, which they did in March 1968, encouraged by a further grant of $31 mn. from the government in funds for research and a further $7 mn. in the form of purchasing shares. A tacit Buy National policy has, since 1965, been promoting the sale of ICT and English Electric computers to government departments and universities. Backed by this help ICT has retained some 40 per cent of the British market, the same proportion as IBM. With English Electric included, the new International Computers Limited will have half the British market.

In France too, the government is spending $100 mn. on *plan calcul:* its attempt to build up the French-owned Compagnie Internationale d'Informatique. The West German Government is backing Siemens and Telefunken with development funds to the tune of 100 mn. DM ($25 mn.) each, orders, and low interest loans.

What chances have these three separate national policies of succeeding?

ICL at present has no largescale bases in the major markets of continental Western Europe, and lacks both the men and the capital to establish them. Hence the immense resources of a company like IBM and General Electric tell critically, and though by 1967 there was a pause in the American commercial offensive, as General Electric sorted out the troubles of its Bull operation, and IBM patched up the harm done amongst its customers by the painful difficulties of the 360 series, the strategic considerations outlined above will tell in the end.

In France the *plan calcul* will certainly produce a range of second generation computers, but it is by no means certain whether it will match up to the next generation of American computers which will appear by then; and there are many signs that the effort on software will not be competitive.

As for Siemens and Philips, there is no doubt that they have the resources to develop computer hardware, at considerable cost, and, in some of the many process applications they are already involved in, they will succeed. But Siemens, like English Electric in the past, is at present technologically tied to RCA, with which it has a ten-year agreement. Only time will show whether, in the next generation, it can profitably go it alone.

One thing is clear: the defensive national policies developed by three European governments each damage the efforts of the others. 'Buy national' policies, for instance in the French or British government markets, add to the mutual difficulties of companies like ICL and Siemens in establishing a Europe-wide marketing base comparable, for instance, to that of IBM. Indeed, American-owned companies which produce in, say, France or West Germany receive higher priority in public buying than European companies exporting from outside. As for development costs, while there may well be a case for the existence of more than one European-owned computer company, the present triplication of effort, on a national basis, may well be slowing the rate of development and diminishing the prospect that any one European-based company will eventually succeed in establishing itself as a genuine rival to IBM. Is it possible to move on to a truly 'European' policy, which will bring to an end the triplication of government-backed research and development effort, open the separate markets up to European-based computer companies and foster the development of companies of European scale?

Building a European computer capability does not just mean manufacturing computer 'hardware'. It means developing the skills in programming which can enable Europeans to apply computer systems to the wide range of applications which is beginning to emerge. Because computer systems will become so intimate a part of the entire organization of society—government, industry, education, science—it is essential to have this vital skill available on the spot in Europe, and because of its immense significance for society there is a powerful political case for having at least some component of the industry European-owned. IBM is not merely American-owned but a near-world monopoly. A powerful competitive European computer enterprise would be an asset, not merely to Europe, but to the Atlantic community as a whole.

The development of such a European-based industry is becoming easier now that computer technology has stabilized. The hard place to catch up is not in the construction of central processors but in software.

A first initiative to bring together European computer development was taken in 1964 when the British and French governments attempted to finance and support, jointly, the development of a large computer by ICT and the French firm CITEC. The companies got to know each other, but after a period the French Government decided that its resources were too limited to finance both this and its own national computer development programme. It plumped for the *plan calcul* and the computer Concorde was dropped. In any case, a wider strategy is needed.

First and most important, government purchasing policies need to be brought together, so that instead of 'buy national' policies, there is an element of 'buy European'. Initially, this could merely mean removing any element of discrimination against other European countries in public buying; more ambitiously, the governments could get together to analyse their future requirements and use these as an instrument to encourage rationalization of what the companies do and especially of new applications. For instance, most European governments will be interested in the application of computers to hospitals, to education, to the payment of society security benefits, and to transport planning. Why not team up to place development contracts for such new applications, using such contracts, where this seems sensible, as a means of bringing together the different national computer firms.

A second obvious area for common policies is compatibility—of high level languages, codes, and electronic interfaces. In part this is a question which cannot be decided at a European level. But the major European governments could, most usefully, agree to a common policy to put to the American Government as a world policy. Such a policy might, for instance, press for the adoption of the International Standards Organization (ISO) code, with an eight bit word, as a world standard.

This would require some changes by IBM, as well as by other manufacturers. IBM has hitherto dictated computer standards regardless of governments or anyone else. But there is no reason why IBM's judgement should be perfect for all time, any more than Mr Brunel's railway gauge proved right a hundred years ago. In America the Federal Government would like to see the ISO code adopted.

The creation of a computer common market in public buying could be backed up by more positive action in the form of common development projects at a European level. For instance, why not develop a European system of information, storage and retrieval for the whole of science and technology, linking the major European universities and research centres together? Euratom, as we have seen, already has such a system in the limited nuclear field, but like most existing European projects, it uses an IBM machine. Why not make the development of such major European information systems a tool for stimulating new capabilities in the European computer industry?

Yet, as in aviation, nuclear power and other fields, the heart of a European policy must be an industrial strategy. The real answer to IBM is to develop European companies capable of competing with it. As in other key sectors, the major European states will all want some stake in such a company or companies, so such companies will have to have an element of multinationality with ownership and control split, somewhat, between different European nation-states. Yet to compete, such companies must be fully integrated operations. Struggling consortia cannot expect to compete effectively with IBM.

Complications are also created by the existing links between some European companies and American ones. English Electric and Siemens have marketed RCA computers and based their own on them. Even the French CII has begun by manufacturing computers under licence from the small American firm Scientific Data Systems. A concentration of European computer firms must either give up such links, or retain them, excluding itself perhaps from the American and other markets, or find a means to do a reverse takeover, of, say, SDS or RCA's data processing division.

Finally European governments have an interest, not merely in promoting an indigenous computer industry, but in a degree of effective competition. It would probably be wiser to promote the development of at least two major European computer groups, in competition with the Americans. Such different groups might usefully tend to concentrate on different types of application, so that there is a degree of specialization as well as competition between them.

Such considerations suggest a structure rather different from what will emerge if concentration at the national level takes place first. If there were no national prejudices and pressures involved a structure on the following lines might have made most technical and commercial sense.

One European company might have been formed from a merger of ICT, the French CII, and perhaps Telefunken and an element from Philips. ICT brings its existing strong software capability, the CII is an unknown quantity, but certainly can contribute capital and a number of good men. Telefunken has barely entered the market yet, but its early TR4 computer was impressive, and it is now building up its effort. Above all it has a powerful communications capability; it is of course already one of the West German Government's 'favourite sons' in the computer field. Philips brings a vast marketing network and a vast internal market as well as its own late-starting effort in the computer field. This European company might specialize, particularly, in the fields in which ICT and CII have been successful: data processing, scientific and commercial applications and the like.

A second European group might have been formed by Siemens and English Electric, both based on RCA technology and both with capabilities in process-control. Indeed the thought of a merger of these two companies' computer activities opens up a wider prospect. The two are also significant on the nuclear power chessboard and play key parts in the fast-breeder programmes of Britain and West Germany. The two companies of course have many other overlapping areas of activity, from power stations to communications. So why not a total merger between the two? The difficulties are, of course, family ownership, and the need for some equality (English Electric is a smaller company). All the same, the strategy, in terms of meeting world competition from a European base, looks correct.

Two strong European groups of this kind might be able, more effectively, to take the offensive in the American market either by, in one case, acquisition of RCA's computer enterprise or by buying into other smaller American computer enterprises, or simply by a marketing attack.

Unfortunately the main pressures by governments have been towards single national enterprises—not such a balanced European pattern. And the British Government's success in bringing about the English Electric-ICT merger makes a different solution inevitable. Plainly International Computers Limited (ICL), if it seeks European partners, will have to choose between Siemens and Telefunken. And since, of these two companies, Siemens is farthest ahead and most intent on carving out a place in the European market on its own, Telefunken will probably be the most suitable West Germany partner for ICL. An ICL-Telefunken partnership indeed might be an interesting model in many ways, because of the complementary character of the two companies. ICL is bound to provide the nucleus of the software and hardware development in the first place, and probably the management leadership. But Telefunken can provide a world marketing network and a communications capability which ICL could never achieve on its own; in the burgeoning communications side of the business it could be expected to lead.

The initiative for such mergers may well come from the companies, but since European governments have decided to involve themselves in the computer industry, they will have to play some part. The pressures in Britain for a merger between English Electric and ICT, and in West Germany for cooperation between Siemens and Telefunken will have to be succeeded by encouragement for the more European and more commercially attractive mergers we have discussed. In all the companies concerned, it is probable that mergers or combinations at the European level would be at least as welcome as combinations with traditional rivals at home—if not more so.

Integrated Circuits

While, in computers, the stabilization of the overall design of central processors makes it relatively easy for Europeans to squeeze in, at least in hardware, it is far more difficult for Europeans to get a competitive share of the new area of dynamic change, the minute integrated circuits which are assembled together to make up a computer processor. The computer industry is increasingly dividing into three major areas: the development of programmes to apply to an ever-widening range of applications, the design of computers themselves, and the design of components.

As advances in physics, chemistry and engineering develop the components—so that today a thousand minute circuits can be grouped together on a silicon chip a square inch large—the component manufacturer is invading the design of the computer itself. It is here that the technology is changing fastest. Before much of industry has even learnt to use a 'first generation' computer, the component manufacturers have produced, first, a pin-headed sized circuit on a chip, next, a thousand circuits on a small disc, and now, experimentally, a computer made from a package of such chips. The applications of such integrated circuits, and the possibilities of cost reduction and improved reliability in radios, television, telephones, communications, and so on, are immense.

Here, American technology is ahead and advancing at dramatic speed. The technology of the three American leaders, Texas Instruments, Fairchild and Motorola is probably a year ahead of their best European competitors. Indeed these firms have some 90 per cent of the European market, and the signs are that for Europeans to get into it profitably is about as easy as boarding a moving express train.

For here a price phenomenon typical of fast developing industries is apparent.

In the initial stages of the technology, A, prices are high and profits large. In period B, as the diagram shows, the technology is advancing rapidly and prices are falling fast. In C prices stabilize at a low level. Technologically, if you have missed out at A, it is easier to get into the market in C, because the technology has stabilized (as in computers), but established firms already have a big

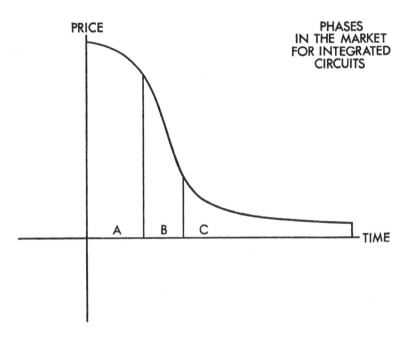

PRICE

PHASES
IN THE MARKET
FOR INTEGRATED
CIRCUITS

A   B   C

TIME

hold on the market. In B (microcircuits today) the market is still mobile, but it is fiendishly difficult to catch up with the leaders' technological and cost lead. Europeans have tended to be at a significant disadvantage in this matter in several advanced industries because the market for many products (e.g. colour television as well as microcircuits) has developed first in the US, giving American firms the best chance to get in during period A. The decision whether to struggle in later during period B or C is a far harder one.

The worst formula is to do what British firms have done; at least seven different companies have tried to get into the microcircuit market, mainly to safeguard their traditional internal markets for more conventional components. Most are far too small in scale. At best three or four companies in Europe (GEC? Cosem? SGS? Philips? Siemens?) might be capable of building up a capability during period B and fighting their way to a profitable place in the market when prices stabilize.

An interesting solution has been found by the Italian firm SGS. Until October 1968 Fairchild had a minority (33 per cent) holding, so Fairchild's dynamic technology was transferred fast. Good management, however, has been provided by Olivetti and Telettra, the other Italian shareholders. SGS has been carving out a rapidly growing share of the European market, based on American technology but without American control.

Here an important distinction must be drawn between the computer and integrated circuit industries. In computers a single firm dominates the world market, obliging European governments to seek to build up effective countervailing industrial groups. In integrated circuits, however, there is fierce competition between at least three leading American producers, and there are of course powerful buyers (such as IBM) with an opposite interest from those of the component manufacturers; hence Europe is in a position to exploit the forces of competition. The dangers of 'domination' by a single large remote company are small. Europe has an interest in building up some kind of indigenous profitable integrated circuits industry if it can. But it has an even larger interest in ensuring that it gets access to America's swiftly advancing technology in this field. The best formula might well be to promote more effective European competition against such firms as Texas Instruments by the formation of an industrial group of three or four companies pooling development work at first and later moving on to a rationalization of production (you make transistors; I make resistances) in the semi-conductor and integrated circuit field. The big European conglomerate companies which see integrated circuits as an integral part of their overall business might not be suitable members. But SGS, Cosem and Ferranti might fit together well.

This is a case, indeed, where Atlantic anti-trust action would probably be valuable. The crucial European interest is to ensure that computer manufacturers, especially IBM, do not acquire a hold over the component industry. Some ways in which Atlantic anti-trust action or rules might be applied are described in Chapter 15.

The formula—make the best use of American investment; discipline it by Atlantic anti-trust rules; acquire a share in control of it where practicable; and build up a few effective European countervailing groups—is one that applies in many other industries.

CHAPTER 12

THE CHUNNEL AND BEYOND

Near the white cliffs of Dover, the moss-covered outworks can still be seen of the original borings drilled in 1878-83 for a channel tunnel. The original British and French tunnel companies had worked for three years and bored for over a mile at each end before Mr Joseph Chamberlain, then at the Board of Trade, slapped on an injunction to stop the work. What would happen, said the War Office and the soldiers, if an invading foreign army outwitted the watching fleet and popped up through the tunnel?

The islanders were still wary and suspicious in 1924. A Royal Commission reported in favour of the tunnel, but it was defeated by seven votes in the House of Commons. Behind the failure was a more ingenious veto from the Committee of Imperial Defence in the form of a gratuitous advertisement for the tunnel. If there were a Channel Tunnel, said the committee, it would have such success that the harbours on the south coast would wither and their personnel disperse. In the event of hostilities the 'capillary points' would tend to be too weak to feed Britain and supply munitions overseas. Like the cinque ports before them, they would silt up, at least metaphorically, and Britain would be left only with its single, efficient lifeline to a perhaps hostile continent.

French generals did not share the view of the reluctant islanders. Marshal Foch declared in 1921 that a tunnel could have shortened the First World War by two years. General de Gaulle has long been, in his own words, a 'tunnelist'. But the British military veto was not lifted until 1955, when Mr Macmillan, then Defence Minister, answered in reply to a question in the House of Commons as to whether the government might have military objections: 'Scarcely at all'.

The channel tunnel company, which had been leading a shadowy existence ever since 1880 and whose chairman was Leo D'Erlanger, grandson of the chairman of the original company, took its opportunity. Needing fresh capital, they turned, in early 1956, to the Suez Canal Company, whose term was expected to run out in 1968. Arab nationalism shortened the time scale, for within a few months the Suez Canal Company was out of Suez. Together with an enterprising group of American financiers, they formed the Channel Tunnel Study Group in 1957 (25 per cent UK Channel Tunnel Company, 25 per cent French Channel Tunnel Company and International Road Federation, 25 per cent Suez Canal Company, and 25 per cent Tech. Studies Inc., New York).

The Group's consultants studied until 1960; the Group then reported to the governments that the economic case for a channel tunnel was stronger than ever and asked permission to go ahead.

One striking piece of evidence in favour of the tunnel was that in 1960, as in 1967, or for that matter 1882, abundant private capital was prepared to invest in the project, in the belief that it would yield an economic return. The Rothschilds backed the original channel tunnel company and are still involved in it, together with Barings, Lazards, Schroders, Morgan Stanley and others. And when, in February 1967, tenders were at last put out to competition by governments for the financing of the enterprise, three competing consortia embracing many of the leading merchant banks in the western world put in bids.

The railways in both countries have also shown great interest. On the British side the Chatham-Dover Railway which became the Southern Railway and then British Rail, on the French side the SNCF, have been the principal shareholders of the British and French channel tunnel companies from the start. The railways have always seen the tunnel as a cheaper competitive means of transporting railway wagons than ferries. Now, of course, it offers a highly competitive method of attracting freight and passenger traffic from ship, hovercraft and air. The commercial potential of the tunnel has been shown by the fact that the argument over its financing, between governments and private financiers has, at any rate in Britain, been complicated by the government's feeling that it does not want to be left out of a potentially highly profitable affair.

These hopes are built on solid geological foundations. The channel at Dover is one of the easiest stretches of water to tunnel in the world. Its bed is flat and shallow (at the most 60 metres deep). There is soft chalk, easy to bore, but the strata are hard enough to keep out most of the water. A channel tunnel would be no longer than the Northern Line Tube in London, from Cockfosters to Morden—but there would be little hard rock or shifting sand to penetrate or shore up, as in the London tube or the far more difficult Mont Blanc tunnel.

An alternative proposal, for an immersed tube entrenched in the sea-bed, would be a much more awkward and heroic enterprise, involving fourteen changes of gradient and curve and very difficult dredging at a depth of 60 metres. Old fashioned tunnelling, as on the Victoria line or the Paris Metro—of which the technology has not changed much since the last century—seems the best way. It could be done by any one of a dozen British or French tunnel contractors.

The channel tunnel will be a railway tunnel. Cars driving on a road raise much bigger ventilation problems, and have frequent accidents which could impose the huge extra cost of an additional maintenance lane. And in any case, a larger number of vehicles can travel through the tunnel on fast trains, leaving at intervals similar to the London tube, than could drive under their own power.

The economics of the tunnel are as encouraging as the geology. Between 1952 and 1960 the number of passengers crossing the channel each year rose by 146 per cent (to nearly 8 mn.), and vehicle traffic by 203 per cent (to 442,000 vehicles). UK trade with the Continent grew by 31 per cent between 1952 and 1957 and since then it has more than doubled. This massive growth can be expected to continue as the European economy becomes one. When the channel tunnel project was broached afresh in 1960, some critics still argued that new alternative methods of transport, like the hovercraft, might be more efficient. Now, it seems increasingly likely that all the methods will be necesary. The channel tunnel will replace much of the existing ferry capacity as it phases out, and some air traffic. But it will also generate new traffic. All types of link will continue to expand. In Western Europe, as in America, the airlanes, and still more the airports and the routes to airports, are becoming increasingly congested and traffic is still easily disrupted by bad weather, technical faults, and so on. There will be a growing, sheer physical need for better fast ground transport links.

The tunnel looks cheap. In 1962 the Study Group estimated that the cost of expanding port facilities and constructing ships and aeroplanes to take a volume of traffic comparable to the tunnel would range from $462 mn. to $560 mn. over a period of 50 years, nearly double the $360 mn. cost of the tunnel and its terminals.[1] They estimated too that operating and maintenance costs over a period of fifty years would also be twice as large: some $1,400 to $1,700 mn. compared to the tunnel's $630 mn. Since then almost all the figures have roughly doubled, through inflation, but the relation between the tunnel costs and costs for other forms of transport has not changed.

Costs to users would be correspondingly lower, perhaps 50 per cent lower for freight, and 30 per cent lower for railway passengers and vehicles. The train journey from London to Paris would be cut to 4 hours 20 minutes, little more than the time for air travel from the city centres. Liner trains might directly link British industrial centres with Paris, Cologne, Frankfurt, Basle and Milan. The channel tunnel, in short, would pay users, the entrepreneurs and the two nations. Moreover, it would be cheaper to build than a bridge, which would create risks for channel shipping and might be blocked by fog.

Why, then, has it taken so long to get moving? Partly because governments—or at any rate the British Government—take time to make up their minds. The French Government came out for a fixed channel link in 1961. An intergovernment committee was then set up, and the British came out in favour in 1963.

The debate then began over financing. The channel tunnel group asked the governments to guarantee a bond issue to finance the tunnel, mainly in order to facilitate bond issues on the US market. And the French Government accepted from the start the value of enlisting private capital. Britain's Conservative Government however, was inclined to press for straightforward government financing. The Labour Government, more aware it seems of other tremendous demands on public capital, has accepted the principle of private financing, while sensibly maintaining that some share in running and profiting from this communal facility shall go to the state. In the end private enterprise is to find the capital to build the tunnel through a bond issue. The railway operators will lease the facility, paying a royalty. The debate still goes on over the question how much of this rent should be fixed and how much should be a

[1]Channel Study Group, *Why Britain Needs a Channel Tunnel*, 1962, also Channel Study Group, *Channel Tunnel*, Report of the Delegate of the Group.

varying royalty carrying the prospect of both high profits and high risk.

The two governments are putting out both finance and engineering responsibility to tender; the Channel Tunnel Study Group will then have to compete to get the job. The finance groups will be responsible for technical planning of the enterprise. The actual tunnelling will be done essentially by specialist subcontractors.

It will not be the first great common transport link in Europe. The Mont Blanc tunnel, costing $60 mn., was an Italian-French venture. The canalization of the Moselle, financed and executed two thirds by France and one third by West Germany, cost $188 mn. Denmark and Sweden are now planning a technically far more tricky tunnel beneath the Skagerrak. The channel tunnel however does, perhaps, have the greatest political significance, bridging not only the widest strip of water but the widest political gulf. And because of its impact on one of the densest transport routes in Europe, it opens up much wider questions about the planning of European transport as a whole.

The tunnel, after all, is a totally different kind of enterprise from the north-east corridor study in the United States described in Chapter 2. There, an attempt is being made to examine the transport needs of a whole, highly congested region, to explore and predict the impact of a series of different kinds of transport systems, ground and air, and to analyse the possible patterns of population and economic activity which will be generated by the different systems. In the channel tunnel, by contrast, all that is happening is that one of Europe's worst bottlenecks will be widened.

The tunnel, however, will have a major effect on industrial location and transport at either end. It is true that the Channel Tunnel Study Group rather cheerfully predicts that even at the worst times, tunnel traffic will not represent more than 15 per cent of traffic along Britain's A20 or M2. Nonetheless, in Britain in particular, it will exert a powerful pull; industry will tend to concentrate near the end of the tunnel. Road as well as rail routes to the north, round London, will have to be constructed (the British Road Federation has called for motorway links to the M1 or M4); the pull to the south-east will be increased.

There will be similar, though less acute problems on the other side. (The French *Union Routière* has called for motorway links towards Belgium, West Germany, Paris and Rouen.)

The two countries could solve many of these problems on a

o

national basis. For instance, a Thames tunnel, opening up East Anglia to the channel tunnel and encouraging industrial development there, and providing an easterly link with the Midlands, would do much to ease the problem of congestion in London. A direct link with any new London airport (Stansted or Foulness?) would be valuable too. One interesting idea is to site the main container terminus far inland. But here one runs up against a really awkward problem. While the British railway gauge is the same as the Continental gauge, British tunnels are smaller. So a great deal of expensive engineering work would be necessary to enable Continental-sized liner trains to go straight through to the Midlands.

All such measures are, in any case, reactions to the decision to build the tunnel, not parts of a broader strategy for the development of Europe. It is this which will be needed, increasingly, if our tight-packed region is to make the best use of the huge investments in transport, and the new transport system and methods which are being developed.

There is a need, at once, for a longer look at both the economics and planning implications of different kinds of European transport systems, and at possible future technical developments, on which the economics depend.

An existing organization, the Conference of European Ministers of Transport, might well be the body in which an initiative on planning might be taken. Hitherto this body has concentrated, in the main, on short-term practical questions, such as licensing and transit across frontiers. But there is no reason why it should not branch out into wider fields, at least until an enlarged European Community effectively takes the task over.

In density of population and industrial activity, north-west Europe is rather similar to north-east America. But the patterns of trade and transport are more complex. What is needed, in Western Europe, is an 'arterial study' of the traffic pattern up the great spinal cord of Western Europe, from Liverpool, through London, the Low Countries and the Ruhr, to Milan and Rome. The study must of course embrace the major lateral routes—to Amsterdam and Paris, to Hamburg and Berlin. It should analyse existing traffic patterns, the future potential, and the impact on industrial location and the pattern of development of different kinds of transport system. It should study, too, the development of alternative arterial systems— like a westerly spine linking Toulouse, Brest, Bristol, the West Midlands and Liverpool—which would helpfully redistribute industry and population away from the present heartland. The results of this systematic approach should eventually shape government policies on road, rail and airport development.

It is true that cooperative work on certain conventional means of transport already takes place. A European motorway network is already emerging. The Continental railways already plan, purchase, and run jointly a number of major common services, like the Trans Europ expresses. Eurofinance, a joint financial company, raises money on the capital market and purchases rolling stock for the railways of most of the major West European countries (though not Britain). But these common services and activities do not amount to joint planning of transport systems.

The analysis of different types of new systems must reach beyond the classic transport systems of the present: road, rail and conventional aircraft. The airlanes are getting increasingly congested; and the wretched passenger, flipped to Paris in 40 minutes, too quick to bolt a meal, spends two to three hours at the two ends getting to his destination. Yet conventional railways are still too slow. And the roads still lead, in the cities, into nightmare bottlenecks.

Vertical-lift, however, could transform the efficiency of aircraft, lifting people from city centre to city centre, provided—and it is a massive proviso—the problem of noise can be overcome. Or again, even the efficiency of conventional aircraft could be massively improved, if really fast ground links to airports could be developed—with customs and passport formalities either abolished, or executed on the moving vehicle. Still better, what if far more effective surface transportation systems can take the passenger all the way to his destination?

A 'systems' approach to the major transport arteries of Western Europe must consider and compare the possible economic and social implications of such differing types of transport systems, and plan to introduce whichever system looks like paying off.

Such an overall economic and land-use plan should be backed by judicious joint development of the new techniques in certain key areas. Of course there are many types of surface transport equipment which can be left to individual companies, countries and even municipalities to develop. Europe does not need, collectively, to take an interest in every kind of new travelator, or even electric car. Yet the time has plainly come when European governments ought to be putting more into backing new kinds of surface transport, if European countries are not once more to be left standing by the new state-backed programmes in America—and this in an area of far greater economic and social interest than the space race. Yet there is no sign that any individual European government is prepared to back surface transport development on the scale needed, after other demands have been met. The sums needed are far smaller than what is being spent on, say, the aircraft industry, but, when placed on top of other needs, the case is strong for a common effort.

Certain governments have already made a start. The British Government has spent $11 mn. on developing the hovercraft, the French Government another $9 mn. on M. Bertin's air-cushion train. In 1965 the Ministry of Technology proposed a joint effort to the French. The proposal was unfortunately rejected.

It is not too late to reverse that decision, and indeed to place it in a wider European framework. Full use of the hovertrain principle will be made only if there is an effective and suitable means of propulsion. The propeller used on the Bertin train is noisy and disturbing. At Imperial College, London, however, Professor Laithwaite has been itching for some years, to apply the simple, elegant principle of the linear electric motor, which could whisk hovertrains smoothly and speedily up to 300 mph. After years of obstruction from British Railways. and tempting invitations from America, the NRDC has at last (in 1967), granted $5.6 mn. for development of a linear electric motor hovertrain. Here, surely, British and French skills could be usefully combined. The most sensible solution would be a straight merger between Hovercraft Development and the Bertin company.

Should such an advanced principle be sensibly applied to the channel tunnel? Few arteries, after all, are better suited to a new and really high-speed ground link than the London-Paris route.

The difficulty is that the power needed to drive a train through a tight-sealed tunnel multiplies, because of growing pressure, in geometrical proportion to the speed. So, though speeds of say 120 mph can be reached with relatively ease by a train in a tunnel, a 300 mph train would require either gigantic power, or a far larger tunnel, to let the air rush by and so reduce the pressure. In a short thirty mile tunnel like the one planned, a 300 mph train would only lose ten minutes if it slowed down to 120 mph. But for longer distances the economics would go awry.

Another principle, however, might solve the problem, that of the air-breathing engine. A tube train which progresses by sucking in air and shooting it out behind might, in the future, prove economic for underground transport. It might be an answer for a second later tunnel beneath the channel, if this proves economic.

At present air-breathing trains of this kind are being developed only in the United States. Europeans are waiting and watching to see what happens. Here is another illustration of the need for a wide ranging European programme. A common programme for development of different means of surface transport might place contracts for the hovertrain with one company, and for the air-breather—or further development of monorails—in another. Or, at an earlier less supranational stage, several governments could agree on a division of labour in this field, with a guarantee of cross licensing if one or other succeeds.

There are similar attractions in trying to develop a range of different types of new city transport systems on a European basis— continuously moving belts to which the individual's moving vehicle is attached, and many other kinds of travelator. In this field there is, again, room for individual experiment by particular companies, nations and cities. Yet, if there is to be a relatively expensive programme for developing different types of hardware, there is a good case for an organized division of labour between European countries. In short M. Gueron's 'community of prototypes', proposed for nuclear power, could be applied here too.

As the joint programmes of technological development—for vertical-lift aircraft, for hovertrains, and so on—bore fruit, and experience with prototypes gave precise guidance about future performance, the material would be provided for the broader planning of the transport system. Such planning will inevitably imply, increasingly, systematic community thinking about the regional location of industry, population, and leisure areas. Even a question like the level of air fares within Europe, and hence the volume of air traffic (discussed in Chapter 9) of course has wide implications for amenities, land use, and economic development.

Transport in short, is by nature international, and thus, within Europe, European. As techniques advance, and traffic multiplies explosively between the nations, both the technical methods used, and the policy choices made become increasingly common questions which have major social, economic and political implications for the region as a whole. Inside the European Community, the common transport policy, insofar as it existed, has been concerned mainly, like the Rome Treaty as a whole, with creating a single common market with common competitive conditions throughout. What is now needed is a more dynamic and positive approach: the active and deliberate joint planning of the major transport arteries of Europe.

CHAPTER 13

WIDER HORIZONS

In each of the sectors so far analysed, the facts of life have obliged Europeans to make a start on joint endeavours. But there are many other areas of science where united Europe is but a need.

The Oceans

In oceanography, each of the three largest European countries has begun to examine its existing rather limited efforts and to move on from there to develop a national programme.

France has gone furthest, inspired by men like Cousteau who have been fascinated by the world beneath the sea. For many years, of course, institutions as varied as The French Navy Survey Department, the Sea Fishing Scientific and Technical Institute, and many other ministries and universities have been exploring particular aspects of the sea. By 1961, awareness of the common scientific problems and potential of the ocean led to an effort of coordination. The Délégation Générale à la Recherche Scientifique et Technique (DGRST) was charged with the development of a national oceanography programme and set up a committee on the exploitation of the oceans. It undertook an inventory of existing work and helped to finance team research between the many universities and other agencies engaged in oceanography, bought heavy equipment, like ships, for the joint use of different agencies, and set up a small training programme (which has trained about 100 people at all levels).

This small beginning was followed, in 1967, by the creation of the Centre Nationale pour l'Exploitation Oceanographique (CNEXO) to coordinate the work of the 500 oceanographers working in different centres and ministries in a common programme. Unlike the DGRST, which had to work on the recommendation of a scientific committee, composed of the very people—like university professors—whose work was at stake, CNEXO's Director and Council of Administration have the power to decide on policy themselves after 'consultation' with the science committee. Unlike the American Oceanography Commission, CNEXO has money (some $30 mn.) to be spent on research over the period of the Fifth Plan (1966-70). Its credit granting power thus give it real authority over the programme of ministries and institutions. And it is explicitly empowered to promote not merely research, but 'exploitation' of the oceans.

CNEXO plans to use its limited resources on a selected list of priority questions—the movement of tides and currents, exploration of the French continental shelf, some experiments with sea farming —and the further development of submarines and diving vehicles in which Commander Cousteau has pioneered the way.

The trouble is that by contrast with the American effort ($428 mn. in 1968), even this French programme ($6 mn. per year) is minute. The scientific explorations, though valuable, are deliberately limited in scope; one deep diving submarine is to be built, but there are obvious limits on what can be spent on expensive, large equipment —say for mineral exploration, or even fish farming.

The nascent oceanography programmes in Britain and West Germany are equally limited. In Britain some fourteen ministries and institutions are engaged in oceanographical research; in 1967 a consultant was engaged to investigate these activities and make proposals on coordination. In West Germany there are a variety of programmes in different universities and institutions; useful work has been done on meteorology, the study of the sea-bed and biology; the Forschungsgemeinschaft is seeking, in some measure, to coordinate these efforts and limit duplication. But the total spending on oceanography in West Germany is probably no more than $6-7 mn. per year. There are small, specific efforts in other countries, like Italy—where the Naples marine fauna research station has been open to scientists from all countries for nearly a hundred years—but no national programme anywhere.

The contrast between the tiny scale of resources devoted by any single European nation to oceanography and the big needs of a really comprehensive programme thus underline the case for a joint European effort in this field. It is enhanced by the common nature of the problem; the sea belongs to all.

Already, at the level of fundamental research, there is much ex-change of information between researchers in different countries. Indeed a variety of common programmes for research have been carried out on a bilateral basis between different European countries and between European countries and the United States. Yet, at the level of exploitation, for instance, of North Sea gas, the procedure adopted has been to carve up the sea-bed between the countries that surround it, like so much cake. Can a more effective joint European policy be developed in the vast area between pure scientific re-search and ultimate commercial exploitation, the field where the high costs of long-term development are found and where govern-ments have to pay part of the bill?

The common interest in one vital area was brought home when the *Torrey Canyon* split open on the rocks off Land's End, spilling oil on to the shores of Brittany and Cornwall and, still worse, provoking the governments into flooding the beaches and the inshore sea with detergent which destroyed far more sea life than the origi-nal oil. International efforts have since been made to agree on new routing arrangements for channel shipping. But no programme has been undertaken on oil and other pollution, with a view to develop-ing a range of anti-pollution measures and an agreement on which should be used. Here is a first item for a European oceanography programme.

The exploration of the continental shelf round Europe is a second area. Of course it is sensible for France, Britain, or Norway, say, to explore the shelf off their shores. The fact remains that a common programme is needed to study the European sea-bed as a whole, with a pooling of techniques and information, and joint efforts in areas between more than one country. Gradually a bank of infor-mation about geological formations, sea life, currents and possibili-ties of mineral exploitation could be built up at a common European centre.

A third potential area for common action, linked to the second, is more fundamental research. The results of work on tides, currents, the heating of the sea and its effect on sea life, the chemistry and biology of the deepest oceans, could increasingly be brought into a common programme. Of course individual universities and enter-prises must be left free to pursue exciting avenues which interest them. The worldwide exchange of information—especially with the United States—must be encouraged too. Nonetheless, a better use could certainly be made of European resources, if the pure research efforts of European countries in this vast and complex field were part of a common programme, spearheaded by deliberate joint research programmes on key problems.

A fourth area for common effort is fish or 'sea farming'. Here, too, there are areas for national or entrepreneurial effort, and others, like conservation, for a wider world, or North Atlantic approach. It is in the development of new equipment, and of large-scale experiments in fish farming (netting the channel, heating the sea-bed, electric barriers) that high cost makes a common European effort sensible. If the common agricultural policy is to provide 'common funds' for common 'structural improvements' to European agriculture, why not common funds for the developments of new fishing techniques, and perhaps even common technical assistance to the starving undeveloped world.

A fifth area in which such integration seems necessary is developing equipment for the four other fields. Individual countries can build survey ships and even submarines. The difficulty is that different types of equipment are needed for different tasks—deep ocean exploration, mineral exploitation, manipulation at great depths. There is a strong case for a rational distribution of development contracts at a European level, so that development work is divided up between different contractors, and the cost of equipment and of learning in this new expensive field is shared between members.

With national programmes in their infancy, it is tempting to suggest that the way ahead for Europe is to start at once on a European oceanography programme, without wasting time first on constructing national bureaucracies and interests which later have to be overcome. The sooner a European oceanography authority is set up, with common funds to back it, the better. A logical way to do this would be to follow Laurence Read's suggestion and finance the fund from royalties from sea-bed resources, such as gas.

Molecular Biology

A second exciting area in which a common European programme has been proposed, but not yet executed, is molecular biology, the new key life science concerned with the exploration of the chemical and physical nature of the cell and the key chemical substances which compose living things—proteins, nucleic acids. What the explosion of nuclear physics was to nuclear power, telecommunications, solid-state physics and electronics and our knowledge of the cosmos in the first decades of this century, molecular biology may be to agriculture, medicine, chemistry, and our knowledge of living things in the next thirty years. Our knowledge of heredity and of cell behaviour, as well as of wider biological functions—supra-cellular activity, the nervous system—have already been revolutionized, opening up a fascinating prospect of understanding, guiding and controlling life itself.

Many of the key discoveries in this field were in fact made in European laboratories. In particular Cambridge and the Pasteur Institute have made key contributions, reflected in the list of Nobel prizes won by Europeans. But, as with nuclear physics in the early postwar years, a growing number of bright European molecular biologists have been emigrating to America, attracted by the better conditions of research, the stimulating intellectual atmosphere of the universities, and more liberal funds. Once more the initiative in a crucial scientific field is tending to move across the Atlantic.

The exciting work already done in Europe proves that it has the human resources to reverse the trend. But they are not properly mobilised. Molecular biology, like many areas of science, springs from a mixture of disciplines: chemistry, biology, physics, maths. A successful centre for molecular biology is, in short, a centre which can mobilize a team of people with a wide range of skills. Yet as things stand, no European laboratory or group of laboratories covers more than about a third of the field; there are only two or three which do as much as this.[1] Large size, found at present only in American universities, is needed to create such 'centres of excellence'. And if the efforts of molecular biologists in smaller European centres are to be used to the full, there must be freedom of movement between centres and a far greater coordination of research.

It was with such needs in mind that the leading European molecular biologists founded the European Molecular Biology Organization in September 1963. The quality of this group is as high as the one which created CERN, and indeed CERN has helpfully fostered their enterprise. The EMBO group rapidly persuaded the private Volkswagen Foundation to provide a grant, for a limited experimental period, to cover the cost of fellowships, courses and administration. Using these funds EMBO can, within 24 hours, move a research biologist in Europe, who has precious cells which he wants to examine

[1]See EMBO, The European Molecular Biology Organization, obtainable from Dr R. K. Appleyard, University of Brussels, 67 Paardestraat, St Genesius-Rode, Belgium.

on someone else's equipment. Dr Appleyard, the British secretary of EMBO, happens also to be in charge of Euratom's programme on radiobiology. He has used a part of his $16 mn. Euratom research budget to build up centres of excellence at Naples, Leyden and Brussels in molecular biology and to encourage cooperative programmes between them and the stronger centre at Paris.

The main aim of EMBO is to broaden these pilot efforts into a far bigger and more systematic programme, and for this they need effective government support. This wider programme would establish post-doctoral fellowships in one country for scientists from another, and provide grants to a range of centres on condition they worked together on a common programme, or to a centre which appointed staff members from another member country.

At present European work in molecular biology is splintered between a multitude of small centres. What is needed is the development of, perhaps, one or two big ones to which the small ones can be linked, with profit to the efficiency of both. Help for such a movement is the top priority. As the hub for this effort, a European molecular biology laboratory would be established, of sufficient scale to become a 'a centre of excellence' in its own key field, comparable to CERN. No one claims that such a central laboratory is dictated by the need for some giant piece of equipment as in the case of CERN, though big computing facilities are needed. The key common facility needed is a research centre of sufficient scale to bring together the several teams of people, including some of the best ones, from a wide variety of disciplines.

EMBO's proposal[2] is for a laboratory of some 570 people, of whom nearly half would be professional research scientists and engineering staff, working in perhaps a dozen teams.

Only about 10 to 15 per cent of the staff would be permanent appointments; the rest would come for shorter spells, so that experience of working together at the pinnacle of European molecular biology feeds back, continuously, into other existing universities. Symposia and advanced training programmes for molecular biologists would be another by-product of the research at the European laboratory. It would in short do for molecular biology what CERN has done for high energy physics: raising the general level of European effort, attracting the best brains back from America, encourag-

[2]See European Conference on Molecular Biology, Document CEMB 68/31E. Proposal for a European Laboratory of Molecular Biology, prepared by the Council of EMBO, 1968.

ing greater movement between, and higher standards in, existing universities. The one big difference is that there would be no big machine. The total cost of running the laboratory once it is established is put in the region of $10 mn. per year, of which the main items are amortizing buildings and equipment (some $4·2 mn. per year), salaries at $4 mn. for the staff of the centre and $1·5 mn. for visitors and fellows. The sum is not exorbitant. EMBO has won a degree of support from European governments; it is time they took the plunge.

One serious doubt is whether Europe's molecular 'centre of excellence' should be based on one of the existing university centres or should be entirely new. The French Government have already proposed a site near the French national computing centre; the British have suggested Cambridge. Probably Cambridge has the strongest case, because of the quality of the work done there. But if a national centre is indeed to become a European 'centre of excellence' fulfilling all the tasks proposed by EMBO, a large number of vital conditions must be fulfilled. The host country will have to make available certain facilities, in return for the benefits it will enjoy through the presence of this powerful European group of scientists. Guest countries will have to be given a proper say in running the enterprise. Most important, the creation of a major European 'centre of excellence' in one country in one sector of science, with all the benefits it brings in jobs, prestige and 'fall-out' into other fields, must be matched by the creation of corresponding centres in other countries in other fields of science.

In molecular biology, it is conceivable that both Cambridge and the Pasteur Institute might be built up into twin centres of excellence for Europe. Out of their work might spring, in the future, some other major projects which would require expensive equipment. Cancer research is one such field; others can be found in the field of agriculture, for instance a project on pathological viruses. Major experiments in biological control of pests (two are being carried out on olive flies in Greece and Italy) can cost much money. So, indeed, can a large primate centre (i.e. a large collection of monkeys, on whom genetic experiments can be done). All this suggests another major objective for European policy in molecular biology: there should be a systematic effort to link fundamental research work with practical applications in fields like agriculture and medicine. Special fellowships should be granted to bring people with practical experience of pest control, or hospital analysis, or the pharmaceuti-

cal industry into the pure laboratories, and for taking funda-
mentalists into the field. The major centres should be required to
provide a certain amount of service to the regions which surround
them—links with industry and so on.

A successful European policy for molecular biology thus has much
wider implications. Like the choice of a site for the 300 GEV accelerator, or a major nuclear research establishment, the choice of a
location for a great centre in molecular biology ought to be part of a
wider European policy to distribute such scientific assets fairly
throughout Europe. Applied research and policies to help the regions
must also form part of a wider policy too. Indeed, a closer look
shows that there are many other fields of science and technology
where needs similar to those of molecular biology apply.

Common research programmes, for instance, in which several
centres are linked together might be applied to solid-state physics
and cryogenics (the physics of low temperatures) or, particularly
perhaps, to multidisciplinary fields like the study of surfaces or
ceramics and non-conductors.

In applied science a special programme might be developed to
study ways of 'making the desert bloom', or other technologies of
crucial interest to developing countries.

Helping Mobility; Better Communications

Merging research efforts in all these ways raises a number of
common needs. Throughout the universities and research institutions
of Europe, barriers to movement thwart cooperative efforts and
often make it easier to go to the United States than move between
two European countries. In some countries, for instance France,
foreigners may not take up professorships. Different social security
and pension arrangements provide grave obstacles to movement. In
many countries absence abroad for a year or two jeopardizes promotion prospects on return. The hierarchic atmosphere of some
European universities contrasts with the team approach and mobility
which tempts able Europeans to America. Three immediate needs
therefore stand out: to harmonize social security benefits and make
pensions transferable; to permit individuals to be members of more
than one university in more than one country; and to persuade the
leading academic bodies in the different countries to encourage their
members to make experience abroad an asset rather than a bar to
promotion.

The effects of bad communication are manifold. In some European universities researchers are so isolated that they repeat work already done elsewhere. Accelerators (for energies over 10 MEV) have been built by people who have never seen those built by others.[3] Advanced instruments are often redevised in the laboratory, when better designs and experience could be bought, copied, or learnt by proper contact with fellow researchers elsewhere. Research workers often lack the stimulus of contact with other interesting people doing similar work. Too often, in European universities, research methods have a pre-industrial revolution flavour which may look romantic, but is hardly efficient. The universities, which were once the only centres of research, are often insulated from the new centres in industry and other institutes.

As Mladjenovic puts it, there are 'in general few mutual analyses of situations and suggestions for further development. There is no systematized "inventory" of specified knowledge, skill and talent, which would be available to a larger community'.

To break out of this situation, new instruments are needed. In matters of research, money is usually the most powerful catalyst available, money, combined with analysis and knowledge, and used as a judicious instrument of joint research enterprises, mobility and change. A European equivalent of America's National Science Foundation[4] would serve this need.

A European Science Foundation

A European Science Foundation would carry out a permanent inventory of Europe's scientific activities and capabilities, at least in those areas where no European organization (like CERN or EMBO) already exists to do the job. It could of course draw on national science policy organs for information, where these could help. It would chart research programmes already in course of execution. And it would provide analysis of science policy needs and choices, for the decision-making organs we shall describe in the next chapter.

It would work out means for solving the technical problems of movement of researchers (social security, etc.) and if necessary contribute funds to do so. It would, like EMBO, finance fellowships for

[3]See paper to Conference on science policy, 1967, Strasbourg University, by Professor Mladjenovic of Institute of Nuclear Sciences, Belgrade.

[4]P. Piganiol, *Développement de La Recherche Scientifique et Coopération Scientifique au sein de la Communauté Européenne*, Unpublished Paper, 1964.

researchers and lecturers, moving from one country to another, and back research programmes, provided they were part of a 'network' programme or *action concertée* involving several centres, which the foundation considered worthwhile. In such programmes, it would not only make grants conditional on a joint effort, but provide money for travel between centres, require regular joint symposia which would reflect the state of the work, and generally provide guidance on the management of such joint efforts. It would give special backing to interdisciplinary studies, and to joint European summer schools and seminars covering particular areas of research.

It would plan and assist financially the development of 'centres of excellence' in a particular field, where European scientists from many countries would work together. In this it would not only seek to build on existing strengths but also to ensure a measure of balance between countries; if Nancy were to become a centre of excellence in metallurgy, Rome could get, say, solid-state physics and so on. The 'centres of excellence' would be linked with other small centres and would tend to guide joint programmes.

If, as has happened in high energy physics, oceanography and molecular biology, the scale of potential joint operations were to outgrow these means, a separate agency could be created with its own budget, responsible to the highest decision-making authority (see Chapter 14).

A useful first step towards the harmonization and linking of programmes by different countries in common fields would be the permanent appointment, on the different national science councils (say in medicine for instance) of members from neighbouring countries.

A European Degree

At the undergraduate level, an immense amount plainly has to be done to make possible the free movement of young people throughout the universities of Europe. Many bodies, from the Cultural Committee of the Council of Europe to the Ministers of the European Community, have at one time or other concerned themselves with this. Slow progress is being made towards establishing a certain 'equivalence' of degrees, so that a French or Dutch degree, say, is acceptable in West Germany. Yet, understandably, there is also a fear that too much uniformity could inhibit progress. The sensible solution accepted, for instance, by the West German Rectors' Conference, would be to recognize 'comparable' degrees, even if the content varies. To get this right means looking closely at degrees in different countries to see whether certain quality standards are attained. The Council of Europe has in fact agreed to set such standards and test the content, teaching methods and material conditions of the courses. Studies have begun on biology and history, and will be followed by others. Already common tendencies—to try to form a broadly-trained biologist, able to handle the interdisciplinary perspective now opening up—are apparent.

The progress towards a more permissive market for graduates in Europe is useful, but it is tortoise-like and limited. Far more dramatic progress towards the formation of European-minded engineers, scientists and so on, could be made to spring from a political act. If a decision were taken to make all degrees in Europe dependent on spending one year in another European country, the universities would very rapidly adjust to the new situation, and a massive step would have been taken towards an education system which really produced citizens of Europe. Of course initially this will be declared impossible. In practice, if a deadline three years hence were set, the universities would soon find a way to adjust curricula. A common financial pool would be needed to help even out the financial burden. Here some awkward problems would be posed by the different methods of financing used in different countries. But none of these obstacles should prove insuperable. So radical a move should prove a tremendous catalyst of innovation in curricula, forcing many university private worlds to recognize the existence of a wider world from which they can learn. The learning of foreign languages, incidentally, in Britain in particular, would be put in perspective and exposed for what it is: the acquisition of a simple preliminary skill necessary, like the ability to read, for living in the modern world.

A small common agency will be needed to act as catalyst and instrument of the harmonization of examinations, the financing of student movement and the development of curricula. Initially this work will continue to be done by the Cultural Committee of the Council of Europe and by OECD. Eventually, it might be done more effectively by the European Science Foundation, or by a special agency attached to an enlarged European Community.

Applied Research

In private industry research associations in European countries often cover common ground. They should be encouraged to develop common programmes in those main areas where a direct competi-

P

tive problem is not involved. In steel, prompted by the European Coal and Steel Community, something of this kind has already happened.

Public research laboratories and the laboratories of nationalized industries are another area where common programmes would be valuable. The different national building laboratories, and some atomic energy establishments are often working on similar studies of materials. Their work could be coordinated into a common programme. This might be done, initially, by simple decision of the governments, or, on a more continuous basis, through the catalytic efforts of a central agency, prodding the different laboratories into action by granting funds for common programmes and movement of research workers.

In the same way one can see no commercial competitive reason for secrecy in the research programmes of the nationalized railways. Why not pool their efforts—and in mining research too?

There is a case too for some kind of common European equivalent of the British National Research and Development Corporation to back joint development of innovations in industry and elsewhere— like joint work between two companies on fuel cells or, far more grandly, on air-cushion trains. This European Technology Fund would have the task of exploring, constantly, the possibilities of joint development work. Its work in development should be linked to two other major functions: the development of common standards, and common public buying policies. We shall return to these key issues in a later chapter.

As with science very large projects—like ground transportation schemes—might be executed by hived-off special agencies or by special agreements between governments. But there is no doubt that a more general European instrument, with its own funds, is needed too.

The European Science Foundation, and the Technology Fund concerned with applied research and development, would, in short, like the National Science Foundation in America, act as balancing wheels of a European science and technology policy, filling in gaps not covered by specialized agencies, providing studies and information, serving the special European need for mobility, financing 'centres of excellence' and joint research and development programmes. But, again like its American sister, the European Science Foundation cannot be the steering wheel, or sometimes even the main motor of European policy for science and technology. The great political decisions of a science and technology policy—the choice of major goals, which involve heavy spending, and decisions on the location of really big projects—must be taken at the top. In the next section we turn to the commanding political institutions of a European science and technology policy and to some of the choices they will have to make.

PART FOUR

A STRATEGY FOR EUROPE

CHAPTER 14

A EUROPEAN SCIENCE AND
TECHNOLOGY POLICY

The proliferation of organizations and endeavours described in Part II of this book arouses a mixture of hope and fear for Europe. On the one hand, dramatic successes like CERN, more modest achievements like Euratom's fusion programme, and the major movement of political consciousness and will reflected in joint aircraft projects, manifest Europe's growing willingness to unite its efforts in science and technology. On the other, resurgent nationalism, cumbersome and inefficient institutions and the total absence of an overall policy threaten to waste resources, erode the will to act together, and leave Europe exposed and vulnerable to the challenge of America. Certainly the present chaos of European organizations for science and technology cannot be allowed to last much longer. Ad hoc bilateral projects, duplicated organizations, loose cooperative arrangements which fall apart at the seams with depressing regularity, absence of parliamentary control, may be excused as the first faltering steps of a child learning to walk. But it is time now for Europe to start growing up. To respond effectively to the American challenge Europe must now rationalize and strengthen its organisations, learning from the successes and failures of the past, fill in the wide gaps in its common endeavours, and seek to bring them within the scope of an overall strategy.

So long as Britain and other West European countries are not united in a supranational community, a degree of improvization will continue to prevail. All the same progress can be made. In the major sectors, effective common agencies exist, or must be created. CERN must go on. EMBO must be given life. Even without Britain ESRO and ELDO must be amalgamated into a common space agency with a common programme. The European aviation conference proposed in the Plowden Report should be held and a common advanced projects agency set up to plan for the future, and work towards common requirements policies. Euratom's useful work must go on, and there can be discussions at industrial level to explore integration of work on fast reactors and other fields between Britain and the Community. The Ministers of Transport can get on with some common planning. The European computer agency could be set up. The Science Foundation should be established covering the whole of Western Europe. Work on common industrial standards can go on, inspired by the extremely useful tripartite (Anglo-German French) committee which has been doing practical work on this question for the past three years.

The trouble is that the more ad hoc organizations there are, the weaker the management and also the political control over their activities; the resulting hotch-potch of results has no resemblance whatever to a common strategy. In each separate organization or project, decisions are a compromise between separate government positions. Those positions are themselves the result of an internal compromise between different ministries, pressure groups, and so on, and the European programmes are further drained by the national programmes which governments take out as an insurance policy. How totally different Europe's decisions on space would look, for instance, if the entire space expenditure of Western Europe were planned collectively, and this total had to take its place within a common strategy of priorities for Europe as a whole. In the past France has given space high priority, Britain a low one with other countries somewhere in between. The result has been an awkward compromise, very different from the possible results of a joint European decision on priorities, measured against other collective needs —atoms, EMBO and the rest.

The sooner the many managerial agencies that are coming to life are brought under a collective decision-making body, the better. And of course the natural framework is a European community enlarged to bring in Britain and others. The Six have already begun to hold meetings of Science and Technology Ministers. This will be ineffective unless developed further. The Commission also needs a strong science and technology directorate, headed by a Commissioner. Let us call him the Commissioner for Science and Technology; here too an evolution has already begun. The partnership between the Council of Science Ministers and the Commission should form the steering wheel for Europe's science and technology policy; the equivalent, in terms of Community Europe, of the American President and his Office of Science and Technology.

The Council of Ministers and European Directorate of Science and Technology ought to be assisted by a European Science Advisory Council, drawn from the best scientific brains of Europe. Its task would be to help in establishing scientific priorities and, if necessary through subcommittees, to conduct scientific investigations into new problems, fields of common action where things are going wrong (such as Euratom), and so on. For instance, if such a body existed now, it should be given the task of reporting on the best form for a European oceanography organization, and on the main programmes such a body should initially carry out. A start has been made in the Community on some of these functions in the *Groupe Marèchale*, a mixed group of national and community officials who have been studying the scientific needs of the Community and making proposals. But this body is modest and over-weighted with national officials. In the period while Britain is outside the Community, there is a case for bringing Britain into it (as in the Benelux proposals) and perhaps for asking the scientific academies of Europe to set up a joint advisory council themselves.

It is important to define and limit the tasks of the central steering agency of a European science and technology policy. When Euratom was originally set up it combined the functions of executive agency and policy-making body; this has been one of the causes of its difficulties. Management has been up to the neck in politics; clearly defined objectives, and the means to achieve them, have been hard to come by. Such a hotch-potch of politics and management must be avoided, as European integration extends to wider fields of science and technology. The management agencies must be given clearly defined executive reponsibilities, and each placed under the direction of a single man. They must have clear responsibility for placing contracts on a competitive basis where they are engaged in this kind of activity, with the one key qualification that tendering may have to be by consortia where this catalyst for industrial integration seems desirable. They must be given rolling five-year budgets, where possible, and told to get on with the job. The European Science Foundation, like the specialized agencies, will also operate mainly in this way, not making big decisions about science policy, but executing, within an agreed budget, its many tasks.

Plainly, in the major sectors, there will also have to be specialized

Councils from the member states guiding particular agencies. CERN's Council, for instance, which might be described as a subcommittee of Europe's future Council of Science Ministers, will carry on. European Ministers for Aviation will also meet from time to time in connection with aviation matters, and so on.

The central function of a future European Directorate and Council for Science and Technology will be to make choices about science and technology policy, and of course promote the efficiency of the evolving process of integration. Making choices, or indeed operating at all, is not going to be easy, for some of the member countries, as we have seen, do not really have a national science and technology policy and hardly take deliberate choices themselves at home. To contribute properly to a European science and technology policy the member states do not need elaborate programmes of their own; indeed these can be an obstacle. But they do need to possess at least a body as effective as, say, Belgium's Conseil National de la Politique Scientifique, capable of performing an accurate inventory of the country's scientific and technological activities, possessing certain instruments, and able to speak with authority in the counsels of Europe.

As for the central body itself, it will be no more than a talking-shop (like OECD), if it is not backed by money, political authority, and a real community approach.

What kind of choices about science policy will Europe have to make as it looks to the needs of the 1970s? Choice in science policy means deciding which are the areas where the investment of men and public funds is most likely to yield a large social, economic, political and scientific return. In our discussion of particular sectors we often found it was not possible to make definite judgments on key joint projects, because such choices mean priorities; an individual project cannot be judged alone.

In our discussion of several of the sectors we found too that big savings could be made by cutting wasteful duplication in the form of national programmes. Nuclear power, especially fast-breeder reactors, and space, are obvious examples of this. In CERN too, though the proliferation of national accelerators is not really wasteful, it must now be kept firmly in check, lest it strangle the Giant Machine. In the nuclear field there are important opportunities to transfer skilled laboratories and men to new areas. Within the individual sectors there are important opportunities for the application of cost-benefit analysis. The case for a large number of separate national

TABLE L

Priorities for Europe: an illustration

	Priority	Comment
Funds for a European Science Foundation	1	High overall scientific return for relatively small sums invested.
EMBO laboratory	2	High scientific return in one of the two most important areas of science, for relatively small investment.
Computer systems and software development	3	The most important single area of technology, affecting the whole of industry and society.
Rationalized fast-breeder reactor development programme	4	Expensive but, *with an integrated European programme,* existing resources of manpower and facilities could be used to achieve a European world lead in the principal future source of energy. Without European rationalization, however, far more doubtful economics.
Ground transportation schemes	5	A high social and economic return on investment, in a field where Europe has particularly acute needs.
Development of series of medium-range high density airliners	6	This is where the biggest aviation market is inside Europe itself; European technology can easily cope.
CERN's 300 GEV accelerator	7	Expensive and not immediately useful, but essential to maintain Europe's most successful common scientific endeavour in one of the two key areas of science.
Major oceanography programme	8	Yields are long-term, costs could be high, but big eventual returns.
Advanced military aircraft development programme including VTOL and swing-wing technology	9	Expensive; costs very hard to control; ultimate requirements uncertain; this becomes essentially a politico-military argument. Does Europe require to possess *control* of the most advanced military aviation technology? A complete nuclear armoury is already beyond its reach.
Supersonic airliner programme	10	Expensive; dubious commercial return; sonic boom problem still unsolved. Main arguments are huge possible balance of payments cost if competition compels buying American; role of advanced technology in whole aviation industry.
Programmes of rocket and satellite development with a view to a European direct transmission system	11	Cheaper to buy American. May be impossible to catch up with American lead. Huge investment required for uncertain commercial-industrial benefit. Crux is again political. Does Europe require to have some *control* over crucial means of communication and propaganda.

Financial resources needed

1. Say $100 mn. annually. Existing total national pure science budgets are some $600 mn. annually.
2. Annual cost only $10 mn. including amortization.

3. Existing competing *National* programmes of Government research and development grants expected to cost some $180 mn. between 1967 and 1972 (in addition to R & D by companies). If these resources were used in a common European programme, no additional resources would be necessary.
4. Three triplicated national R & D and prototype programmes for sodium-cooled reactors to absorb $1,500 mn. by 1974. With total rationalization (i.e. only one sodium prototype, with further developments), it should be possible to develop a second reactor-type (gas-cooled) in addition, for a smaller total bill (say $1,200 mn.) for both types together.

5. Say $50 mn. annually for a group of prototypes.

6. Airbus and engines will cost $500 mn. to develop up to 1973; smaller shorthaul aircraft, say $200 mn. (engines already developed) till 1976–7; peak annual spending on two projects $150 mn.
7. $316 mn. spread over ten years. Peak annual cost of construction and operating $67 mn.

8. Up to, say, $100 mn. annually (could cost much more). National programmes total some $15 mn. annually. Could be financed from sea-bed royalties.
9. $700 mn. to be spent over eight years, mainly after 1970.

10. $1,400 mn. spent between 1963 and 1973. (That is, annual average of $140 mn., annual peak of $300 mn.)

11. Total annual space budget of $300 mn.—$400 mn. Existing national programmes cost $100 mn. annually; existing European programmes cost $110 mn. annually. New joint programme for applications satellites and further launcher development would raise joint programme to some $250 mn. on top of national programmes.

programmes as a support for a European programme is often based on the slenderest of evidence. Careful analysis should show what is the cheapest method of achieving a given European objective and where duplication or poor communications waste resources and jeopardize the goal.

There are other areas, however, like aviation, where there is not much more room for curbing purely national expenditure. And in other sectors, such as space, even if there is a proper curbing of national programmes, it will be hard indeed to find the means for a European programme which keeps pace with the galloping technology of direct transmission and the rest. Choices about priorities have to be made. Are Concorde and its successors the best investment for $1,400 mn. and more of research and development funds? Should priority be given to a $1,000 mn. space programme (over five years) or to a major effort of oceanography, or to the 300 GEV accelerator, or to all these things?

Table L shows the possible cost of some of the European programmes already described, together with guesses about possible national programmes in the same fields. Both pure scientific and applied technological projects are deliberately included, for when the decision to spend is made, they should be compared and evaluated together. Obviously a choice of priorities in these fields is an immensely complex business. But, on the evidence briefly assembled so far in this study, the projects might be placed in the categories of priority illustrated in Table L.

Perhaps it will be possible to carry out all these European objectives if national programmes are properly controlled. No doubt there will be certain cases, say oceanography, where the choice is not between all or nothing, but simply how much to do and how fast. No doubt careful analysis will throw up different answers. But it is at least important that, when the maximum rationalization within each sector has been achieved, the decisions on what to do next should be seen as a question of priorities for Europe; and that the choice should be made deliberately, weighing up the different factors involved. The British decision to get out of space, for instance, like the French decision against the VG aircraft, was made not on the basis of a joint European analysis of priorities, but of a purely national budgetary problem. The repercussions of these decisions on others show that they exemplify how not to behave.

A research and development strategy for Europe ought to be guided by a long-term plan, which would be continually adjusted to take account of the changing scene. There should be rolling five-year budgets for each major sector, with annual budgets within this framework.

The major instruments of a European science and technology policy have already been described. They are the Management Agencies, the Science Foundation, and the Technology Fund. The Fund and Foundation in particular will only be effective if they have large sums behind them and a real delegation of managerial authority.

Nor will the joint funding and planning of European research and development get far without real integration at the industrial level: the lesson of computers, aviation, nuclear power and all the major sectors considered in this book. The development of powerful European industrial units, and an industrial strategy to promote them, is the subject of the next chapter.

CHAPTER 15

AN INDUSTRIAL POLICY

It is at the level of industrial application that Europe's innovations have often been overtaken by American rivals. A European science policy will not be much use without an industrial policy designed to foster the devlopment of powerful industrial companies that can exploit and market European inventions fast. In nuclear power, aviation and computers, for instance, this was and is the compelling need.

The Common Market and its extension to Britain is, of course, of first importance. It is the open continental market of America which has engendered companies of continental scale. But now that the tariff barriers in Europe are eroded, other barriers—such as different patent laws and standards—emerge as barriers to trade and industrial rationalization like rocks exposed by a falling tide.

Patents

In the field of patents, the Common Market's draft convention has been held up for some years by Holland's refusal to go ahead unless Britain and other countries are in too. Here the crucial need is to make one country's patent procedure acceptable to others, so that there is no need for each invention to be patented in, say, twenty different countries. When patent offices have a backlog of several years work, as they do today, this can mean not only massive duplication of effort and waste of skilled manpower and money but great delay. For innovating companies, large and small, the present patent set-up is a massive burden.

Creating a European patent law means finding a happy mean between different types of system. In Britain and West Germany there is a full examination of each patent and a chance to lodge objections. In France patents are simply registered and there is no testing and approval process. A compromise would probably be best for a European patent law, with patents simply registered automatically, and an examination if an objector lodges a claim that he had conceived the idea first. Such a system, with a patent lodged in one country recognized in another, would dramatically cut the costs and time consumed by patent law. The patent might apply provisionally for the first five years, during which time an application for examination could be made. After that the patent would provide complete protection; though to encourage the dissemination of knowledge, compulsory licensing ought to be granted after a period of, say, five years, or longer depending on the time it takes to develop a particular product.

Patents are much less important, today, than they were twenty years ago. The best firms innovate regardless of patents and make their money not by technical monopoly, but by keeping ahead. One innovating firm (say firm A) may patent merely to insure itself against a competitor (say firm B) who might take a patent later in order, unfairly, to extract royalties from firm A. There is a powerful case for abolishing the system altogether. But if it is to survive, it had better be simple, international, and limiting the exclusive right to inventions to the shortest possible period of time.

Standards

Differences in industrial standards are an even more direct barrier to trade. Different standards of safety and so on have been such obstacles that trade in electrical consumer goods within the European Free Trade Association has grown surprisingly little in the period of tariff reduction. Different licensing regulations on the maximum speed of tractors, colouring regulations for food, different plugs for light bulbs and varying building regulations all stand in the way of trade.

The Brussels Commission has been working steadily in this field and has produced common standards for a list of state-regulated areas, from food colouring to refrigeration and thermally insulated articles. Since February 1966, a tripartite Franco-German-British group has been setting in motion an effort of standardization for the wider Europe. Personal trust, and a realization by both France and Britain of their common interest in proper European standards led to this. The tripartite committee meets four times a year, discusses difficult products, reaches agreement where possible, often by giving one of the three the lead in setting a standard, and then decides which international organization to work on to win general acceptance for the common line.[1] A subcommittee, which also brings in Belgium, the Netherlands and Italy, is working out common standards for electronic components, as well as common test and inspection procedures. In machine tools and vehicle safety, the West Germans have been given the lead in setting common standards; in machine tools the aim is to achieve standard units, permitting interchangeability, common lubrication, maintenance procedures and coding, and common acceptance procedures. In building and construction, Britain has the lead, since it has already established metric modules. Non-ferrous bars and sheets, threads, tolerances and fasteners, units of stress and energy, and electric standards generally, all come within the general scope of the committee. It is, in short, setting the ground rules for the integration of European industry—a complex, tedious process vital to Europe's bread and butter.

A Common Market in Public Buying

Despite this slow reduction of technical barriers one major network of barriers still divides up even the Common Market. Buying in the massive public sector, in most European countries, is still organized on national lines. National power companies, hospitals, education authorities, road building authorities, ministries buying office equipment, above all the defence industries or the purchasers of telecommunications equipment all apply Buy National policies in varying degree. The four major British telephone companies, for instance, have for years sold under a cosy market sharing arrangement with the Post Office. The French Electricity Authority has only once bought foreign in the last ten years to break up a particular strong French price ring. The result, especially in heavy industry, has been to foster and defend national industrial structures and an excessive number of relatively small companies, and to slow down the evolution of European-wide firms.

A common market in public buying is therefore crucial to the

---

[1]The organizations include CEN, the European Standards Committee; CENEL, the European Electrical Standards Committee; ISO, the International Standards Organization (World); IEC, the International (World) Electrical Standards Committee; ECE, the UN Economic Commission for Europe (motor vehicles); and OECD, which deals with agriculture and agricultural vehicles.

development of companies of European scale. The Rome Treaty makes no specific mention of this; but plainly it is an essential part of any policy to enforce Article 7, which bans 'discrimination on grounds of nationality'. The trouble is that most of the protectionism in public buying is of a subtle kind; though a foreign product might be cheaper, technical specifications of the domestic product are said by the purchasing ministry to be more favourable; or a particular public authority simply does not invite foreigners to tender at all.

It should not, however, prove impossible to draw up Community regulations to open up the public markets of all the members simultaneously, and this the Brussels Commission is trying to do. Such common rules would require a growing proportion of all public buying (perhaps with a few key sectors in defence omitted) to be opened step by step to common tender for partner countries over a period of three or four years. It would also describe and forbid certain kinds of covert protective practice. Bit by bit the structure of European industry would adapt to the requirements of a wider market.

This simple liberal recipe is probably the best and most efficient means of adapting the industrial structure to continental scale. If Volkswagen could tender to the British police, on equal terms with BMC, if ICL could do the same for computers in France, if Siemens & Ericsson could bid for telephones in Britain, there is little doubt that major shifts in the market would take place; the most efficient producers would grow. Rolls Royce would almost certainly become Europe's only producer of large aero-engines; and the Dassault company might find a larger market, notably in Britain, for its supersonic military aircraft.

Why 'European Companies'

Yet obstacles to the optimum distribution of resources in Europe would still remain—in particular, in the form of differing national legal and fiscal systems. The emergence of transnational companies that can match in Europe the rival giants in the United States is frustrated, it is said, by different national company laws. The stock answer, to create a 'European Company Law', which will enable such European companies to be formed, lies ready to hand, and the Brussels Commission has been working for some years on a formula for a European company statute.

Unfortunately, a closer look throws disconcerting light on the purely legal arguments for this panacea. In the first place there is no single company law in the United States. The US giants must take pot-luck, establishing themselves under the company law of New Jersey, Texas or California. They do benefit, however, from other common facilities, like the splendidly developed US capital market. No less important, large US companies are taxed in only one place by the federal tax man; they are not obliged, like today's transnational European companies, to pay taxes in six different places and undertake a delicate balancing operation as they seek to reconcile, say, six different tax systems with the requirements of optimum decisions on profits and investments.

Though the US does not have a single corporate law, it does have a single law of contract, or rather a single system of day-to-day law, culminating in a single Court of Appeal on commercial cases. This means that a company based in one state and operating in another (where it perhaps has a legal problem with a bad debtor) is subject to a single code of law in its contracts, sales, debts and everyday business. This is a crucial unifier of the business environment.

Even more disturbing to the conventional notion that a single European company law is a key to the emergence of 'European' companies is the fact that many companies in Europe, particularly American ones, already operate across frontiers most effectively. IBM, for instance, integrates both production and research in several European countries and the United States. Its component factory in France produces components for IBM computers made in many countries. So does the memory factory in Britain. IT & T is systematically integrating research in several European countries. General Motors is to produce transmissions for all its European car factories in Strasbourg. Many European companies too, like Philips, Olivetti, Siemens, Dunlop, Nestlé, Brown Boveri, Ericsson and so on have operations in several countries which extend far beyond mere sales and include a network of more or less integrated manufacture and research.

All these companies, however, though international in the character of their operations, are based in a single country. Both managerial power and ownership are rooted, in the case of IBM, IT & T, or General Motors, in the United States. Philips, Olivetti and Siemens are run from Holland, Italy and West Germany. When Europeans complain that there are 'no European companies', what they are saying is that there are no companies in which ownership and controlling power are distributed between several countries, with no single one predominant, and that this, together with other obstacles, is an important factor preventing the evolution in Europe of large companies.

Within the Common Market, the national-based companies with operations in many countries can be expected to become increasingly 'European' in character as time goes on: by issuing shares in many capital markets, by employing people of many nationalities and promoting them to the top, by absorbing small partner companies in other countries with whom they have worked during the transitional period, by catering increasingly for the tastes and markets of all Europe. But for such companies the centre of gravity may still be in one country.

Is this absence of the company based in several countries really detrimental to Europe's industrial structure, and if so, why? After all, in the United States and Britain, takeovers as well as mergers are a common way of combining. Why should not European companies attain a continental stature by takeover and by the simple process of competing freely in a common public and private market?

One danger is the nationalist flavour which creeps in despite the apparent international character of the market. Especially if concentration continues as at present on a national basis, there is a real danger that in, say, the motor industry, each major country will come to be represented by a single company, which will tend to be backed by national prejudice and public buying policy, however well concealed. This is not the way to create an optimum economic pattern in the market; nor is it, politically, the way to unite Europe.

Nor will integration by takeover satisfy the need for speed. As the barriers fall and a single European market emerges, the industrial structure of Europe has to adapt from national to continental scale in a relatively short time. Firms like General Motors, IBM or Standard Oil have grown to their present stature in America over a period of fifteen, thirty or even fifty years. European companies cannot afford to wait so long, which is what growth by internal expansion and acquisition involve. Because of their sheer size, financial resources and technical lead, large American companies are in a position to put together by acquisition a number of major European units in a short space of time and thus create 'European companies' of a stature to match the emerging common market. If European companies are to grow fast to continental stature, they will sometimes have to do so, not merely by the large devouring the small, but by agreement to combine. They are under pressure to take short cuts to growth.

Q

Here there is an important distinction between what appears to be optimum size within a European oligopolistic equilibrium (say in the motor industry) and the optimum size needed to compete with far larger American firms. In the short haul, the major European motor companies—BLMC, Volkswagen, Fiat, Renault—are easily large enough to compete with each other and with American subsidiaries in Europe in terms of large-scale production facilities. In the long haul, in world competition with General Motors, it is much less certain that they are, individually, large enough to compete with the financial resources their American rivals can put into marketing and development if they wish. Thus it is the American challenge, above all, which pushes even the larger European companies to combine.

A subtle political factor also obliges Europeans to move on from the mere expansion of nation-based companies in advanced industries to the further stage of creating companies with control and ownership shared by several countries.

Public authorities like to buy from their own national industries; so far the Common Market has not broken this down. If there is to be a common market in public buying—a major thesis of this study and of this chapter—the buyers will still want to see a distribution of power and ownership in the industries they buy from which gives their country some industrial stake in key fields. This predilection must not be allowed to prevent the emergence of an effective common market. It would be better for Sweden and West Germany, for instance, to supply a large part of the telephone market in Britain and Britain the lion's share of Swedish and West German aero-engines than for all three countries to attempt, fussily, to keep uneconomical domestic producers alive. But it is unrealistic to imagine this division of labour going to extremes. For political reasons the large European countries at least will continue to want some stake in key defence industries. They will want a share in new industries which promise to contribute crucially to economic growth or to have a major social impact. They may also want some share in the basic industries which provide material for the country's basic communications system. Strong and efficient European companies are needed in which many nations have a stake, if this desire for some local source of supply is to be reconciled with large scale.

Certainly, in the defence industries, European companies with several national components may be essential to the emergence of a common defence market. For British, French and West German military authorities, still suffering from inherited tribal loyalties, it would be a great deal more easy to buy their tanks and aircraft from one or two competitive common suppliers than from another country.

How can Europe develop, not just companies with international operations, but companies with a base of power and ownership in several nations?

Agfa-Gevaert: the Siamese Twins

Much can be learnt from those rare birds, the multi-based European companies which already exist. There are in fact three: Royal Dutch Shell; Unilever; and the newly created Agfa-Gevaert photographic combine, born in 1964. These three companies have a common structure; each is formed from a carefully balanced combination of two large national companies. And of the three Agfa-Gevaert is the most interesting, because it is new, and presents an up-to-date case study in overcoming the existing obstacles to merging across European frontiers.

The Agfa-Gevaert combination was a classic European response to the challenge of American scale. Kodak's massive size already dominated the world market for photographic films; neither of the two leading European companies, Agfa, a subsidiary of West Germany's giant Bayer chemical corporation, and Gevaert, a Belgian company, could see any hope of mustering alone the financial resources to match Kodak's advancing technology, financed by heavy spending on research. Kodak's research and development expenditure was roughly equivalent at the time of the merger to Gevaert's turnover. Photography is going through a technical revolution, with the introduction of Xerox-type copying and many other new techniques. In this industry, like others therefore, size was becoming technically vital. Good men were needed as much as money. Economies of scale in marketing and production, rising costs of materials and labour, all suggested that combination was essential for strength.

The merger was helped by the absence of serious alternative partners. In the European photographic industry Agfa-Gevaert dominates; there was a reasonable balance of strength between the partners, once the German partner had been strengthened by the absorption of Bayer's other photographic interests at Leverkusen, and by the absorption of six other small companies in which it had a share.

More convenient still, there was a fair degree of complementarity between the two potential partners, with Agfa strong in amateur films and Gevaert specializing in the technical and industrial field. Once the two merged they had a balanced coverage of the whole market. Geographical good fortune favoured the match too; the two main factories are a mere two hours and ten minutes apart, so that executives can and do step in their cars and, after a drive of one hour and five minutes, meet for a conference at the aptly named Euromotel at Herstal, near Liège.

In June 1964, after long talks and preparation, the two companies merged, forming two 50-50 operating companies on either side of the frontier. Each of the parent companies, Agfa AG and Gevaert Photo-Producten NV, now holds 50 per cent of the shares of both the Gevaert-Agfa company at Antwerp, and the Agfa-Gevaert company at Leverkusen. Each of the two sister companies is headed by a board composed of five Belgians and five Germans. The twofold board is a fiction, for the directors are the same men in each case. The board meets alternately each month in Antwerp and Leverkusen and from there on down operations of the merged companies are integrated in varying degrees. Joint committees on production, research, administration, sales, and planning were set up to undertake the process of integration and to plan future policy. Thus, though the two operating companies exist, there is in fact only one enterprise, with uniform advertising, policy rules and so on.

The merger has already brought some striking economies. Predictably enough, it was in research and marketing that the biggest economies of scale have as yet appeared. In research a common director has been appointed, based in Antwerp, with a German manager in Leverkusen. Research on amateur products is done mainly in Leverkusen, and on technical and industrial products in Antwerp. Gradually basic research is being integrated into a single programme. The joint effort is now probably at a level comparable to that of Kodak, though at one third the cost. Each company has brought its own contributions and innovations to the research programme.

In sales there has been a complete integration of marketing networks, with all branches integrated into 22 subsidiaries scattered throughout the world. The Antwerp company now controls marketing of technical and professional products throughout the world (including West Germany), and Agfa the marketing of amateur products everywhere. Budgeting, however, is split along geographical lines, for one sales operation could hardly be controlled financially from two headquarters. Antwerp has financial control over the United States and Europe, with the exception of West Germany, Spain, Italy and Switzerland, where Agfa was strong. Agfa controls the budgeting in these countries, Asia and Africa.

The marketing system is not perfect. Unlike the research side, there are still two sales directors on the board, and inevitably there are occasional conflicts of interest, and administrative friction between the regional breakdown of budgetary control, and the functional division of marketing and servicing, with technical products controlled from Antwerp and amateur products from Leverkusen. Nonetheless there have been dramatic improvements in productivity. Sales since the merger have risen by an average of 6 per cent per year, but manpower in the marketing network has been cut by 25 per cent. The inevitable problems of organization are not so different from those of many national-owned companies.

The rationalization of production is moving more slowly than in marketing. But it has been helped by the inherited division between Antwerp's expertise in technical products and Leverkusen's knowhow in the amateur field. Paper manufacturing is now concentrated in West Germany; the making of professional cinema film and X-ray film in Antwerp. Integration of production would probably move faster if a single production director were in charge. Nonetheless, within three years, a remarkable degree of integration has been achieved, and with it higher productivity. The real limiting factor has been the usual emotions and personal problems of a merger between two major companies and two nations, not external factors, like tax systems or law.

Gevaert brought to the merger a world outlook (90 per cent of its sales before the merger were outside Belgium), and a modern approach to marketing and management systems, as well as its research effort in the technical field; Agfa brought its name, the big West German market, and the resources of brains and finance which Bayer could provide.

Why Twin? the Legal Labyrinth

Why did the Agfa-Gevaert group choose the curious doublebarrelled formula for its merger? Has this caused problems? What have the legal and fiscal difficulties been, and what measures, including a European company law, would remove the difficulties, rendering such a merger even more efficient, saving expense in lawyers and management time—and in short facilitating the formation in Europe of large industrial units with a continental base?

The first answer, given in Agfa-Gevaert's public utterances and literature, is conventional enough. Agfa and Gevaert, it is said, were obliged to form two companies because of the differences between West German and Belgian company law and the absence of a European one. The trouble with this answer is that other companies, particularly American, manage to operate in several countries without such tricks. Why, one must ask, could not the two companies when merged simply form a single company based in, say, either Belgium or West Germany, or if this were too painful to national sensibilities, in Luxembourg, and run their activities in the other countries as subsidiaries or branches? It is only when we ask this question that the real obstacles to European mergers and even takeovers appear.

There is first a detailed legal difficulty. Belgian jurisprudence, for instance, regards 'location' as a key factor in a company's identity. To move out of Belgium, a company must have the unanimous consent of the shareholders, and since, in the Gevaert case, there are a very large number of small shareholders, the chances of such consent were in this case nil. Minority blocking rights of this kind vary from country to country in Europe, but they exist, in some form, in all.

In the case of Agfa-Gevaert, there was also a special objection to the constitution of a joint holding company in, say, even Luxembourg. The Agfa group of companies is a 90 per cent subsidiary of Bayer Leverkusen. Gevaert, on the other hand, has a large number of small Belgian shareholders. In any joint annual general meeting or 'assembly', the monolithic Bayer holding would have been sure to dominate. The double-barrelled company ensured that the Gevaert shares were kept together and that there was thus true parity. Here we begin to touch the heart of the matter: the anxiety to retain, in the new company, a balance of political power.

Under present national Belgian and West German laws (and for that matter French and Dutch ones) a local company cannot be absorbed by a foreign company in one single move, and in West Germany and the Netherlands even a merger between two local companies cannot happen in this way. Such mergers require the legal 'liquidation' and 'reconstitution' of the company which moves. This costs money, first of all in lawyers' fees; for German lawyers will certainly be needed by the emigrant Belgian company to carry out the 'reconstitution' under West German law, as well as Belgian ones to organize the liquidation. Legally, in short, merging in one country and setting up a subsidiary in another is perhaps even more complex than the creation of Siamese twins. For in the twinning arrangement there were no liquidations, only the constitution of two new companies.

Moving means bills from the tax man too. For Belgian law imposes a special liquidation tax on the difference between public capital value and liquidation assets (i.e. on the hidden fixed assets etc. realized at the time). In Belgium, international mergers have not been helped by the fact that, to facilitate mergers at home, the liquidation tax of 30 per cent was abolished on domestic mergers in 1965, but not on international ones. In both West Germany and Belgium, the new reconstituted company would have, in addition, to pay a registration tax when it was formed.

An odd anomaly adds to the fiscal burden: Belgium and West Germany have, as yet, no double taxation agreement, so if the merger took the form of the establishment of a parent company in one country, say Belgium, and of a giant subsidiary in another, say West Germany, the profits of the West German subsidiary might be taxed twice. Some community countries (France, Belgium, Italy) still impose a degree of double taxation on domestic subsidiaries, and the rates of profits tax vary in every country.

A more fundamental difficulty concerns the taxation of capital gains realized at the time of liquidation. In addition to the liquidation tax, most community countries impose a substantial capital gains tax on such assets. Most also give tax relief, or at least allow companies to spread the burden over a period of years, when such mergers take place internally. But they rarely do so when the assets are transferred from the country. After all, if the assets are removed, a source of future revenue is lost for good. A company seeking to migrate to merge, must thus first pass through a legal and fiscal labyrinth.

A European Company Statute

How much would these difficulties be overcome by the efforts being made in Brussels to harmonize laws and taxation and draft a 'European company statute'?

Progress in fiscal harmonization would obviously be a big help. The Commission in Brussels has already proposed the harmonization of the tax on assets at liquidation at the rather low level of 0·5 per cent. This would both remove discrimination between local and European mergers and helpfully lower the rate.

A common double taxation convention is also needed. Article 240 of the Rome Treaty provides for non-discrimination in the taxation of guest companies owned in other member countries. A double taxation agreement or convention would plainly have to provide that profits of subsidiaries would be taxed no more and no less than national parent companies.

Harmonization of corporation or profits taxes, except for agreed regional policies, is a further desirable step, not so much to promote European mergers, as to ensure that there are no distortions in the location of emergent companies and of investment generally. The proposed Community-wide introduction of an added value tax would remove any distortions in indirect taxation.

Finally, the Commission has urged a harmonization of capital gains taxes on assets realized at liquidation, so that there is no major deterrent to capital export. By thus chipping away at fiscal differences, the Commission is slowly making it easier for European mergers and concentration to take place.

The introduction of a European company statute would be a further assistance, though not the panacea sometimes implied. If Agfa and Gevaert, for instance, had been able to combine together as a single 'European company', with a statute recognized in all Community countries, their initial legal problem would have been somewhat diminished, and they would have been able to present a single set of company accounts. But just how meaningful the change was would depend on several other factors.

For a start, while a European company statute would have placed ownership and company structure under a single law, most local business activities—purchases, sales, credit, contracts—would still come under the local laws of the countries concerned. Here the Benelux customs union has moved further down the road of harmonization than the Common Market. But even Benelux still has some way to go. In the Common Market major differences in legal practice have still to be bridged—between laws based on the code Napoleon, for instance, and the quite different West German Burgerliches Gesetzbuch. Many industrialists feel it may take 50 years to achieve harmony. Here there is a major contrast with the United States. Under the system of common law, commercial cases really form part of a single system, with the peak of the pyramid at federal level. Until harmonization is achieved within the Common Market,

European companies will be obliged to employ local national lawyers and fight out cases under different laws.

Nor, of course, will a European company statute in itself overcome the fiscal differences between one country and another. Until these are harmonized, the activities of a 'European' company will continue to be taxed at different rates in different countries unless, that is, 'European companies' were taxed under a special tax system of their own. Yet, so long as national systems varied, the new 'European' system would inevitably be either more or less favourable than the tax system of any individual country—say Belgium, West Germany or France; a new and undesirable element of discrimination would thus be introduced. The establishment of a 'European company statute' would helpfully increase the pressure for fiscal harmonization, but not in itself satisfy it.

Even if taxes were harmonized, a 'European company' would not automatically enjoy the crucial benefits of direct taxation at a single source. The governments of, say, France, Belgium and Italy cannot be expected to accept the Dutch, say, reaping the full tax return from a 'European' company based in Holland but operating in the other countries. Taxing European companies at a single source will be possible only if the revenue goes to a European budget which provides for the balanced reallocation of expenditure to Community purposes or amongst the members. Yet being taxed at a single central point would be a great help to the Continent-based company, seeking to centralize its company financing and allocate resources rationally throughout Europe. Even in the United States there are still some state income taxes on companies and their subsidiaries. But the main burden of taxation is imposed at the federal level.

If a European company statute cannot in itself bring centralized financing, harmonized taxes, or even common contract law, what are its advantages? One concerns the operation of the capital market. A 'European company statute' ought to be a model in its requirements for the presentation of information about companies. There should be a standard profit and loss account in a form which would facilitate storage, retrieval and processing of information in the electronic proprietary information systems of the future. Investing and dealing in the shares of a combine such as Agfa-Gevaert would be facilitated if shareholders were investing in the shares of a single company instead of in the shares of one parent of a Siamese twin.

Much more than a European company law is of course needed to stimulate the development of a vigorous European capital market. The freeing of issues in the member countries, to open up markets to one another, the removal of restrictions on investment by institutions in equities, and the many other proposals set out in the Segré Report to the Europe Community in 1966,[2] are all needed if the European capital market is to develop a strength comparable to America's. The 'European company statute' is no more than one expedient—and not the most important—in this essential process.

The more one examines the detailed obstacles to mergers between European companies, the more apparent it becomes that a European company law will not in itself remove them. The fiscal and legal walls piled up by centuries of separate national developments can be removed only by systematically chipping away at differences, as the Rome Treaty intended, and working steadily and systematically towards a common fiscal system, a common budget, and a common system of law applying, not merely to a select band of 'European companies', but to all.

The main significance of the idea of a 'European company statute' is indeed psychological and political; both as a catalyst of this broad process, and as an encouragement to companies to combine, thus overcoming the real, but certainly surmountable existing legal and financial difficulties, and taking advantage of the continuing process of harmonization as it goes forward. Certainly the Agfa-Gevaert example bears this out. Why, in the last analysis, did the two companies choose to twin, and not set up a Luxembourg holding company, or simply merge as a West German or Belgium firm? The tax and legal obstacles were serious, but psychological factors went deeper still.

We have seen already how the Gevaert directors could not have accepted a single company assembly in which the monolithic Bayer shareholder would be sure to dominate. That practical difficulty was reinforced by the deeper national feelings of old Europe, which cannot be wished away overnight. The Gevaert company, built up originally by a single entrepreneur, and then financed increasingly by many small Belgian investors, was the pride of Flanders. Neither it, nor Agfa, was prepared to countenance a merger which amounted to absorption by the other. Agfa-Gevaert's twin arrangement, like the 'European company', is essentially designed to permit a merger in which one national identity is not swallowed by the other, but both share in something larger.

[2] *Le Développement d'un Marché Européen des Capitaux*, European Economic Community, November 1966.

If all this is true of photographic films, how much deeper are the tribal loyalties and political considerations which must be overcome in politically sensitive fields like aviation, nuclear power, and computers!

In the defence industries, or related ones like aircraft, even small countries like Sweden do their best to maintain a national capability. Elsewhere in public purchasing—from electric power equipment to office equipment—it is the normal assumption that public authorities 'buy national'; a practice which the Common Market has, as yet, done little to break down. It is true that this attitude is often interpreted to include foreign manufacturing subsidiaries in the country. Nonetheless, at least amongst the major West European countries, total dependence on foreign suppliers for equipment for the nation's infrastructure is, at present, unacceptable.

All this applies, not merely to industries almost wholly dependent on public customers (telephones or electric power in Britain and France) but to other major industries. An Italian or American takeover of the British motor industry, or a West German takeover of the French, would be unacceptable politically. 'Key' advanced industries, such as computers, are already being systematically promoted on a national basis by the French, British and West German governments all of whom wish some part of the industry to be under home control.

These national minded political attitudes are less potent in Holland, Belgium and Italy, than in Britain, West Germany and France. It has been said that the first three suffer from a 'protectorate' mentality, while the three large powers are all afflicted with the mythology of the ex-great power. Certainly, when it comes to foreign ownership, or indeed to partnership with other major industries, the citizens of the smaller countries have fewer sensibilities than the ex-great powers. It is the Flemings in the Agfa-Gevaert partnership who speak German, and are prepared to tolerate and humour an occasional Germanic stiffness or rigidity; the Dutch in Royal Dutch-Shell and Unilever who speak English and know how to humour the pretensions of the islanders. All the same, even the smaller countries are well aware of the political significance of power in industrial combinations. In the entire European merger movement it plays a major part.

All this implies, not that European industry must remain in a state of national division but that, in many cases, there is a need for industrial companies with roots in several countries; to put it another way, if two major companies in European states see potential profits in combining, the best form of combination may often be the merger, in which a balance of power and ownership is retained (as with Shell and Agfa-Gevaert), rather than the takeover. Fiat and BMC might well one day form a European company, with a balance of ownership and directorships on the board. Bayer and Rhone Poulenc might do the same same. In none of these cases could one expect a merger in which one of the founding companies would dominate.

Especially in sectors where the public buyer is important, and especially in the advanced industries, such as aviation, Continent-wide companies will have to be composed from a judicious balance of national elements. The development of a common market in public buying, from railway equipment to radar, will probably not be possible without conscious encouragement by governments of multi-national companies with a base in several states.

Two conclusions can be drawn from this analysis. First, it can be done. Though there are legal and fiscal obstacles to multinational combinations across frontiers, none is sufficiently awkward to prevent a complete merger of European companies across frontiers today. And at present this applies as much to a combination between a British and Continental company as to one within the Six. Industrial companies which have the will to bridge the difficulties can do so now—with considerable rewards, as the Agfa-Gevaert example shows.

Second, the major obstacles to such combinations have hitherto been psychological and political. Such obstacles, especially in the public sector, may need to be overcome by the combined will of governments and firms. If such determination were forthcoming—if the British and French governments, for instance, were to encourage a merger of BAC and Sud Aviation—or the British and West German governments to encourage Siemens and English Electric to get together, or the French, Dutch, West Germans and British a computer combination between ICL, CII, Philips and Telefunken, there is little doubt that things would move faster than they do today. Of course companies must ultimately choose their partners, and decide whether to invest expensive management time in mergers or other joint activities instead of in their own internal expansion. But if governments were to give vigorous support to European mergers, instead of paying lip-service while in practice they jam on the brakes, it would be a great help.

Companies themselves can do a great deal. One reason why so few have moved is that so few European companies plan properly ahead. Short-term considerations almost always militate against a merger or cooperation with another European firm. It costs management time and money, and obliges all kinds of people to think, and re-examine accepted ways of doing things. It is the long-term considerations which often dictate a combination. If a company looks ahead ten years, sets a target of, say, 400 per cent growth, and then recognizes the reality that it has no hope of achieving this from its own re- sources of men and money, it may then begin to look realistically at what could be achieved in combination with the resources of another European firm. A strategy can then be developed: first, a series of initial steps—buying from each other, marketing certain products together, joint development of a future range; next, perhaps an exchange of shares and certain joint production operations; finally the merger. Or, if the company really plans ahead with its future partner, it may decide that the best thing is simply to plan for a merger straight away.

Action is also needed at the Community level. So far, while there has been much talk of European companies, all the action has been national. The conventional wisdom has been that, once national mergers have taken place, the resulting giants can be stuck together to make a European monster.

The trouble is that the pieces which emerge from national re- shuffles are not necessarily suitable components of a European struc- ture. In computers and aviation, for instance, we have already seen how concentration into large national units could face Europe with a most unpleasant choice between an industry divided up into separ- ate national monopolies or a single European monopoly, challenged only by competition from the United States and American firms. The sooner thinking and action to promote concentration starts at a European level, the sooner mistaken national policies which place obstacles in the way of an optimum European structure can be avoided.

Such a European industrial policy would aim to combine the benefits of scale with competition; dual objectives which are far easier to attain in the continental market of all Europe than in a small European nation-state. In the case of computers, for instance, we suggested the development of at least two major computer groups each with a base in several countries, quite apart from the American companies that operate in Europe.

Strategies of this kind can be promoted, in part, by public buying policies. If common management agencies require groups, or companies, based in several European countries, to tender (as ESRO does) consortia will be encouraged. The governments could do the same; if, in telecommunications, for instance, common standards were set and the decision made that, after a certain date, orders for major systems and exchange equipment would only be placed with companies or groups with a base in more than one country—but that, apart from that condition, competitive conditions would apply, dramatic progress towards a common structure might take place. If this move were backed by the placing of joint development contracts with such European groups or corporations, the move would be accelerated. The wider the number of industries in which such policies are applied, the better the chance of a viable and permanent industrial reorganization. In Europe's present half-baked state, impermanent consortia tend to be formed in response to contract conditions like ESRO's. But consortia, with their built-in inefficiencies, are too often merely machines for sharing out the work. The virtues of enterprise—rapid innovation and its application in the market place—are to be found, not in consortia but in full-blooded companies, run by modern management methods to achieve profits and growth. These will emerge if industry sees that a common European public market is here to stay.

A European Industrial Marriage Bureau

The encouragement of such enterprises requires a more effective European instrument than mere influence from public buying policies. A European corporation or bank should be created similar to the British Industrial Reorganization Corporation, to promote cross-frontier mergers. Such a body could invest, perhaps temporarily, in a new joint company, to enable a merger to take place. It could provide consultancy on the problems of combining, and perhaps place a director, experienced in such problems, on the combined board. It would, in short, act as a marriage broker, and back its mediation with money and management skills. Like the British IRC it would be an independent agency, and it could be set up now. Once there is a Community which includes Britain and other countries it could be brought under the general supervision of the Commission's industrial directorate.

This directorate, created when the three executives were merged, in 1967, will have to work closely with the competition directorate to elaborate a policy on competition and mergers. The Rome Treaty's

Articles 86 and 87 are purely concerned with preventing price rings and other restrictive practices. This makes good sense, but must be tempered by the need to develop companies of optimum scale.[3] In general, Europe must seek to prevent oligopoly from becoming monopoly by encouraging more than one major producer to be active in a particular sector. Transatlantic competition can be a help here too. As trade barriers fall, and the world becomes one market, some kind of Atlantic anti-trust rules or policies will be needed increasingly, to curb the worldwide corporation and enable American and European authorities to give expression to their common need—to prevent domination of their markets by particular large firms.[4] For instance, it would be in the interest of the United States for one or more European computer companies to become strong enough to challenge IBM in the American market itself. And it was probably in the interest of Europeans for IT & T's merger with the American Broadcasting Corporation to be restrained by the anti-trust authorities in America, so that this, the largest American employer in Europe, did not acquire even greater leverage and power.

Size, as we saw in our analysis of the American challenge, is not the sole source of US strength. Does Europe need, deliberately, to find means of promoting dynamic, small enterprises in advanced technology? Does it need, in particular, to develop new sources of risk capital? This is probably more a problem and opportunity for the merchant bankers, and for private capitalists, than for governments, together or apart. The further development of the European capital market and the integration of London with Continental markets could be a help too. Large European companies might well also follow the lead of their American rivals, and set up special subsidiaries with the task of financing innovating small firms. Conceivably there might be room, too, for certain special official measures, comparable to those of the Small Business Administration in the United States. It might be an aim to allocate a proportion of public orders by European governments and common European Agencies to small businesses, as in America, provided they can achieve certain standards of competitiveness. A special department of the European Technology Fund might be given a fund of risk capital to invest in small advanced technology businesses—par-

[3]D. Swann and D. L. McLachlan, *Concentration and Competition—A European Dilemma*, Chatham House and PEP, European Series No. 1, 1967.

[4]See Christopher Layton, *Transatlantic Investment*, Atlantic Institute, Paris, 1967, for a further elaboration.

ticularly perhaps in the neighbourhood of university centres of excellence. Difficulty in obtaining such risk capital is still an awkward obstacle to the dynamic young European firm.

In all these departments of European industrial strategy central agencies must at first work closely with governments; the European Industrial Marriage Bureau would join with, say, IRC or IRI capital in the provision of joint capital to a new European company; it would work with governments when a European merger in a crucial industrial sector is at stake. But the more effective the common policy becomes, the more it will touch the very heart of political and economic power in Europe. Far more than the merely permissive act of creating a common market, common industrial policies mean a pooling of political power. The big amounts of money involved, the pressure to work towards common policies in defence, the implications of common planning for industry and education, all increase the need for political union. Above all the need grows for effective parliamentary control. If international projects slip out of the hands of national parliaments, the European Parliament will have to be strengthened, by giving its science committee the right to investigate the common science and technology agencies, by granting it some real share in Community decisions, and, one day, by direct elections.

CHAPTER 16

EUROPE AND ITS PARTNERS

Far more than the mere creation of the Common Market, a European industrial strategy touches the interests of the outside world. American companies leaping over the Common Market's tariff barriers have been the first beneficiaries of European unity. If Europe sets out, deliberately, to create strong industrial groups capable of competing with America, for the first time American commercial interests could be hit hard.

Just as CERN placed European high energy physics on an equal footing with America, so the formation of strong European companies could do the same. Chemicals, where European companies are already comparable in size to their American rivals, and match them in research, provide a model. In computers, or aviation, the measure of success of European industrial strategies is whether they can do the same, recapturing a major proportion of the European market and then successfully and peacefully 'invading' the United States.

Some myths ought at this point to be exploded. It is hard to imagine, for instance, what is meant by a 'technological Marshall Plan'. In those areas where there is a technological or managerial gap between Europe and America, it is private American industry which, by its skill in applying new technologies, has won a lead. No amount of government activity or talking will persuade powerful industrial companies to share knowhow gratis with their competitors. The one way to strengthen the position of European industry is to create powerful industrial companies whose own research and position in the market enables them to bargain more effectively with their American opposites in the trade in knowhow. This means better prices for licensing, fewer limitations on marketing by the

R

purchasing company and perhaps a more thorough effort by the licensor to make sure the client acquires all the knowhow he needs. After all, if a company is selling knowhow to a major partner, from whom it expects to buy back knowhow in return, it makes an effort to ensure success. Equally, the purchaser of knowhow cannot make the most of complex technology unless he has a powerful research and development effort of his own. A more fruitful and rapid flow of knowhow across the Atlantic to Europe depends on building strong partners at the European end.

European governments might help this process, indirectly, by the development of common buying and development policies in advanced industries. If, in aviation for instance, there were a common market in aircraft materials and parts, an effective 'shadow tariff' of some 10 per cent on the purchase of commercial aircraft, and a joint requirements policy, fostering the development of a series of common aircraft to fulfil common European defence needs, the European Community would be well placed to bargain with the United States to reduce the effect of the Buy American Act, and allow European sales of defence equipment to America. A bout of transatlantic bargaining in public buying should follow the successful Kennedy round. Eventually, there might be a systematic attempt at a division of labour in the Atlantic defence market with some products developed and produced in Europe and others in the United States.

There is a difficulty here. The rigours of the Buy American Act are partly due to America's balance of payments deficit, worsened by the Vietnam war. Many Europeans would reply that the answer is to stop the war. That might certainly produce a dramatic change in America's balance of world payments. But even before the war became a heavy drain, aid and military assistance added a heavy burden to the US balance of payments. If there is still a deficit, the best answer is not more US protectionism but a greater European contribution to capital exports and aid to the developing world.

American Direct Investors

The most delicate decisions for Europe concern, not trade, but policies towards American companies already established in Europe. Should there be limitations, or taxes, on American direct investment? Should there be discrimination between companies owned by Europeans, and those owned by Americans, if both manufacture and operate in Europe? So far in this study we have examined positive responses to the American challenge: help by governments to the formation of large European-owned companies; and better provision of risk capital for small ones. A degree of favouritism in public buying, at European level, may be necessary to serve these ends. But this does not mean excluding or throwing out American companies. It means striking a proper balance, in which Europe keeps control of some competitive countervailing companies in powerful industries, and monopoly or domination by a single firm, European or American, does not arise.

In certain sectors, it is well to recognize the crucial role American companies play and will continue to play, and to ask whether European interests might not be better served by a policy of participation in existing US companies than by one of trying to keep them out.

IT & T, for instance, will probably remain Europe's largest supplier of telephone equipment. Based, as it is, in most of the major European markets, it will probably be the first 'European' company in this field. As the Post Offices struggle slowly towards common requirements and common technical arrangements, IT & T will be a powerful, useful catalyst. It has already begun to persuade the British and French Post Offices, for instance, to buy certain common items of equipment, made in the other country.

Yet, in the case of IT & T, American legislation prevents the company from selling more than 20 per cent of its shares to foreigners—on the grounds that it is a communications company concerned with the basic infrastructure of the United States. Is this perhaps a case for the establishment of a holding company in Europe (IT & T Europe) bringing together the IT & T companies in Europe and permitting Europeans to invest in a larger proportion of the equity, than they may do in IT & T America?

The idea of a European holding company for US companies in Europe is a valuable one. US parent companies rightly say that, as the Common Market takes shape, it is necessary to integrate their European operations. Why not do so via European holding companies—Ford Europe, Monsanto Europe, and so on—in which Europeans have a meaningful share in both ownership and control?

There is a need, indeed, for an advisory Code of Good Conduct—drawn up at European level—to be given to would-be and existing American direct investors as a guide to action. The threat of legislation, if they failed to follow its advice, would be a good incentive. Further suggested measures to guide American direct investment in Western Europe are discussed in *Transatlantic Investment*.[1]

In Chapter 15, we discussed the need for an Atlantic anti-trust policy as a means of disciplining the overmighty worldwide firm. Clearly, there is a common American and European interest in preventing a single firm from dominating any one sector; a joint policy between the European Community and the Department of Justice in the American Administration to prevent takeovers which might have this effect would make sense. Unilaterally, the Department of Justice took a step in this direction early in 1968 when it stopped Gillette's take over of the US subsidiary of Braun, the German razor firm—on the grounds that this would dangerously strengthen Gillette's already dominant position in the shaving market.

An agreement between the OECD countries, or bilaterally between an enlarged European Community and America, on rules to outlaw discriminatory pricing, certain kinds of loss-leading, price agreements and market-sharing, would also be helpful. In a genuinely competitive market, the benefits of American investment will be harvested. In a market made rigid by cartels and other restrictive practices, the giant firm has a standing invitation to use its financial resources and monopoly profits to expand by acquisition; the small up and coming firm has no comparable weapons.

As a European science and technology policy emerges, major joint research endeavours with the United States should be easier. Once a single European Space Authority exists, with a proper programme, why not take up the American proposal for a joint probe of the planet Jupiter? Why not try to divide the supersonic transport market rationally between European medium-range and smaller aircraft and American long-range machines? In oceanography, once a coherent European programme exists, a joint programme with America and Russia might seek to explore the deepest ocean depths. In all this a measure of equality is a precondition of partnership.

Eastward Horizon

A European science and technology policy must seek, increasingly, to involve Russia and the countries of Eastern Europe.

Here a distinction should be made. East European countries harbour towards Russia many of the anxieties which West Europeans sense towards the United States. Both feel overshadowed by a giant partner. The smaller East European countries too are beginning to

[1]C. Layton, *Transatlantic Investment*, Atlantic Institute. See Chapter VII, Partnership in the International Corporation and Chapter IV, Towards Fair Competition.

sense that one day they, too, might form part of a wider united Europe. Certainly Yugoslavia, which was a member of CERN until the financial burden became too much, is keen to participate in European scientific cooperation.

East European countries should therefore, where possible, be brought into Western Europe's specialized scientific and technological agencies, perhaps, if the lawyers want a formal difference, as associates.

There is room, too, for specific deals providing technical assistance to particular countries. In the nuclear field, for instance, Eastern Europe will need power stations. Common research programmes and construction of power reactors would pave the way for exports and wider industrial collaboration.

Western Europe's relationship with Russia must be different in character. In CERN, while Yugoslavia was a member, Russia is a major partner, on a basis of equality with CERN as a whole. While the small states of Eastern Europe should be seen as prospective future participants in a Europe Technological Community, Russia should be seen as a partner for the Community, comparable in potential to the United States. In all this the Scientific Directorate of OECD could play a useful mediating role.

Facing the Future

These immediate industrial needs are, however, overshadowed by the huge future problems which scientists and technologists must tackle at world level, and which require partnership between the three industrial giants, Europe, America and Russia. Satellites, computers and other new techniques are beginning to permit systematic control of weather. Already some 40 companies are working on this in the United States. But the weather in northern Siberia or Africa will not be changed without affecting temperate Europe, at present the favoured garden of the world.

One day the explorations and burgeoning techniques of the oceanographers might permit the slow heating of the sea from nuclear power stations sunk beneath the ocean, bringing a gigantic multiplication of ocean life and food from the sea. Or, on the other hand, continuing uncalculated exploitation of the sea could exterminate key species, on which the fishermen rely. The blue whale may soon follow the way of the dinosaur.

Dangers indeed already threaten the balance of plant life, through Man's ruthless exploitation of his environment. Strong and germ resistant strains of crops are bred from the crossing of different strains. The tougher ones come from less developed, wild parts of the world, where modern agriculture has not yet been introduced. As the tractors, and the agricultural advisors with their sophisticated crops, conquer these less developed regions, the wild seed beds of our crops of the future disappear.

Then again, there is the silent Spring, the extermination of species by pesticides, causing lasting damage to both humans and animals, and stimulating the insect world to respond by evolving new and tougher species immune to man's attack.

As man burns increasing quantities of energy, dumping carbon dioxide into the atmosphere, the heat balance of the world's atmosphere is slowly being changed; some scientists believe that this could raise temperatures of our atmosphere by some 3 to 4 degrees in the next 50 years. That would be sufficient to start melting the Arctic ice cap. Over a period of anywhere between 400 and 4,000 years the sea level of the oceans could be raised 400 feet, flooding most of the world's inhabitable land and cities.

In the underdeveloped world, a frightening prospect of starvation, misery and political upheaval stretches for decades ahead. The world's population, which has taken 50,000 years to reach its present size, will double in the next 30 years. Thus the rich continents of the northern hemisphere have the task, not only of helping to try to contain explosive population, and of meeting starvation with food from the sea and agriculture, but, more systematically than hitherto, of applying modern technology to the needs of the underdeveloped world. An intermediate technology means, not palming off old western machines, but a systematic effort to develop products and processes suited to the immediate needs of developing countries and capable of being taught to them fast. One enterprising western company has, for instance, developed an extremely simple plant for producing modern radios. It sells a complete plant as well as instructions and trains the customer.

Man's technology has not only given him the power to exterminate all life on earth in a few hours. It has also given him the power to destroy or make anew the environment he lives in, or, one day, to emigrate to other planets. A constructive partnership of the powers —Russia, America, Europe, Japan—which already command advanced science and technology, is essential to confront these needs. Such a partnership is not possible while Europe remains a divided, weak protectorate.

CHAPTER 17

CONCLUSION: MORALS FOR BRITAIN

In autumn 1966 the British Prime Minister proposed the creation of a European Technological Community. The challenge America's technology poses to European industry made this a political trump card in Britain's attempt to join the Common Market. Yet in the 18 months that followed this proposal little was done to give it substance. The Six moved slowly towards a common science policy. But Britain remains outside the Common Market. And European cooperation in science and technology remains coloured by 'adhocery' and nationalism.

In November 1967 the Prime Minister substantiated his suggestion. He declared that the British Government was prepared to harmonize company and patent laws with Europe, to back the formation of European companies, and to initiate, together with industry, discussions in key sectors, like atomic energy and computers. He also proposed a European Institute of Technology, which was perhaps meant to combine the qualities of a Think Tank with those of the Industrial Marriage Bureau and Technology Fund. Speaking to the Council of Europe, Lord Chalfont, Britain's chief Common Market negotiator, also talked of common development work in the fields of surface transport, computers and atomic energy. Just what, asked some of our Continental neighbours, did these proposals mean?

For while it is clear enough, in Western Europe, that Britain has a technological contribution to bring to the European Community, by the middle of 1968 it was still not clear just how it would be brought. Europeans have recognized that in nuclear power, computers and aviation, Britain has a large capability, and that her research and development expenditure is two thirds that of the Common Market as a whole. But if Britain were merely to join the Common Market, the 'contribution' Britain brings in R & D might merely be felt in the form of vigorous British exports—a prospect which might well fill many Continentals with alarm. If there is to be a real common interest in British participation in the European Community the practical ways in which European science and technology, including British, can be pooled for the good of all must be spelt out clearly, and initiatives taken to get the process moving.

In earlier chapters of this book we set out the following proposals:

1 Push ahead with the construction of a giant 300 GEV accelerator, under CERN, so that European high energy physicists can remain in the front rank—on a par with the United States.

2 Invest Britain's nuclear knowhow in fast-breeder and other reactors in the creation of European companies. Shares in the companies would be based on the original investment by contributors, measured in terms of either capital or knowhow.

3 Create a mixed company to run joint European nuclear fuel enrichment facilities at Capenhurst and Pierrelatte, for peaceful purposes, with finance from several countries and a sharing of technology.

4 Move on from the present ad hoc series of bilateral or trilateral aircraft projects to develop a long-term strategy. Hold the conference of aviation ministers suggested in the Plowden Report and set up a small, permanent aviation planning group to harmonize military requirements, conceive joint development programmes, pool the efforts of national research laboratories and foster an industrial strategy. Such a strategy means encouraging the formation of a number of European companies, or divisions of a European aviation industry (Sud Aviation and BAC Weybridge; Dassault and Wharton; Sud helicopter and Westlands); fostering a division of labour in avionics to reduce duplication when new equipment is financed by government development funds; working on bread and butter problems like industrial standards and common contract procedures.

5 In space a major effort must be made to overcome the divisions between the different European organizations and rationalize their work. ESRO and ELDO must be merged into a common European Space Authority. A long-term space programme must be drawn up which takes into consideration the probable development costs of both launchers and satellites, for particular ob-

jectives, such as direct transmission satellites. An effort must be made to squeeze and rationalize national space programmes, so that the sums Europe does spend on space are devoted to the chosen goals. If Europe decides to develop particular types of communications satellites—say a regional television system, or later a direct broadcasting system—these should be managed by a new joint company, backed by private and public capital, which would take over negotiations in the world communications body—Intelsat.

Europe also needs a much wider policy to rationalize and develop its communications system. The Post Offices must be made to work together to develop common standards and common requirements for equipment, notably in such expensive fields as electronic telephone exchanges. There must be a European communications policy.

6 In the computer industry the need is to combine the splintered efforts of European countries and create one or more powerful European companies, with a strong position in the major European markets and the ability to compete effectively in the United States. Two possible groupings could be envisaged: (a) a commercial data-processing company based on European technology and perhaps grouping the British ICL, the French CII, a Philips element and perhaps Telefunken, in other words a European competitor to IBM; (b) a group centred round Siemens which may retain its close link with RCA, and would be stronger in process-control.

Governments should encourage this process of industrial integration by working out joint requirements in computer systems, agreeing on a common policy for the standardization of data coding and high-level languages, and using the financial help they give to development to promote European companies, instead of purely national ones. This information systems policy will be intimately linked with communications policy.

7 The channel tunnel must go ahead. The time has also come for a much wider joint planning of Europe's transport system. Economic, social and technical assessments are needed of the existing and potential major transport corridors in Europe, in order to develop long-term plans which place the development of new transport systems—whether by air, or by new fast ground routes—in the wider context of the planning of industrial concentration and regional development in Europe. Com-

mon programmes for the joint development of new types of ground transportation are also needed.

8 A European oceanography programme, guided by a common agency, should be initiated, to cover four main areas: basic research, exploration of Europe's continental shelf, exploitation of food from the sea and minerals, and equipment.

9 The European Molecular Biology Organization should be given financial backing by governments. One or more major centres of excellence should be developed together with a systematic programme of joint research, and fellowships for research workers moving from country to country.

10 A European Science Foundation should be created, and given the general tasks of drawing up an inventory of European scientific research and the resources available, organizing and financing centres of excellence, and joint programmes of research linking several centres (or *actions concertées*), fostering mobility of research workers, and promoting new joint research efforts in areas where there are gaps.

11 To accelerate mobility of undergraduates, European governments ought to take a political decision that all university degrees should be dependent on European students spending a year in another European country.

12 The management agencies of various kinds described under proposals 1 to 10 above, ought each to be run on modern managerial principles under a single director. They should be given long-term (say, five-year) rolling budgets and clear-cut goals, and encouraged to place contracts on a competitive basis. They ought to be brought, as soon as possible, under the guidance of a European science and technology policy, one of whose main tasks would be to decide scientific and technological priorities for Europe. The appropriate seat for such policy decisions once Britain and others are in an enlarged European Community, would be the council of this Community. The Ministers of Science and Technology would meet, backed up by Scientific and Industrial Directorates of the Commission and advised by a European Science Advisory Council.

13 In addition to the Agencies already described, the Commission and Council should have two other agencies under their guidance: a Technology Fund, which would finance joint development programmes outside the special fields already described,

and an Industrial Marriage Bureau, which would act as a catalyst of industrial mergers across frontiers.

14 To accelerate the development of European companies which
can match the giants in the United States, enlargement of the
Common Market, and the development of a complete economic
union, including common company and patent laws, harmonized taxes, and common standards, are of course urgent. Above
all, a common market in public buying must be developed too.

'Buy national' policies, whether overt or through covert administrative preferences, are the biggest single obstacle to the
formation of competitive European companies, especially in
the advanced industries. A 'buy European' policy, based on
genuinely competitive tendering, and designed to promote the
emergence of multinational industrial groups, is essential. It
should be backed up by the placing of jointly organized development contracts.

15 Large and strong European companies will be able to bargain
more effectively with American companies for knowhow; a Buy
European Act makes possible a transatlantic bargain to
diminish the effect of the Buy American Act. An effective European anti-trust policy must lead on to Atlantic anti-trust
measures too. Technological and scientific cooperation with
the United States and with Eastern Europe and the Soviet
Union will be more fruitful once Europe is effectively pursuing
its own scientific and technological goals.

The achievement of this Grand Design for European science and
technology plainly depends, in some measure, on whole-hearted
British participation in the European communities. It is tempting
for some Britons to take the view that British knowhow and 'secrets'
should be used as a bargaining counter for getting into the European
Economic Community and should not be shared until this happens.
But technology and American competition cannot wait for such
diplomatic niceties. Industry simply does not work in this way.
The time to prepare for a European computer industry is now,
before a new generation of computers comes to life in 1972-73. A
rational European fast-breeder reactor programme has to be developed before the beginning of 1969. The decision on the 300 GEV
accelerator cannot be indefinitely postponed, for major members
(like France) are under pressure to spend the money on national
projects instead. Britain's technological cards can be played
effectively now, before the Community evolves its own science and

technology policy, and before a new Treaty takes shape. Hold the card too long, and a new game may have started, with different trumps.

Instead of seeking to make the withholding of an ill-defined technological 'contribution' a form of threat, to extract membership, there is a powerful case for Britain pushing integration, in science and technology, with the Continent as fast as possible now. The creation of strong European companies across the frontiers, of common programmes in computers, nuclear power and the rest, could set up such pressures for more far-reaching integration that British membership of the Common Market could well become unavoidable within five years. The Common Market itself is only on the threshold of industrial integration. If Britain deliberately joins in the process from the start, exclusion from the customs union must become an anachronism.

If such a process is to gather speed, the British Government has a number of clear-cut decisions to make, both about specific industrial or research sectors and about the general character of integration in technology it is prepared to accept. Is the British Government prepared to encourage, say, two major British nuclear enterprises, in which the AEA might have shares, really to merge with European companies to form common enterprises? Is it prepared to share the technology of the Capenhurst enrichment plant? Will it, in computers, give priority to the creation of powerful European companies or does it regard European 'cooperation' as a marginal addition to the policy of national concentration it has pursued so far? Will it encourage the formation of European companies in aviation? Will it back EMBO? When this book went to press no positive action had been taken on any of these questions, and in space and over CERN's 300 GEV machine the British Government had spoken a decisive 'no'. More than words is needed if British talk about European technology is to be taken seriously.

It may seem hard to put such questions—as the French often do—when in aviation British ministers have gone very far indeed in their backing for particular joint projects. The tragedy of the collapse of the variable geometry aircraft project between Britain and France was indeed that, had it succeeded, it would have committed both the British and French governments to integrate both strategy and military technology in the 1970s. In the military field it would have provided just the sort of test of commitment which the French often demand. The decisions have still to be taken in the other sectors where there is in fact a much better prospect of a commercial return from joint European endeavour. And in the end the British Government must decide how far it is prepared to accept the political commitment which joint funding and joint strategies for science and technology imply.

Given a little encouragement a British government of any political party might go a long way. But France, on its side, also has a decision to take if it wants to help build Europe. Plainly a Community policy concerning the very sources of power in the modern world flatly contradicts the idea of a Europe of States. In practice France has, so far, tried to combine the pursuit of national power and European unity by seeking to make French efforts the hub of European ones. France has Europe's largest space programme, so it leads in communications satellites. France offers CERN's 'giant machine' or EMBO a site—advancing the cause of European science and France as well. In a field such as oceanography the French cooperate bilaterally with Russia, America and any other partners they can find. In colour television they use Russia as a lever on the West. But the time comes when the attempt to play power politics with technology becomes incompatible with the idea of a Community strategy. Certainly it is not possible for each of the three major West European countries to be top dog at the same time. During their years of tutelage and recovery, the West Germans were generally ready to accept French or American leadership in their various partnership arrangements. The era when West Germany could be treated as a strong but meek retainer is coming to an end.

France, in other words, like Britain and West Germany, has to come to terms with the idea of a partnership of equals—not necessarily, of course, in every separate technology project, but in the overall balance of a European science and technology policy. Time is short. Though the desire for European integration still has far deeper roots in West Germany than in the two old European nation states, years of tutelage in nationalism from France and Britain have inevitably fostered a revival of German national feeling too. In high energy physics and nuclear power, for instance, there are Germans who, encouraged by their country's reviving power, are sorely tempted to add to the duplicated uses of European resources by going it alone. They will turn to Europe only if their partners show a real will.

How much can the principle of equality be applied to the other West European countries? Realities dictate that once the three

larger countries agree on a common project or policy, this will decide the policy for Europe. Initially, the large states must make the
running in matters like common policies on computers, nuclear
power and aviation. But such a system has its dangers, in frustration
and restiveness of the smaller countries which, rightly, will not be
content with a satellite role. The kind of balance struck in the European Communities (where votes are weighted in favour of the larger
countries) or in CERN (where there is straight majority voting, but
where the lead of the major powers tends to be followed) is needed
as Europe seeks jointly to become a new technological great power.

Can the ambitious programme summarized in this chapter be
achieved without a far deeper change in European political consciousness and will? Even in the present dispirited condition of the
European Communities, industry can act to cross frontiers; new
agencies (like EMBO) can be set up and particular schemes carried
out. But it is plain that a state of affairs in which France systematically sabotages Euratom and British membership of the Communities; in which Britain repeatedly sends a torpedo into the European
space organizations; and no government is prepared to take the
political step implied by a Buy European Act is quite irreconcilable
with the development of a full-blooded European science and technology policy and advanced technology industries of continental
scale. If the European states are really to rationalize the use of their
resources, spend large sums of money jointly, choose priorities together, merge their defence industries under a single defence policy,
create common companies which no longer have roots in any one
country, they must recognize the implication—the development of
strong common political institutions.

To Jean-Jacques Servain Schreiber, the only effective way to meet
the challenge of America is to build a United States of Europe. This
may seem Utopian today. But even in the long period before the
vision is realized, it is clear that Europe cannot make efficient use
of its resources in science and advanced technology unless it develops Community-style institutions to guide science and technology
policies and manage industrial strategies for the whole of developed
Western Europe.

The American challenge has stirred the dazed political consciousness of Europe, or at least of European industry. But that new
awareness has still to be translated into political facts.

STATISTICAL APPENDIX

TABLE 1

US DIRECT INVESTMENT ABROAD ($ mn.)

	1950	1957	1961	1962	1963	1964	1965*
Total	11,788	25,394	34,667	37,225	40,686	44,386	49,217
Canada............	3,579	8,769	11,602	12,133	13,044	13,796	15,172
Latin America........	4,445	7,434	8,236	8,424	8,662	8,894	9,371
Europe............	1,733	4,151	7,742	8,930	10,340	12,109	13,894
of which:							
Common Market	637	1,680	3,104	3,722	4,490	5,426	6,254
Belgium-Luxembourg	69	192	262	286	356	455	585
France	217	464	860	1,030	1,240	1,446	1,584
West Germany	204	581	1,182	1,476	1,780	2,082	2,417
Italy	63	252	491	554	668	850	972
Netherlands........	84	191	309	376	446	593	698
Other Europe	1,096	2,471	4,638	5,208	5,850	6,683	7,639
United Kingdom	847	1,974	3,554	3,824	4,172	4,547	5,119
Switzerland	25	69	388	553	672	948	1,116

*Preliminary figures.
Source: US Department of Commerce.

TABLE 2a

THE BRAIN DRAIN

(Proportion of professional, technical and kindred workers migrating to the United States)

Migrants from	(1) Total migrants FY 1966*	(2) Professional, technical and kindred	(3) Col. (2) as % of Col. (1)
Europe	125,023	12,059	10
North America	127,340	8,633	7
Asia	39,878	5,931	15
South America	25,836	2,527	10
Africa	3,137	598	19
Oceania	1,820	291	16
Total	323,034	30,039	9

TABLE 2b

(Qualified scientists and engineers as a proportion of professional, technical and kindred migrants to the United States)

Total	(1) Total Migrants 323,034	(2) Professional, technical and kindred 30,039	(3) Col. (2) as % of Col. (1)
of which:			
Natural scientists and technologists ..		10,774	36
Medical and related fields		7,722	26
Teachers		4,477	15
Other		7,066	24

*FY = Fiscal Year, 1 July 1966–30 June 1967.

Source: Tables 2a & b; *Some Facts and Figures on the Migration of Talents and Skills*, Bureau of Educational and Cultural Affairs, US Department of State, 1967.

TABLE 3

THE FLOW OF KNOWLEDGE

Balance of payments in licensing and knowhow ($ mn.)

West Germany	Receipts	Expenditure	Balance
1963	54	159	−105
1964	66	174	−108
1965	80	195	−115
1966	77	201	−124
Britain			
1964	91	95	−4
1965	110	108	+2

By industry	France 1963 Balance	West Germany 1963 Balance	Britain 1964 Balance
Chemicals	−9	−15	+15
Electrical engineering	−22	−18	−4
Mechanical engineering	−7	..	−21
Vehicles	−2	..	..

	Balance with USA 1963		
Germany	Receipts	Payments	Balance
Chemicals	19·3	33·8	−14·5
Electrical machinery	10·7	29·0	−18·3
Steel, machinery, vehicles	2·5	16·2	−14·1

Source: Board of Trade Journal, December 1966 and July 1967; Deutsche Bundesbank Report, February 1967.

.. Not available.

TABLE 4

SPENDING ON RESEARCH AND DEVELOPMENT

(Source of finance in ten countries)

Country	Year	GNERD [a] $ mn.	Government %	Business enterprise %	Private Non-profit %	Higher education %	Abroad %
France	1963	1,299	64	33	n	—	3
West Germany	1964	1,436	41	57	1	—	3
Italy	1963	291	33	62	1	4	1
Belgium	1963	137	24	71	} 1		4
Netherlands	1964	330	40	54	3	—	3
Total EEC [b]		3,493					
United Kingdom	1964-65 [d]	2,160	54	42	1	n	3
Sweden	1964	257	48	49	1	1	1
Total EEC, UK and Sweden		5,910					
Switzerland	1963 & 1964	150	..	..	..	..	..
Other W. Europe [e]		111	59	37	1	—	3
Total W. Europe		6,171					
Japan	1963	892 [c]	28	65	3	4	..
United States	1963-64 [d]	21,075	64	32	1	1	2

Source: The Overall Level and Structure of R & D Efforts in OECD Member Countries. OECD Paris, 1967.

[a] GNERD — Gross National Expenditure on Research and Development.

[b] Excluding Luxembourg which is very small.

[c] Official exchange rate gives a figure for Japan that is very low when set against manpower comparisons (one quarter of QSE number employed by US).

[d] Financial years.

[e] Norway, Austria, Greece, Spain, Ireland.

n – Negligible.

.. Not available.

TABLE 5

SPENDING ON RESEARCH AND DEVELOPMENT

(Main goals in nine countries)

Country	Year	Defence, atomic, space		Other industrial goals		Other areas	
		($ mn.)	(% of R & D)	($ mn.)	(% of R & D)	($ mn.)	(% of R & D)
France	1963	584	45	403	31	312	24
West Germany.........	1964	244	17	790	55	388	27
Italy	1963	61	21	140	48	90	31
Belgium	1963	5	4	102	74	30	22
Netherlands	1964	17	5	198	60	116	35
United Kingdom	1964–65	864	40	950	44	346	16
Sweden.........	1964	87	34	118	46	52	20
Total 7 European countries		1,862	31	2,701	46	1,334	23
Japan	1963	27	3	517	58	348	39
United States.........	1963–64	13,280	63	5,486	26	2,319	11

Source: CSP. ISY R & D Preliminary Analysis. OECD Paris, March 1967, unpublished, Table III & OECD published figures for ISYRD.
Notes as for Table 4.

TABLE 6

DISTRIBUTION OF INDUSTRIAL R & D[b] BY INDUSTRY IN WHICH PERFORMED[a] ($mn.)

Industry	United States			United Kingdom			France		West Germany	
	1959	1962	1964	1959	1962	1964	1962	1964	1963	1964
GROUP A										
Aircraft and missiles	3,028	4,520	5,100	308	396	388	147	164	129	131
Vehicles	866	921	1,059	33	34	..	14	34		
Machinery	946	1,021	1,051	70	82	i12	34	32		
GROUP B										
Electronics	1,161	2,690	1,837	84	243	216	137	155	228	249
Electrical equipment	1,079	486	1,115	71		74		35		
Instruments	353		483	21	26	29	..	..		
GROUP C										
Chemicals	1,221	1,556	1,162	109	130	164	89	73	222	285
Drugs			238			28		25		
Petrol refining and products			410					18		
GROUP D										
Ferrous metals	75	249	113	9	32	33	17	8	45	68
Metal products	124		152	10		18		21		
Non ferrous metals	64	76	78	10	13	13	..	8c	7	14c
Rubber	111	137	159	9	13	14				
GROUP E										
Transport							48	3	..	..
Energy	..	672	..	..	49	38		68	4	5
Construction								1		
Utilities		237	318		18	68	13	14	14	16
Services										
Other non manufactures										
Total	9,028	12,565	13,275	734	1,036	1,195	499	659	649	768

Prop. of GNERD.

(a) Since this table includes R & D work done in industry only, some expenditure (e.g. on aeroplane and electronics work performed in government laboratories) do not appear.
(b) Includes public corporations and research associations performing industrial research.
(c) Including some plastics.

Sources:
National Institute Economic Review, May 1962, NISER, London, 1962. C. Freeman and A. Young, *The Research and Development Effort in Europe, North America and the Soviet Union,* OECD, Paris 1965.
United States: *Data on Science Resources No. 10,* NSF, Washington, December, 1966.
Britain: Ministry of Technology, *Statistics of Science and Technology,* London, 1967.
France: *Recherche et développement dans l'industrie française 1964,* Paris, 1966.
Germany: *Wissenschaftsausgaben der Wirtschaft,* 1964.
.. Not available.

TABLE 7

HOW TRADE FOLLOWS RESEARCH AND DEVELOPMENT

*A comparison of competitive trade performance in
18 US industries with research and development*

Industry	US Exports as % of exports by ten leading industrial countries 1962	Scientists and engineers in R and D as % of employment January, 1961
Aircraft	59·52	7·71
Office machinery	35·00	5·09
Drugs	33·09	6·10
Other machinery	32·27	1·39
Instruments	27·98	4·58
Chemicals, except drugs	27·32	3·63
Electrical equipment	26·75	4·40
Rubber	23·30	2·95
Motor vehicles	22·62	1·14
Petroleum refining	20·59	2·02
Fabricated metal products	19·62	0·51
Nonferrous metals	18·06	0·69
Paper and allied products	15·79	0·47
Stone, clay, glass products	15·22	0·60
Other transport equipment	13·71	0·46
Lumber and wood products	11·68	0·08
Textile mill products	10·92	0·29
Primary ferrous metals	9·14	0·43

Source: D. Keesing, *The Impact of Research and Development on United States Trade*, International Economics Workshop, Columbia University, February 1966.

TABLE 8

THE EDUCATION GAP

(Percentage of age group entering full-time higher education)

Country	1958–59 British degree level	1958–59 All levels of higher education	expected 1968–69 British degree level	expected 1968–69 All levels of higher education
United States	20	30	40	55
Sweden*	10	12	15	19
France*	7	9	15	18
USSR	5	5	30	30
United Kingdom	5	8	8	16
West Germany	4	7	11	16
Netherlands	3	6	7	16

Source: Report on Higher Education (Robbins Report), Cmnd. 2154, HMSO, London, 1963.

*Table No. 1 on p. 4 of the *OECD Observer*, No. 33, Paris, April 1968, The Impact of Science and Technology on Social and Economic Development, suggests that the Swedish and French figures for British degree equivalents and all levels are overestimated in the Robbins Report. The OECD figures for 1964 give percentages about the same as the United Kingdom and West Germany.

TABLE 9

USA: GROWTH OF FEDERAL SPENDING ON RESEARCH AND DEVELOPMENT ($ mn.)

	1960-61	1964-65	1966-67	1967-68*	1968-69*
General scientific research	588	1,324	1,620	1,967	2,096
Atomic physics and nuclear energy (AEC expenditure)	986	1,505	1,462	1,486	1,599
Space research (NASA expenditure)	401	4,171	5,933	5,600	5,300
Defence research	5,654	7,517	6,735	7,168	7,682
Other objectives	110	175	266	299	379
Total	7,739	14,692	16,014	16,520	17,056

Note: Totals do not check due to rounding.
*Estimates.
Sources: NSF Annual Report, Federal Funds for Research Development and other Scientific Activities, 1967. GPO Washington, 1966. Special Analyses of the Budget, 1968. GPO Washington, 1967.

TABLE 10

UNITED KINGDOM: GROWTH OF GOVERNMENT SPENDING ON RESEARCH AND DEVELOPMENT ($ mn.)

	1961-62	1962-63	1963-64	1964-65[a]	1965-66[b]	1966-67[b]
General scientific research	172	204	234	283	367	447
Atomic physics and nuclear energy	151	153	148	149	160	170
Space research	..	..	35	30	52	66
Defence research	687	720	749	714	710	700
Research in universities	60	75	87	105	123	137
Total	1,070	1,152	1,253	1,281	1,312	1,520

[a]Provisional.
[b]Forecast.
Source: Report on Science Policy. Cmnd. 3007. HMSO London, May 1966.
..Not available.

TABLE 11

FRANCE: GROWTH OF GOVERNMENT SPENDING ON RESEARCH AND DEVELOPMENT ($ mn.)

	1959	1960	1961	1962	1963
General scientific research	80	107	124	191	238
Atomic Energy Commission	65	65	76	215	255
Space research	—	—	3	17	30
Defence research	174	226	295	304	291
Other bodies	27	33	36	81	102
Total	346	431	534	808	916

Source: Reviews of National Science Policy, France. OECD, Paris, 1966.

— Nil.

TABLE 12

WEST GERMANY: GROWTH OF FEDERAL SPENDING ON RESEARCH & DEVELOPMENT ($mn.)

	1962	1963	1964	1965	1966	1967 forecast
General scientific research	93	95	102	116	162	208
Atomic physics and nuclear technology	78	84	106	114	148	180
Space research	3	13	35	35	43	70
Defence research	102	137	162	175	189	251
Research in universities	25	33	34	37	40	44
Total	301	362	439	477	582	753

Source: Bundesbericht Forschung, 1967. Budesminister für Wissenschaftliche Forschung, Bonn, 1967.

TABLE 13

HIGH ENERGY PHYSICS: SPENDING ON RESEARCH AND DEVELOPMENT IN EIGHT COUNTRIES IN 1966 ($ mn.)

	France	West Germany	Italy	Belgium	Netherlands	EEC	United Kingdom	Sweden	Seven countries	All members of CERN	USA*
Total budget for HEP	38·3	23·2	13·8	1·9	2·3	79·5	36·5	2·1	118·1	125	146
Total contribution to CERN	7·7	9·3	4·5	1·4	1·6	24·5	8·8	1·6	34·9	40	..
CERN contribution as a proportion of total budget %	20	40	33	75	70	31	24	76	30	32	..

Sources: ECFA Report for 1967 (CERN 700 ; CERN/ECFA 67/13/Rev. 2), Table VIII. 89th Congress Subcommittee on Research Development and Radiation. Hearings of the Joint Committees on Atomic Energy (First Session. High Energy Physics Research), Appendix 23.

*1965–66 Fiscal year budget. AEC expenditures.

..Not available

TABLE 14

HIGH ENERGY PHYSICS: PROJECTED SPENDING ON BUILDING AND OPERATING LARGE ACCELERATORS ($ mn.)

	Total	1967	1968	1969	1970	1971	1972	1973	1974	1975	1976	1977	1978	1979	1980	1981
The 200 Bev machine (United States)																
Construction	280	10	30	50	73	75	30	12								
Operating		3	4	5	6	15	23	35	45	51	58	60	62	64	64	64
The 300 Gev machine (CERN)																
Construction	316	1	2	5	20	51	55	53	51	41	36					
Operating					1	4	6	9	17	27	32	69	69	77	85	93
The 800 Bev machine (United States + CERN?)																
Construction	800			1	1	5	35	70	95	115	125	130	125	70	27	
Operating		2	2	3	3	4	5	5	6	8	14	25	40	65	85	95
World Totals																
Construction	1,396	11	32	56	94	131	120	135	146	156	161	130	125	70	27	
Operating		5	6	8	11	23	34	49	68	86	104	154	171	206	234	252
Construction *plus* operating		16	38	64	105	154	154	184	214	242	265	284	296	276	261	252
The 70 Gev machine (Russia)																
Construction	100	15	10													
Operating		8	12	20	22	25	30									

Sources: ECFA Report for 1967 (CERN 700 : CERN/ECFA 67/13/Rev. 2), Table IX. 89th Congress Subcommittee on Research Development and Radiation. Hearings of Joint Committee on Atomic Energy (First Session, High Energy Physics Research), Appendix 25, Table I. PEP Estimates.

TABLE 15

SPENDING ON NUCLEAR ENERGY AS A SOURCE OF ELECTRIC POWER ($ mn.)

	Year	France	West Germany	Italy	Belgium	Nether-lands	EEC	Euratom Budgets	United Kingdom[b]	USA
National civil nuclear R & D	1962	266	91	37	11	10	415		134	535[c]
	1964	414	133	30	13	17	607		132	687[c]
	1966	438	179	45	14	19	725		140	707[c]
Contributions to international nuclear research	1962	25	25	19	7	6	82	71	..	..
	1964	30	37	28	13	8	116	94	..	..
	1966	47[a]	49[a]	34[a]	15[a]	10[a]	155	126	37(ENEA)	..
Nuclear power stations	1962	45	9	50	8	..	112		203	..
	1964	60	17	14	12	..	93		238	..
	1966									
Military nuclear expenditure	1962	154	—	..	—	—	154		..	835
	1964	428	—	..	—	—	428		61	995
	1966								78	890
Total expenditures on nuclear technology	1962	490	125	106	26	16	763		..	2,696[d]
	1964	932	187	72	38	25	1,254		..	2,739[d]
	1966									2,440[d]
Contributions to international nuclear research as a percentage of total expenditures	1962	5	20	18	27	38	11		..	..
	1964	3	20	39	34	32	9		..	..
	1966	..	..	..	..	..	..		..	..

a Extrapolated from 1966 total Euratom budget and national contributions to 1964 budget. (Euratom contribution.)
b Budgetary years April–April.
c Assume one third of reactor development is for military operation.
d AEC net cost of operations.

Source: Reports of UKAEA; Data on Science Resources, No. 10, NSF EEC Commission Washington.
.. Not available.
— Nil.

TABLE 16

MAIN AIRCRAFT COMPANIES IN EUROPE IN 1966

(Classified by size of employment)

Company		Approximate turnover ($ mn.)	Employment
Hawker Siddeley	UK	550–600	40,000–50,000
British Aircraft Corporation ..	UK	400–450 ⎫	
Rolls Royce[a]	UK	350–400 ⎬	30,000–40,000 each
Bristol Siddeley	UK	250–300 ⎭	
Sud Aviation	F	250–300	20,000–30,000
(none)			15,000–20,000
SAAB	S	150–200 ⎫	
SNECMA	FF	150–200	
Nord Aviation	F	150–200 ⎬	10,000–15,000 each
Fiat	I	75–100	
VFW	G	75–100 ⎭	
Westland	UK	75–100 ⎫	
Short Bros.................	UK	75–100	
Dassault[b]	F	150–200 ⎬	5,000–10,000 each
HFB	G	30– 40	
Fokker	N	75–100 ⎭	
Dornier	G	30– 40	
Bölkow	G	30– 40	
Breguet[b]	F	50– 60	
Handley Page	UK	30– 40	
Messerschmidt	G	20– 30	
Potez	F	20– 30 ⎱	2,000– 5,000 each
Fabrique Nationale	B	20– 30 ⎰	
MAN	G	30– 40	
AFU/FFA	SWI	30– 40	
Turbomeca	F	30– 40	
Hispano Suiza	F	30– 40	
Svenska Flygmotor	S	30– 40	
Agusta	I	20– 30	
SABCA	B	under 20	
Piaggio	I	under 20	1,000– 2,000 each
Aermacchi	I	under 20	
Klöckner Humboldt Deutz....	G	under 20	

UK = Britain	G = Germany	I = Italy
F = France	S = Sweden	SWI = Switzerland
B = Belgium	N = Netherlands	

Four American Companies

Boeing (aircraft)	2,000–2,500	100,000
Lockheed (aircraft and missiles)	1,000–1,500	60,000
North American (aircraft and missiles) ..	300– 500	20,000
General Dynamics	600– 800	35,000

Note: Where the company is mainly engaged in aircraft manufacture, the total company employment is used. Where there are substantial other activities the company is classified by the size of the aircraft division.

[a]Rolls Royce and Bristol Siddeley have since merged.

[b]Dassault and Breguet have since merged.

Source: PEP Estimates.

TABLE 17

NATIONAL SPACE PROGRAMMES AND INTERNATIONAL CO-OPERATION, 1966 ($ mn.)

	France	West Germany	Italy	Belgium	Netherlands	EEC Total	UK	Denmark	Spain	Sweden	Switzerland	United States	European Totals
ELDO programme	20·7	19·1	8·5	2·5	2·3	53·1	33·6	—	—	—	—	—	86·7
ESRO programme	7·0	8·2	4·0	1·6	1·5	22·3	9·1	0·8	1·0	1·9	1·3	—	36·4
INTELSAT programme	1·7	1·7	·6	·3	·3	4·6	2·3	0·1	0·3	0·2	0·5	16·5	8·3
Total international programmes	29·4	29·0	13·1	4·4	4·1	80·0	45·0	0·9	1·3	2·1	1·8	16·5	131·4
National programmes	44·0	24·5	2·5a	1·0	2·4	74·4	20·4	0·3	..	0·6	..	5,600	95·7
Total Space Expenditure	73·4	53·5	15·6	5·4	6·5	154·4	65·4	1·2	..	2·7	..	5,616·5	22·71

a 1964 figures.
.. Not available.
— Nil.

TABLE 18

POTENTIAL PARTNERS IN COMPUTERS

	Total company turnover ($ mn.) (1966)	Total employment (1966)	Turnover in data processing[a] ($ mn.) (1968)	Employment in data processing[e] (end 1967)	Number of machines[e] installed in Europe (end 1967)
European companies					
ICL[a]	200[e]	36,000	225	36,000	1,035
Siemens	1,957	257,000	60	6,000	128
CII	20[e]	3,000	20	3,000	138
AEG-Telefunken	1,215	138,100	25	3,000	26
Philips-Electrologica	2,218	244,000	10[p]	2,000	45
Olivetti	505	52,892	40[o]	500	..
Elliott-NCR[b]	..	..	..	..	509
American companies					
IBM	4,247	198,186	3,500	..	3,582
Univac-Sperry-Rand	1,279	93,596	..	..	418
Honeywell	914	64,148	350	15,000	161
CDC	167	11,048	200	11,048	60
General Electric	7,177	350,000	..	..	1,086 (Bull-GE)
				Total	7,880

[a] ICT plus English-Electric Computer Division.
[b] Since incorporated in English Electric Co.
[e] Estimates.
[o] Desk computer and peripherals.
[p] Excluding, Philips' large use of d.p. equipment within the company.
Source: Company Reports; Diebold group; private information.
.. Not available

INDEX